Contemporary issues in public disorder

First the anti-poll tax riot in London, then the urban disorders in Cardiff, Oxford and North Shields; while in the United States there were riots in major cities like New York and Washington, DC. In the early 1990s public disorder returned to the top of the political agenda where it was received with the same type of confusion and misunderstanding that had prevailed during the tumultuous 1980s. The experience of the previous decade appeared to have taught us nothing; public discussion was superficial and emotional, contributing little helpful enlightenment and creating no prospect of policy change.

This book attempts to provide much-needed clarification of the key contemporary issues in public disorder. The 'flashpoints model' is used to explain that public disorder is most likely to occur where a group perceives that its rights are being violated or denied. The model is applied to a selection of illustrative case studies which are both international and historical in scope, covering British and American inner-city riots, disorderly demonstrations and strike violence. However, because sports spectator violence and the Troubles in Northern Ireland are seen to deviate from the motivational and behavioural patterns associated with other forms of public disorder, they are subjected to separate forms of analysis.

Other perennial issues are closely examined. In particular, Waddington traces the growth of police powers and appraises the effectiveness of existing forms of democratic influence over police behaviour. He also considers the assertion that media coverage has an inflammatory effect and that the media should be discouraged from reporting ongoing disorders. This book will lessen the misunderstanding surrounding public disorder by presenting a comprehensive and reasoned analysis of the key contemporary issues.

David Waddington is Senior Lecturer in Communication Studies at Sheffield City Polytechnic.

Also available from Routledge:

Racism and anti-racism in probation
David Denney

A sociology of crime
Stephen Hester and Peter Eglin

Flashpoints: studies in public disorder
David Waddington, Karen Jones and Chas Critcher

Contemporary issues in public disorder

A comparative and historical approach

David Waddington

London and New York

First published 1992
by Routledge
11 New Fetter Lane, London EC4P 4EE

Simultaneously published in the USA and Canada by
Routledge
a division of Routledge, Chapman and Hall, Inc.
29 West 35th Street, New York, NY 10001

Typeset in 10/12pt Bembo by Michael Mepham, Frome, Somerset
Printed and bound in Great Britain by
Mackays of Chatham PLC, Chatham, Kent

British Library Cataloguing in Publication Data
A catalogue record for this book is available from
the British Library.

Library of Congress Cataloging in Publication Data
Waddington, David P.
Contemporary issues in public disorder: a comparative and historical
approach / David Waddington.
    p. cm.
Includes bibliographical references and index.
1. Riots – Great Britain. 2. Violence – Great Britain.
3. Riots – United States. 4. Violence – United States.
I. Title.
HV6485.G7W33   1992
303.6'23'0941–dc20   92-9367
                                                          CIP

ISBN 0–415–07913–6 (hbk)
       0–415–07914–4 (pbk)

For Mam, Dad and Paul

Contents

Tables and figures

Acknowledgements

Several colleagues and friends made important contributions to this work. I am particularly indebted to my good friend, Chas Critcher, for his invaluable comments on earlier drafts, and for collaborating with me on Chapter 8. Similar thanks are due to John Benyon, who favourably refereed the initial book proposal and provided helpful comments on the final draft.

I am very grateful to the hard-working staff of the Mary Badland library, Sheffield City Polytechnic, for their cheerful support in helping me to research an enormous literature. I am equally grateful to my secretarial colleague, Rita Ridge, for typing up the tables.

Finally, I hope the publication of this book repays some of the enormous debt I owe to my wife, Deb, and our three children for tolerating and supporting me just when I needed them most.

Introduction

A TURBULENT TEN YEARS: BRITISH PUBLIC DISORDER, 1981-91

> I couldn't believe what we were doing: windows were being smashed, police charges dodged, and all the time the police were yelling, 'Get onto the pavement!'. The bottle of some people was amazing. A man in jeans walked up to the police lines, picked up a couple of rocks, stepped back and threw them at the knees of the policeman who seemed to be in charge. Another grabbed a broom and made a show of sweeping away the debris only feet from the police. Pairs of men would sprint up holding dustbins, hurl them and amble back to do it again. A woman stood ten feet away, pelting rocks and laughing...
>
> The crowd was delirious, maniacal smiles all round. This was outside my experience, power surged through me. I was beyond any law the police could impose; they'd charge and I might run, but I would be back again. The crowd seemed to swell. It felt like a bloody revolution. But all the time, the traffic lights changed as usual: *red, amber, green.* People were queuing to buy kebabs at a shop and cokes and 99s at an ice-cream van. And a riot was going on.
>
> (Anon, 1990:11)

These are the candid and articulate recollections of 'Tony', a 25-year-old student and self-confessed 'rioter' – one of the 100,000 people who took part in an anti-poll tax march in London on 31 March 1990. Organised by the All Britain Anti-Poll Tax Federation (ABAPTF), an umbrella organisation for 1,500 affiliated groups, the march involved a series of violent clashes between police and demonstrators, along and at the end of its route from Kennington Park to Trafalgar Square, and afterwards on the streets of London's West End.

That evening's national television news bulletins showed horrendous scenes of violence, including the apparently joyous destruction of shop windows; civilian cars being vandalised and set ablaze; demonstrators jumping for their lives from the paths of speeding police vans; a female protester being pathetically rolled along under the hooves of galloping police horses; police cars with scaffold staves driven through their side windows and, in one case, constables complaining of an attempt to set their car on fire while they were helplessly trapped inside. During a day of incredible chaos, 1,985 separate crimes were reported, 408 people were arrested and three million pounds' worth of damage caused to property (Mason, 1991).

Britain's tabloid press responded with characteristic outrage and vilification. Almost without exception, their headlines focused on the feelings of 'terror' experienced by wretched police officers at the hands of their bloodthirsty assailants:

> Shocked police tell of terror as they faced the fury of rampage thugs: BATTERED BY A MAD MOB.
>
> (*Daily Mirror*, 2 April 1990)

> Cornered cops tell how they faced death at the hands of baying rent-a-mob thugs – LET'S KILL THE BILL: 'They tried to burn us while we were stuck in van'.
>
> (*Daily Mail*, 2 April 1990)

> 4.10: Scaffold pole was pushed in his face. The men of violence were after bloodshed: TRAPPED IN CAR LIKE ULSTER CORPORALS.
>
> (*Today*, 2 April 1990)

Editorial writers, the police and senior politicians attributed the violence to 'criminality', 'wickedness' or a far-left conspiracy of anarchists and rabble rousers. This prompted *The Guardian*'s feature writer, Martin Kettle, to complain: 'In the last 36 hours, we have seen the beginnings of a re-run of the incomprehension which marked the British reaction to the riots of 1981. Rioting may be wrong, but it deserves to be analysed seriously' (*The Guardian*, 2 April, 1990).

The 1980s had been an especially tumultuous decade, marked by successive 'waves' of urban riots in 1981 and 1985, unprecedented clashes between police and trade-union pickets (notably during the 1984–5 coal dispute), frequent disorder at demonstrations, countless examples of football hooliganism and ubiquitous reminders of how the disorder which had accompanied the 1960s Catholic civil rights marches in Northern Ireland had somehow evolved into an intractable civil war.

Any optimism that the 1990s were bound to be more tranquil was quickly confounded, first by the anti-poll tax disturbance, then by riots involving youths from lower-working-class council estates in Cardiff and Oxford between 29 August and 3 September 1991, and by similar riots on Tyneside less than a week later. Alongside the familiar condemnation of the rioters as 'yobs' and 'hooligans' was speculation that drink and the exceptionally hot weather were important contributory factors. The more analytical press articles and television features emphasised unemployment, poverty and 'alienation from authority' as relevant sociological variables.

Public disorder had returned to the top of the political agenda and, in addition to the obvious question of what causes people to riot, other perennial issues temporarily monopolised public attention. Did the media coverage have an inflammatory effect on the violence, and should the press and television be discouraged from reporting ongoing disorders? Were the police tactics too soft or too aggressive? Were we providing them with the necessary training, equipment and legal powers to tackle the rioters effectively? These and similar talking points were ventilated by journalists, politicians and television pundits. But, by and large, their treatment of such issues was superficial, emotive and cliché-ridden, doing little to enlighten and offering no prospect of sensible policy reform. Despite saturation coverage, the issues raised by the events of 1991 soon faded from public awareness, destined to reappear amidst panic-stricken incomprehension with the next 'sudden crisis'.

SCOPE AND STRUCTURE

The primary objective of this book is to replace the recurring confusion and misunderstanding which typifies society's reaction to public disorder with a comprehensive and reasoned analysis of the main issues highlighted by the recent riots and the events of the 1980s. A tried and tested sociological approach is used to explain the various types of disorder which have occurred since 1980, and to help us understand the feelings and motives described by participants like Tony. The book also examines a wide range of topical issues related to media coverage and the policing of public disorder – including the concept of police accountability, a subject seldom raised during the summer of 1991, but one of the most salient and controversial issues of the 1980s.

Many of the ideas underpinning the present approach were developed in the course of research carried out by a team of academics at Sheffield City Polytechnic in the mid-1980s. This team, which included the author, conducted a series of empirical case studies of disturbances or near-disturbances at demonstrations, on picket lines and within communities in South Yorkshire between 1983 and 1985 (Waddington *et al.*, 1989). Despite inevitable variations in the contexts and dynamics of different events, we were able to formulate a general theoretical approach to the study of disorder. This framework, the 'flashpoints model of public disorder', is outlined in Chapter 1.

In the next four chapters, the model is applied to three major forms of civil disturbance: disorderly demonstrations (Chapter 2), riots (Chapters 3 and 4) and strike violence (Chapter 5). In each case the emphasis is both comparative and historical. The comparison is primarily between Great Britain and the United States of America. Like Britain, America has a very long tradition of disorder (Brown, 1970). In 1991, it, too, experienced occasional riots, notably in Washington, DC, and Brooklyn, New York, though nothing to compare in scale with the major disorders of the 1960s, when the United States had its own tumultuous decade (Graham and Gurr, 1969; Gurr, 1989a). Here particular attention is paid to both similarities and differences in the rates, sites and forms of public disorder which have occurred in each nation during the present century.

The historical emphasis of the study is both long-term, identifying the general trajectory of the last hundred years, and short-term, using case studies of particular events to show how and why different kinds of disorder have increased and/or decreased over the last 30 years. Thus each of the chapters is wide-ranging, combining a general historical review which stresses the significance of key contextual or *conjunctural* factors (e.g. the dominant political climate of opinion or prevailing economic conditions), with in-depth analyses of contemporary examples which enable us to closely explore the *dynamics* of disorder.

The focus of the next two chapters is narrower and more specific. The political nature of disorders at demonstrations, in urban areas or on picket lines is an important constituent of the factors which can, on occasion, lead to disorder. Public order is apt to break down in situations where groups perceive that their rights (e.g. to demonstrate, picket or walk freely about the streets of their neighbourhood) are being denied or violated. One form of contemporary disorder, football hooliganism, is rarely related to such an issue or grievance. Here violence tends not to involve the defence or assertion of rights, and is different in origin from the types of disorder previously mentioned. Such behaviour requires a singular theoretical approach. Hence Chapter 6 compares the merits of several established academic explanations.

Chapter 7 discusses the intractable problems of public disorder in

Northern Ireland, where the current 'Troubles' have endured since 1968. The length and complexity of this conflict and the organised nature of sectarian violence might suggest that the situation has escalated beyond 'normal' public disorder into a virtual civil war. However, there are particular reasons for including the topic in the current study. The least important is that Northern Ireland is used as a metaphorical warning of what might happen on the mainland if law and order does not prevail. (Senior police officers are particularly prone to declare that they will not tolerate no-go areas in mainland cities, a reference to Republican community campaigns in places like Belfast and Derry.) More important is the strategic significance of Northern Ireland in the development of intelligence surveillance and paramilitary policing methods which have subsequently been transposed to the mainland (e.g. during the 1984–5 coal dispute). Most important of all, there is a strong argument to be considered that the current escalation of organised violence happened in part because of the way the authorities reacted to the Civil Rights movement of the late 1960s. According to this interpretation, civil war occurs when public disorder becomes habitual, widespread and increasingly violent.

Football hooliganism and Northern Ireland are juxtaposed because, in quite different ways, they deviate from the motivational and behavioural patterns to be expected during riots or at disorderly demonstrations or mass pickets. However, all of these cases raise questions about two major social institutions, the media and the police. They are discussed in Chapters 8 and 9, respectively.

Chapter 8 critically appraises British and American media representations of public disorder, and considers the argument that certain forms of media coverage can help to create the potential for violence. Chapter 9 looks at novel developments in police public-order training, tactics and technology. It explores the possibility that recent extensions of police powers may increase, rather than defuse the likelihood of violence in problematic situations. Finally, it assesses the effectiveness of existing formal mechanisms for exercising democratic control over the police.

The concluding chapter (Chapter 10) reiterates the need to analyse public disorder in terms of an eclectic approach which places equal priority on the contextual and dynamic factors relevant to a specific situation. The chapter consolidates the book's commitment towards addressing matters of topical concern by offering a tentative explanation of the British urban riots of 1991. The penultimate section outlines some possible future trends, while a final section sets out a number of policy recommendations for preventing public disorder.

Such is our agenda for addressing the key contemporary issues in public disorder. We begin by refocusing our attention on our preliminary case study, the anti-poll tax riot of 31 March 1990, the so-called Battle of Trafalgar.

Chapter 1

The anatomy of a riot

The 'Battle of Trafalgar'

In the absence of any single, in-depth study, such as an official report of inquiry, the following description and analysis of the Battle of Trafalgar has been constructed on the basis of four primary sources of information: the Metropolitan police's own 'debriefing' report on the event (Metropolitan Police, 1991); a compilation of participants' accounts, published by ACAB Press (ACAB, 1990); a Channel Four video, 'The Battle of Trafalgar', broadcast on 18 September 1990; and magazine and newspaper articles (e.g. Anon, 1990; Mason, 1991). Any discrepancies in these accounts will be highlighted. The case study is presented in four sections. A brief overview of the principal events is followed by a critical appraisal of academic and lay explanations of the riot. An alternative framework of analysis is then presented in the form of the 'flashpoints model of public disorder'. Finally, this framework is applied to the anti-poll tax disorder, thus dissecting the anatomy of a riot.

THE 'BATTLE OF TRAFALGAR': AN OVERVIEW

The march was scheduled to start at 1 p.m. and to follow a route past Downing Street, up Whitehall to a rally in Trafalgar Square. Despite some barracking of the police by a small core of thirty anarchists, the early stages of the march were overridingly peaceful. Though the head of the march quickly passed through Whitehall to reach Trafalgar Square by 1.35 p.m., a central section of two to four hundred decided to stage a sit-down protest on the road opposite Downing Street, resisting attempts by police and stewards to move them on. Some marchers carried on, but others settled down on the grass verge outside the Ministry of Defence building, using it as a makeshift picnic area or temporary vantage point.

There are discrepant accounts of what happened thereafter. The police report states that officers were forced to intervene because sit-down protesters threw stones, bricks and traffic bollards, and tried to dismantle crash barriers, presumably in an attempt to enter Downing Street. The report further emphasises that increasing congestion was being caused by the sit-down protest. These factors prompted their decision to disperse the demonstrators. The 'Battle of Trafalgar' video disputes two main aspects of this account: first, that a dangerous build-up of people was occurring; and second, that it was the demonstrators who instigated the violence.

As the confrontation escalated and more demonstrators were drawn in, the police used mounted officers to disperse the crowd, some south, and others north to Trafalgar Square. In the square, a carnival atmosphere had so far prevailed: large numbers of people were dancing to samba rhythms or listening to a succession of sympathetic speakers, and humorous banners were draped across surrounding construction scaffolding and nearby tall buildings. But, as more demonstrators arrived, disorder broke out there, too.

It is not entirely clear why or how this happened. Demonstrators allege that the confrontation occurred when a space opened up in the crowd as riot police charged in to be greeted by a hail of stones and bottles. They add that more officers, this time without riot gear, moved in to try and rescue them, but the crowd stood its ground, forcing the police to retreat. The police report emphasises that rioting broke out when officers went to the aid of two police vans at the south-east corner of the square.

In the ensuing mayhem, the police were bombarded with missiles procured from a building site, a workmen's hut was set on fire and South Africa House was stoned and almost set ablaze. Three police vans sped through the crowd at 30 to 40 m.p.h., causing demonstrators to flee for their lives. Mounted police tried to clear the square, driving some demonstrators along Charing Cross Road and St Martin's Lane. However, as the crowd moved off, some of its members looted the windows of West End shops.

As the police became increasingly disorganised, protesters ran through restaurants and climbed on the roofs of double-decker buses. Cars were overturned and set ablaze. At one point, four thousand protesters straggled through the West End, followed by a mere twenty police, so outnumbered they were forced to release their prisoners. Nevertheless, by midnight, most of the demonstrators had left the city centre and order had been restored.

EXPLAINING THE RIOT: LAY AND ACADEMIC ACCOUNTS

In the aftermath of the riot, there was a widespread consensus on the part of the police and politicians of all parties that disorder had been deliberately instigated by a small group of political extremists, comprising anarchists and members of the Socialist Workers' Party (SWP) (cf. *The Times*, 2 April 1990). It is not surprising that this account was given so much credence for, as Martin Kettle pointed out, 'There has never been a riot in British history where someone hasn't claimed that the whole thing was a conspiracy by a minority' (*The Guardian*, 2 April 1990).

Another historically recurring explanation is the 'riff-raff' theory: that rioters are usually drawn from the criminal, deviant and rootless sections of society. However, the American ghetto disorders of the 1960s showed that the typical rioter was a long-term resident of the community; had above-average education for the area; was politically better informed than most; was likely to be politicised (though distrustful of the political system); and was imbued with strong feelings of racial pride (cf. Caplan and Paige, 1968). Fogelson and Hill (1968) further point out that the participation rate in riots in major American cities – excluding those people who merely expressed support – was between 11 and 35 per cent of the ghetto population. Judging from the video, the march was representative of people from all backgrounds, hardly the 'loony left' or 'rent-a-mob' beloved of newspaper editorials.

> Some people were poorly dressed and looked worse fed than their mongrel dogs, some wore the fatigues and black leather that say 'anarchist!' to the media. But the crowd ... was overwhelmingly a *normal-looking* bunch of people, and I only hope that they were marxists and anarchists, because if they were, then they've infiltrated every walk of life in Britain. Every home has got one.
>
> (Anon, 1990:11)

Participants in the anti-poll tax riot admitted to feelings of excitement, power and liberation. Such sensations offer *prima facie* evidence for the view that even rational individuals may sometimes find themselves overtaken by a 'mob mentality' which causes them to behave destructively. This is the underlying logic of the social facilitation approach (Allport, 1924), which posits that individuals in a crowd become trapped in an ever-increasing spiral of excitement and emotionality, caused by their mutually reinforcing reactions.

The deindividuation approach (cf. Zimbardo, 1969) makes the similar claim that the anonymity and loss of self-awareness caused by immersing themselves in a large crowd, causes individuals to act impulsively, aggressively and without restraint. This logic was successfully argued by a British psychologist in mitigation of several black South Africans tried recently for their part in a fatal instance of collective violence (Colman, 1991). However, as Gaskell and Benewick (1987:2) indicate, 'Such individualistic theories appear to explain the homogeneity of the crowd but do so at the cost of predicting bedlam in every crowd, at Ascot and the Lynch mob alike.'

Explanations based on the frustration–aggression hypothesis see rioting as an emotional outburst due to frustration caused by blocked goals or oppressively hot weather (Berkowitz, 1972), or feelings of relative deprivation (Gurr, 1970). Under such circumstances, rioters 'take out' their frustration on a local target of aggression, such as the police or symbols of the establishment. This perspective correlates with the police and dominant press view that the trouble at Downing Street flared up because the rioters were 'thwarted in their attempt to smash barriers and storm the new security gates' (*The Times*, 2 April 1990). Such explanations rest on the unlikely assumption that rioting is merely an aggregated response of scores – perhaps hundreds – of individuals simultaneously experiencing a state of psychological arousal (Billig, 1976).

Almost as a palliative to such approaches, some theorists have explained that crowd disorder is invariably purposive and selective. One perspective of this nature (the 'gaming approach') sees individuals within a crowd acting on the basis of a cost-benefit calculation of the 'pay-offs' accruing from collective disorder (Berk, 1974; Olson, 1965). The benefits to be gained from, say, looting or exacting revenge on the police may be compared with the risks of arrest and injury. A more sociological approach, popularised by historians like Hobsbawm and Rude (1970), depicts collective violence as a way of inducing political concessions: a kind of 'collective bargaining by riot'. However, both these perspectives overlook the fact that many riots (e.g. the urban disorders in Britain in the 1980s) happen spontaneously; and, if demands are formulated at all, they tend to be expressed only when the riot is in full swing (Benyon and Solomos, 1987).

This is not to suggest that actors who riot spontaneously do not harbour common grievances or hold a shared understanding of the appropriateness of their action. Reicher's (1984) analysis of the 1980 St Paul's (Bristol) riot shows how participants operated on the basis of common definitions deriving from their membership of the local community. Residents, both black and white, had long shared a sense of humiliation and indignation induced by their day-to-day experience of signing on the dole, suffering 'exploitation' by local banks and store keepers and encountering harassment by the Bristol police. They felt that they had lost control over their lives, and the riot, sparked off by a police raid on a café frequented by blacks, was a collective reassertion of their autonomy.

The rioters drove the police out of the area, but pursued them only as far as the geographical boundary of St Paul's. Police personnel and vehicles were the only intentional targets of attack, and looting and destruction was confined to buildings synonymous with their resentment, such as banks, social security offices and stores owned by outsiders. Once the area had been purged of any police presence, local Rastafarian youths determined who could enter or leave St Paul's by directing the flow of traffic.

Reicher sets out a 'social identity' explanation of the riot, emphasising that it was the participants' shared understanding of what it meant to belong to a distinct social category, the St Paul's community, which both informed and limited their behaviour:

> The attributes of this concept [the St Paul's Community] are clearly reflected in the crowd's behaviour. The geographical basis is translated into the decision of crowd members not to move beyond St Paul's. The opposition to the police is seen in the selection of police officers and vehicles as the sole targets of collective violence. The notion of control is reflected in the way in which participants took over the area once the police had left, directing traffic through and ... advising [it] not to go down certain roads and checking obvious strangers in the area.
>
> (Reicher, 1984:18)

Helpful though it may be, Reicher's approach needs to be supplemented by explanations both of the social conditions which gave rise to the shared sentiments of the residents of St Paul's and why the riot broke out at this particular point in time rather than another. The so-called deprivation thesis, which highlights such factors as high unemployment, poor housing and inferior social services, is clearly relevant here, but it also fails to explain why rioting breaks out only at some locations and not elsewhere, and on some occasions but not on others (Field and Southgate, 1982).

What these approaches lack is any sense of the political context in which rioting occurs, and of the events and communication processes which precede them. Numerous studies suggest that public disorder is more apt to occur in the context of deteriorating police–citizen relations fuelled by societal perceptions of the targeted group as threatening or unreasonable in some way, rumours of impending atrocities, and the alerting effect of the media on the police and public that something is about to happen. Against this background, forms of police–citizen interaction which go 'beyond the pale' may act as the trigger for public disorder. As Martin Kettle puts it,

> People riot when they have a sense of grievance and when they feel emboldened by circumstances to commit acts of defiance or destruction which require a certain bravery and example. Riots normally start when people witness specific acts of injustice which no longer seem tolerable in the circumstances. Riots frequently then develop discriminately, according to the rioters' shared assumptions of what is, in their eyes, legitimate. This should not mean that rioting is justifiable, only that it is explicable.
>
> (*The Guardian*, 2 April 1990)

It is evident that 'single-factor' theories do not adequately explain such a complicated social phenomenon, and that a theoretical approach which incorporates the full range of relevant variables is necessary. Smelser's (1962) *Theory of Collective Behaviour* is an attempt to meet this requirement. Established within the structural-functionalist school of sociology, Smelser's model posits that society is essentially integrated and self-balancing. Public disorder is an anomolous, irrational and deviant activity engaged in by those groups – e.g. the unemployed, recent migrants and restless adolescents – who are currently experiencing 'social strain', defined as disaffection at the level of norms (as when expectations are not met by society) and/or values (where basic rights are flouted or transgressed).

The explanation rests on the premise that, where social strain is present and conditions are structurally conducive, a 'generalized hostile belief' may develop among the disaffected and thence a 'hostile outburst' occur. Structural conduciveness is characterised by (i) the presence of an agency to which the blame for an unsatisfactory state of affairs may be attached, (ii) the absence or failure of grievance channels, and (iii) the possibility of effective communication among the aggrieved.

It is under such conditions that generalised hostile beliefs may materialise. These are defined as 'magical beliefs (which) distort reality and "short-circuit" the normal paths to the amelioration of grievances' (Skolnick, 1969:253). The danger lies in their tendency to hold groups (notably the police) responsible for a distressing state of affairs who are not actually to blame. The resulting hostility directed at such groups invariably reflects ingroup feelings of their own omnipotence.

According to Smelser, hostile outbursts may be precipitated by a single incident or rumour which serves to exaggerate the generalised beliefs. Specific forms of behaviour enacted by the crowd are likely to be mobilised by the example of individuals who deliberately or unwittingly serve as models, or the lead given by representatives of a formal organisation. How far disorder is allowed to spread thereafter depends on the reaction of the social-control agencies: hostilities are likely to cease where the authorities react decisively by preventing communication among the rioters, blocking interaction between the participants and their leaders, not bluffing or vacillating when resorting to coercion, and remaining committed to impartiality according to the law.

Elsewhere, we have set out the following objections to Smelser's approach (Waddington *et al.*, 1989:169–77):

1 it is unhelpful to look upon society as an integrated whole and public disorder as the irrational activity of people beyond the mainstream;
2 it is equally obstructive to conceive of generalised hostile beliefs as magical or ill-informed: studies of recent disorders show that the police were an actual, not imagined, focus of specific grievances within black ghettos;
3 the model is apolitical and ahistorical, overlooking key differences of culture, values and interests between the police and civilians, and neglecting the importance of prior relations between them; and
4 far from reducing the likelihood of further disorder, decisive police intervention often serves to inflame a situation which might otherwise have been pacified and normalised.

Our own approach, the flashpoints model of public disorder (Waddington *et al.*, 1989), is grounded on empirical research carried out between 1983 and 1985. Unlike Smelser's theory, this approach rejects the underlying premises of structural-functionalism. We none the less accept that it is counterproductive to assume that all forms of public disorder are instrumental and enacted with specific objectives in mind. We consider it more helpful to assume that some collective disturbances are expressive in nature: a collective, but as yet unfocused, manifestation of an underlying sense of grievance or disaffection.

THE FLASHPOINTS MODEL OF PUBLIC DISORDER

The flashpoints model of public disorder was inspired by American theoretical approaches to the 1960s riots which prioritised the relationship between a precipitating incident and a 'reservoir' of grievances (Hundley, 1968; Kerner, 1968), and formulated on the basis of insights and lessons drawn from a series of original case studies. The model has already been applied to a wide range of British political, industrial and community disorders, including the inner-city disturbances of 1981–5 (Waddington,

1987; Waddington *et al.*, 1989). It comprises six integrated levels of analysis: the structural, political/ideological, cultural, contextual, situational and interactional levels. These are now defined in turn.

Structural

At this, macro-sociological level, we refer to inequalities of power, material resources and life chances between different groups in society which form the objective basis of conflict.

> A copy of any non-tabloid newspaper will reveal conflicts whose basis lies in class, ethnicity, gender and sexual politics, region, nation, employment status, age and ideology. Conflict is endemic. Changes in social structure and in values can produce conflict. One need not entertain a theory of conspiracy when technical innovation, 'conviction politics' (i.e. dogma), environmental pollution, economic uncertainty and the break-up of customary community norms are so apparent.
>
> (Fielding, 1991:12)

Objective deprivation is insufficient, in itself, to generate social discontent. Such deprivation has to be *subjectively* recognised before disorder can occur. Typically, this involves a shared perception that a group is being denied some privilege or commodity which it feels entitled to expect from society. The model also acknowledges that *ideological alienation from the state* may provide a similar basis for conflict. This occurs where a group of people (e.g. peace campaigners or anti-apartheid protesters) may not be personally experiencing the effects of inequality, but may none the less consider certain state policies and activities morally reprehensible (Waddington *et al.*, 1989:160).

In liberal democracies, the state is charged with the responsibility of attending to grievances and mediating sectional interests. Latent social conflict is more likely to become manifest when the state seems unable or, worse still, *unwilling* to respond sympathetically towards an aggrieved section of society. Under such circumstances, a dissenting group is likely to become disaffected from the state, feeling that it no longer has a stake in the existing political and moral order. How far this occurs will depend on activities at the next of our levels, the political/ideological.

Political/ideological

This level refers to the relationship of a politically or culturally dissenting group to key political and ideological institutions and how such institutions react to its activities. An aggrieved section of society will try to convey its grievance through conventional democratic channels. Its chances of success will partly depend on its political power – whether it is adequately represented within political institutions, or whether it is effectively disenfranchised and therefore marginalised – and partly on the extent to which the group and its demands are regarded as legitimate.

> Legitimacy refers to the way in which the group's declared ends and the means proposed to achieve them are subject to ideological processes. Through the agency of the mass media, politicians and commentators will represent the dissenting group in a more or less favourable light. At its most positive, the right to protest and on occasion some recognition of the justice of their case will be acknowledged. At its most negative, what the group is trying to achieve and the means at their disposal will be portrayed as a threat to the fabric of society.
>
> (Waddington et al., 1989:161)

This experience of political marginalisation and ideological vilification may increase the dissenting group's willingness to engage in violence as a way of defending or promoting its interests.

The same socially circulating ideas are also likely to affect the way the group is policed. Kilson discusses the tendency of American police to 'pick on pariah groups', reflecting the 'worst localistic anxieties' of the communities they serve:

> Look at police behaviour towards the suffragettes and early feminists – the police mirrored the tensions, took the predominant view and attacked the women. In the early phase they even beat up bourgeois women – women beyond their own status. More recently, adopting the homophobic stance, they beat up people in the gay liberation movement and they beat them up for no reason other than that the localistic and parochialistic pressures said homosexuals were illegitimate.
>
> (Kilson, 1987:57–8)

Jefferson and Grimshaw advance the similar argument that chief police officers develop policies in relation to significant 'audiences'.

> They have to take into account, first and foremost, those audiences to which they are answerable, in various ways, 'in law': principally, the 'law' itself (or, less abstractly, the courts – the body responsible for interpreting the law); police authorities; the Home Secretary; we might call these *legal audiences*. Secondly, they must take into account the views of the local community or 'the policed'; we might call these the

democratic audiences. Finally, they must take into account the views of those under their command – senior officers and the rank and file; what we might call the *occupational audiences.*

(Jefferson and Grimshaw, 1984:66–7)

Thus the 'climate of opinion' engendered by local and national ideological institutions is one of several important factors which chiefs of police take into consideration in deciding how to respond to a dissenting group or organisation.

Cultural

The cultural level of analysis refers to the ways of life and thought which groups develop on the basis of shared material conditions and location within the social structure. Different regional, ethnic, youth and occupational cultures (or subcultures) have their own unique definitions of themselves and other social groups. They have their own ideas of the rules governing appropriate behaviour in specific situations.

As such they provide a basis for collective mobilization and action. They also carry with them beliefs about the rights of individuals or groups. They foster certain characterizations of other social groups and expectations of how they are likely to behave in a given situation. If the groups involved have differing or incompatible definitions of the situation, appropriate behaviour, or legitimate rights, then the potential for conflict is increased.

(Waddington *et al.*, 1989:161–2)

This clearly applies to routine encounters between the police and such culturally or politically dissenting groups as black youths, trade-union pickets or student demonstrators. The police occupational culture has been closely studied by sociologists (e.g. Holdaway, 1983; Manning, 1977; Reiner, 1985; Skolnick, 1966), who generally agree that political conservatism is one of its core characteristics. These authors also point out that police officers anticipate suitable levels of respect for their authority and have highly legalistic conceptions of what constitutes 'appropriate behaviour'. They try to make a dangerous and thankless job more manageable by employing helpful, but crude stereotypes, typifications and recipes of people, places and events. The lower ranks place a high value on solidarity and prize any opportunity for action and excitement. The culture has a distinctly masculine ethos with officers ready to back up their authority with force if necessary.

Police officers generally reserve their most negative attitudes towards those perennially delegitimised groups which 'respectable' society has designated as 'police property'.

They are low-status, powerless groups whom the dominant majority see as problematic or distasteful. The majority are prepared to let the police deal with their 'property' and turn a blind eye to the manner in which this is done. Examples would be vagrants, skid-row alcoholics, the unemployed or casually employed residuum, youth adopting a deviant cultural style, ethnic minorities, gays, prostitutes and radical political organisations.

(Reiner, 1985:95)

Needless to say, the police and dissenting groups will often have incompatible definitions of a particular situation: of how each party should behave and what their respective 'rights' are. While these discrepant viewpoints are potentially problematic, conflict is not inevitable: much will depend on whether both sides are prepared to *accommodate* each other's perspective by acting in terms of a tacitly agreed system of norms prescribing permissible behaviour (Waddington, 1987:209). Thus a 'good, clean shove' might be tolerated by the police and trade-union pickets, whereas throwing stones would not; demonstrators might be allowed to boo and shout outside a town hall, but not to block its entrance; and police might turn a blind eye to black youths smoking cannabis, but not allow the trafficking of a 'hard' drug like heroin.

Contextual

Any one of a host of communication processes may help to provide a context in which a particular incident becomes highly charged or acquires greater significance than it perhaps deserves. Among these, we may include a negative recent history of intergroup relations between the police and dissenting group, perhaps involving a backlog of confrontations which have nurtured animosity and left scores to be settled on both sides.

The prevalence of rumour and discussion relating to past or forthcoming interaction may create an enhanced readiness for confrontation (Hundley, 1968:142). The mass media could similarly magnify the potential for disorder by sensitising the police and public to the possibility that conflict might occur (Cohen, 1980). Comments made by representatives of dissenting groups, articles appearing in their publications, tip-offs to the police or information deriving from covert operations will all structure expectations that violence is destined to occur.

Under such circumstances, the police may choose not to take any chances and organise themselves according to a worst possible scenario. The danger here is that

> While adequate planning and preparation are vital to effective control, they may help create a state-of-siege mentality, increase susceptibility to rumors, and exert a self-fulfilling pressure. This is particularly true when they are found with a get-tough, act-quickly philosophy.
>
> (Marx, 1970:41)

Some of this danger might be offset, at least in the case of demonstrations and mass pickets, by preliminary liaison between the organisers and the police. Discussions regarding the anticipated number of participants and some indication of their 'mood' would help ensure that the police were not taken by surprise or were forced to over-prepare for confrontation. The advance negotiation of 'ground rules' would also help to establish a sense of accommodation on both sides.

Situational

We use the term 'situational' to refer to any spatial or social determinants of disorder relevant to the immediate setting in which interaction takes place. A particular location may be physically more or less conducive to disorder to the extent that it facilitates police surveillance of the crowd, makes the movement of people more predictable and enables them the freedom to leave should the police try to disperse them. The presence of 'targets of derision' (e.g. the embassy of a detested foreign nation, strike-breakers or a controversial political figure) will raise the prospect of disorder, especially where the police choose to intervene. However, the spatial context is always mediated by cultural and social factors. Disorder is more likely to occur at popular locations where many people are likely to be present (Kerner, 1968; Stark, 1972; Sullivan, 1977). Certain locations may also possess symbolic significance, representing territory or 'turf' to be seized or defended (Marx, 1970).

The way that the police and public perceive space is equally important. To the former, a physical location may be looked upon as private property to be protected from trespass or damage, or a clearing to be kept open to allow people or traffic to pass through; whereas the latter may view it as a particularly useful vantage point or a piece of land which they believe they have a right to occupy regardless of what the police might say.

The management of space is another significant factor. For example, where a demonstration is marshalled by its own stewards, its organisers continually disavow violence, there are focal points (e.g. speakers and entertainment) for the crowd, and symbolic channels for the expression of dissent (e.g. the handing in of a petition), disorder is less likely to occur. Similarly, as Stark (1972:131) explains, 'the sheer number of police present, and the nature and amount of weaponry they display, may as critically stimulate what comes to pass as anything the police actually do in terms of using their numbers and their weapons'. A commitment to a low-key style of policing, with reinforcements kept out of sight and crush barriers erected before the crowd arrives, is less likely to provoke disorder. In the event of disorder, there is more chance of the police remaining disciplined in their actions if their tactics are centrally co-ordinated with clear lines of communication between separate units.

The immediate objectives of both sides and the way that each reads the other's intentions will also influence the outcome. Sometimes, demonstrators or pickets may be intent on creating 'maximum disruption' for tactical purposes (Clutterbuck, 1977); alternatively, police officers may deliberately incite a volatile crowd in order to clear a strategically important area while they (the police) have a temporary superiority of numbers (personal communication with Kent police officer). Equally important, however, is each side's interpretation of their rival's motives, e.g. as sinister, illegitimate or unfair, regardless of its accuracy.

Interactional

This level focuses on the quality of interaction between the police and dissenting group. It is at this level of analysis that 'flashpoints' occur.

> We define these as actions seen by the participants as breaking the unwritten rules governing behaviour between groups. A particular action is seen as an index of unwillingness to accommodate to, or wilful infringement of, previously established norms of behaviour.
>
> (Waddington *et al.*, 1987:162)

Disorder may arise from an uncompromising police arrest or forcible attempt to move a crowd; or when crowd members throw bricks at, or charge into, an awaiting police line. Such actions are in clear breach of the 'rules of the game', and are guaranteed to heighten emotions and produce a spiral of recrimination. This is particularly so when they are accompanied by *intensifiers*, a term we use to denote those factors of the individuals involved (whether high-ranking, vulnerable, etc.) or the way in which actions are carried out (e.g. an especially rough or degrading arrest or the systematic beating up of a police officer) which further outrage those present. Such intensifiers offer the clearest sign that one or both sides has no desire for accommodation (ibid.:212).

An escalation of disorder is by no means inevitable at this stage. Much will depend on the nature of subsequent actions. For example, crude and seemingly random instances of aggression on both sides will provide a further indication of their unwillingness to accommodate. Where police action is of this nature, it may unwittingly draw in the previously non-partisan. The pattern of escalation may still be reversed by actions designed to repair the ruptured status quo (i.e. 'pacifiers'), as when trade unionists rebuke a miscreant member of their picket line, or the police instantly release an arrested prisoner (ibid.:215).

The underlying reasons for these activities and the meanings which participants apply to them cannot be fully understood without due reference to our other levels of analysis. This is also true of the various feelings and emotions – e.g. power, liberation, elation and revenge – which must be interpreted, if they are to be adequately understood, in light of the specific grievances held by a dissenting group, their political marginality and their recent exposure to oppressive forms of policing.

ANALYSING THE 'BATTLE OF TRAFALGAR'

Having established our framework of analysis, we now resume our discussion of the anti-poll tax disturbance in London on 31 March 1990. We set out its explanation in terms of the six levels of analysis, beginning with the structural level. It is evident from the 'Battle of Trafalgar' video that the demonstration consisted of a wide range of people, drawn from separate age groups and different social backgrounds, but united in their belief that the 'community charge' – a local tax which demanded the same financial contribution from an 18-year-old school leaver as a wealthy millionaire – was an iniquitous fiscal measure. In the terms used by our model, it was the protesters' ideological alienation which prompted them to demonstrate on the streets of London. However, it would be misguided to look upon the riot solely as an extreme expression of a universal recognition of unfairness.

Another structural variable was significant. It was one particular section of British society – its poor youth – which had most reason to regard the poll tax as a vindictive political weapon. Prominent amongst the rioters were those people The Economist (7 April 1990:16) referred to as 'the vanguard of a semi politicised underclass': groups 'living on the edges of British society' – the young, the unemployed, the homeless (some of them forced to live on the streets of London in cardboard boxes), the 'no hopers'

– for whom the poll tax was intended as 'a hard dose of local civic responsibility'.

While members of this underclass were undoubtedly at the riot's epicentre, the various commentaries suggest that a much broader spectrum of young people was involved. This was not surprising. Here was an age group disproportionately affected by recent government policy (education cuts, student loan schemes, high youth unemployment and the indignity of dead-end training schemes). 'No poll tax!' may have been their rallying cry, but their resentment had a much wider basis. As we shall see, people of diverse ages and social backgrounds were sometimes sucked into the disturbance, but, in essence, this was a young persons' riot. 'It wasn't even about the poll tax; that was just the occasion for it. *It was a young people's riot*, a spontaneous outburst by people from all over the country, that's what made it so great' (Anon, 1990:11, emphasis added).

In terms of the political/ideological level of analysis, here was a powerless and disaffected section of society, aware that no-one within the present political system (with the exception of a score of Labour MPs advocating a policy of mass non-payment) was speaking on its behalf. In the weeks leading up to the demonstration, Conservative politicians had dismissed the growing anti-poll tax agitation and the occasional violence associated with it as a concerted attempt to generate publicity and support for the 'hard-left' Militant organisation.

To differing degrees, young people on the march were tired of being pushed around by indifferent politicians. The riot was not politically organised:

> What happened was more the result of a lack of political leadership. People realised that they weren't on their own and discovered how fragmented, and angry, and disaffected they were. And these feelings manifested themselves in brute force. How can you expect direction and discipline from people who've never had a focal point to aim at? I fear that this was a one-off, as Labour condemned the protest as mindlessly as the Tories. We can't look to them for intelligent analysis or direction. We've gone back to our homes, knowing we've done a great thing but not knowing where to go next.
>
> (Anon, 1990:11)

Journalists who had been present at earlier poll tax demonstrations involving minor confrontations between police and protesters rejected the suggestion that Militant or Socialist Workers' Party activists had deliberately stirred up the trouble:

We were at Lambeth town hall on Friday night [9 March 1990], where 2,000 people gathered to protest and where far fewer people later rioted. Were the rioters outside agitators? No: many were local agitators with no attachment to this country's political system whatsoever. They are part of an anarchist subculture, living rough or in dilapidated squats. For them, a 'community charge' means running full pelt down the street with a brick in your hand and a 'pig' in your sights. They are certainly not members of Militant – an organisation that demands sobriety and discipline.

(Crampton and Jenkins, 1990:16)

This observation is relevant to our cultural level of analysis. It is generally agreed by our sources that both the sit-down protest in Downing Street and the initial spate of window smashing in the West End were instigated by a hard-core group of anarchists. Anarchist groups, like Spartacus, Class War and Crowbar, understand a wide range of political issues, e.g. the poll tax, unemployment, abortion and police harassment, in class terms, and see the violent overthrow of society as the most effective solution.

The violent resistance to the police intervention in Downing Street and the subsequent destruction of property is consistent with this perception. Anarchists also fall into the category of 'police property' and would therefore have been looked upon by the police as 'deserving' targets of aggression. Neither of these cultural factors totally explains the size and severity of the police intervention, or accounts for the wider escalation of the riot. Part of the explanation has to do with those factors already highlighted at the structural and political/ideological levels, and complementary factors at the other, remaining levels.

Several aspects of the communication context were undoubtedly significant. Police preparations for the protest were based on a strong anticipation of violence. *The Times* confirms that:

The police commitment to the demonstration was based on intelligence assessments. These would include reports from a unit within the Special Branch which deals with areas such as subversion. Officers also study recent similar demonstrations and monitor protest meetings, leaflets and posters put out by extremist groups.

(*The Times*, 2 April 1990)

Earlier in the year, there had been clashes between the police and poll tax protestors in London and various other major cities (e.g. Bristol, Birmingham, Bradford and Norwich). In early March, anarchist spokespersons and publications made statements reiterating their support for violent opposition to the poll tax, exhorting their followers to seize the initiative from Militant as the focal point of poll tax agitation, and advising them how to evade or sabotage police tactics (ibid.). Special Branch detectives also claimed to have uncovered an SWP plot to attack 10 Downing Street (*Today*, 2 April 1990). All of the above intelligence is likely to have influenced police preparations.

Prior to the demonstration, regular meetings took place between the police and ABAPTF organisers. However, this liaison did not prove especially beneficial. Due to the disparate nature of its membership, the ABAPTF could not be sure of how many people would be attending, and estimates leapt from 20,000 to 58,000 on the eve of the demonstration. According to the police report,

> The organisers agreed to appoint 2,300 stewards to help police in marshalling the crowd, escorting the march and and assisting with diversions should they become necessary. In the event, although seven Chief Stewards were present, considerably less stewards than promised were in attendance.
>
> (Metropolitan Police, 1991:1)

The immediate situation in which the march occurred further heightened the potential for disorder. The route of the march, itself, through the central streets of the nation's capital, passing several symbolic buildings and locations, gave the police cause for concern (ibid.:11). The absence of effective stewarding and the unruly disposition of some section of anarchists (e.g. destroying tapes and lights designed to regulate the flow of traffic and pedestrians) will have given them further reason to feel wary.

The particular situational objectives of both sides (actual and perceived) clearly affected the quality of interaction between them. Given their intelligence regarding the threat of an attack on 10 Downing Street and/or pre-demonstration statements by anarchist groups, the police may well have interpreted the sit-down protest as the prelude to an organised raid. Evidently, no chances were taken: 'Just a broken window at No. 10 would have been heralded as a symbolic victory', confided one senior police officer (*Today*, 2 April 1990). One other possibility is that the disorder was deliberately instigated as a pre-emptive police strategy. According to one ABAPTF Chief Steward, two police *agents provocateurs* 'spent the entire hour trying to provoke the stewards into the use of physical violence' (quoted in 'The Battle of Trafalgar').

At the last of our six levels, the interactional level, we consider the flashpoint incident which initially provoked the riot. ABAPTF organisers claim that, just prior to the march, they reached an understanding with the police that, in the event of a sit-down protest in Downing Street, stewards would continue to usher the rest of the marchers around them. When the sit-down occurred, as anticipated, marshals appealed to those not involved to carry on moving. Contrary to press reports, most people obeyed them. The police intervention was therefore considered unnecessary and in flagrant breach of an established agreement.

Other key situational factors, chiefly involving aspects of police communication, had a negative effect on the quality of their interaction with demonstrators. The police report concedes that problems of communication within their own ranks, and between police and demonstrators unwittingly aggravated the disorder. Officers working under different lines of command were unclear about, or often unaware of tactics being used elsewhere. There was a lack of co-ordination between the activities of mounted police and police on foot. This general state of confusion was compounded, first, by the loss of several minutes of radio transmission due to interference and the limited life of batteries, and second, the inhibition felt by some middle-ranking officers due to the close presence of senior commanders. The net result was that the police tactics were in disarray and the cause of great frustration to demonstrators.

The report also states that there was no method of auditory communication with the crowd. Senior police officers found themselves unable to ask or instruct demonstrators to move from the area, or to warn them of the introduction of mounted police and short-shield units. Police actions therefore seemed arbitrary and needlessly authoritarian as far as demonstrators were concerned. The attitude of those demonstrators being moved away from Downing Street was clearly one of confusion and exasperation:

> We had nowhere we could go. There were barricades stopping people going (any) further in Whitehall. There were lines of police stopping people going anywhere else and then there were police horses. It was almost like being, it *was* being trapped. We were angry, we were upset; I guess *indignant* is the obvious word.
>
> (male protestor, quoted in 'The Battle of Trafalgar')

Soon, the whole episode was transformed into a simple matter of principle:

> There were no agitators, as such, or anything like that. It was just a feeling that everyone had. There was a lot of really angry people there and I didn't feel that I should leave them there... It got to the point where I wanted to defend the right to be there.
>
> (male protestor, quoted in 'The Battle of Trafalgar')

Gradually, as the confrontation wore on, crowd members became emboldened, first by the actions of the anarchists, and then by the example of their peers and the unlikelihood of getting caught or hurt by the police advances. There was a logic to the selection of targets of attack:

> The London riot was an opportunity for those suffering under the Tories – such as the estimated 70,000 residents of 'cardboard city' – to vent their anger against the Tories and the symbols of 'Thatcherism' which the rich had got used to flaunting in central London – the expensive cars, the ability to dine at the most expensive restaurants and shop at the most expensive stores.
>
> (Lavalette and Mooney, 1990:103)

All present experienced a temporary feeling of euphoria at being above and beyond the law. It was a rare experience: an opportunity to say and do something that was ordinarily denied by an unsympathetic and unyielding political system. As Tony said quite succinctly of his actions: 'I did what I did because I could' (Anon, 1990:11).

DISCUSSION

Table 1.1 summarises the application of the flashpoints model to the anti-poll tax riot. The preceding analysis has shown how the model comprises a credible framework for explaining episodes of public disorder. In due course, this framework will be applied to contemporary examples of British and American urban riots and strike violence. For the moment, we maintain our interest in disorderly demonstrations. It is accepted that the above application is based on a limited range of sources and may be open to possible accusations of a partial interpretation. Further evidence is therefore required of the model's general applicability to disorderly demonstrations.

Most commentators on public disorder arising from political protest have concentrated on explanatory variables residing at what we refer to as the contextual, cultural and interactional levels of analysis. Disorder is said to occur because of inadequate liaison, when 'minority extremist groups' depart from the arrangements made by representatives of the larger group (Mark, 1977), or when police expectations of trouble cause them to over-react to minor incidents (Kritzer, 1977). There is a greater likelihood of disorder where a dissenting group is culturally predisposed to see violence as appropriate in some circumstances (ibid.). Mutually interactive behaviour and its interpretation are seen as significant by Wright (1978:101–16), who discusses evidence to show how the formation of the police, or the speed and nature of their intervention, may impart details of

Table 1.1 An application of the flashpoints model of public disorder: the 'Battle of Trafalgar'

Level of analysis	Evidence of predisposing factor
Structural	
Material inequalities/ inferior life chances	Widespread ideological alienation re poll tax; one section of society – youth 'underclass' – are disproportionately affected by government policies (see poll tax as vindictive and iniquitous)
Political powerlessness	Youth are poorly represented within conventional politics
Relationship to state	State seen as indifferent to young people's needs
Political/ ideological	
Marginality/ vilification	Poll tax protest vilified by government as 'hard left' conspiracy: Labour Party distances itself from active protest
Cultural	
Protesters	Different ages and social backgrounds, but some elements (e.g. anarchists) who see violence as appropriate form of expression or defence
Police	Occupational culture emphasises machismo and solidarity; regard anarchists and militant youth as their 'property'
Contextual	
Anticipation of disorder	Recent instances of anti-poll tax violence; anarchist spokespersons/literature advocate violence; police intelligence suggests possibility of attack on Downing Street
Liaison	Regular and sincere, but organisers under-estimate size of crowd and are not perceived as capable of controlling their members
Situational	
Police organisation	High-profile policing; confused lines of command; poor communication between police units; poor communication between police and demonstrators
Crowd organisation	Ineffectual stewarding arrangements

Table 1.1 (continued)

Level of analysis	Evidence of predisposing factor
Symbolic locations	Vulnerable, expensive city-centre property; key buildings (e.g. Ministry of Defence, 10 Downing Street)
Crowd objectives (actual or perceived)	Sections of crowd perceived as wanting to storm Downing Street
Police objectives	Deliberate provocation of sit-down protesters (by *agents provocateurs*) to pre-empt rush on Downing Street
Interactional Flashpoint	Uncompromising police clearance of sit-down protest in breach of negotiated agreement (breakdown of accommodation)
Escalation	Police tactics seen as heavy-handed and arbitrary; crowd reasserts right to demonstrate
Dominant crowd activity	Selective looting and attacks on persons and property: main targets are police, banks, expensive restaurants and cars (e.g. Porsches)
Dominant crowd emotions	Elation, liberation and satisfaction due to temporary acquisition of power and opportunity to turn tables

their 'mood' to the crowd. These cues are likely to affect the crowd's capacity or willingness to retreat; they may cause it to panic or engage in counter-aggression.

These observations provide piecemeal, though not yet conclusive, validation of the flashpoints model. Significantly absent from such analysis are any references to what we have defined as the key structural or political/ideological variables. The next chapter provides further evidence of the importance of these and the other factors highlighted by our model by reviewing earlier twentieth-century examples of political marches which brought violent disorder to the streets of central London.

One of the protests to be considered in close detail is the anti-Vietnam War march from Hyde Park to Trafalgar Square in October 1968. The international student unrest of this period enables us to make an illuminating cross-reference to a pair of American case studies, the Chicago and

Washington protest marches of 1968 and 1969, respectively, which are the centrepieces of the chapter. A comparative analysis of this contrasting pair, one peaceful, the other disorderly, will be used, alongside an encapsulated account of other examples of twentieth-century American political disorder, to demonstrate the cross-cultural validity of the flashpoints approach.

Chapter 2

Disorderly demonstrations

POLITICAL DISORDER IN LONDON: TWENTIETH-CENTURY EXAMPLES

The following historical review of political disorder on the streets of London over the last one hundred years will show how violence has tended to occur whenever protesters have been castigated as 'subversive', 'unpatriotic' or 'communistic'; when their activities were likely to prove embarrassing to the government, monarchy or 'national reputation'; or when the demonstration was technically illegal, occurring in defiance of a legal prohibition (cf. Bowes, 1966; Critchley, 1970). The first section of the chapter illustrates these general assertions by looking at five categories of protest: the suffragette marches around the First World War, the unemployed and fascist marches of the 1930s, the peace campaigns of the 1950s and early 1960s, and the anti-Vietnam War protests of the late 1960s.

The suffragette marches

One of the first major series of twentieth-century political disturbances to disrupt the central streets of London occurred in the pre-war period of 1910–14, which Dunning *et al.* (1987) nominate as one of the most disorderly eras of the century. As Critchley (1970) explains, this was closely linked to a political climate in which growing inflation and the slackening pace of political reform was causing some groups, like the trade unions and women suffragettes, to lose faith in the parliamentary process and become more strident in their demands. The sense of disquiet evoked by this transformation of attitude provoked a more autocratic style of state control, epitomised by the suppression of the women's suffragette movement.

Dunning and co-workers (1987:46) observe a significant contrast in the tolerant way in which the media, police and political figures reacted to the 'over-boisterous' violence associated with election hustings, compared with their attitude to the violence accompanying suffragette agitation. 'The use of violence by the suffragettes, unlike the violence which was used against them by hostile crowds, was not viewed simply as "over-enthusiastic" behaviour, but as something much more serious which was deserving of condemnation' (ibid.). Jeering, taunting and violence towards the women was reported with lighthearted understatement: the baiting of suffragettes was seen as a form of crowd amusement and the women's flight for their own safety regarded as comical. Yet retaliation by suffragettes was treated severely by the courts.

It was against this background that the suffragette marches in London took place in November 1910. On Friday, 18 November of that year, a deputation of marchers hoping to see the Prime Minister, Asquith, were charged by mounted police and plain-clothed officers as they approached Parliament Square. The suffragettes' own accounts tell of police officers brutally kicking them, and dragging them down side-streets and indecently assaulting them (cf. Raeburn, 1973).

For the most part, the press condemned what they described as the outrageous, communistic behaviour of the suffragettes, whilst gratefully applauding the restrained, 'ever courteous' behaviour of the police (Young, 1988: 282). On the following day, there was a similar clash outside 10 Downing Street in which 153 women were arrested. Again, the women were portrayed as a hysterical, demented mob; the police as patient and good-humoured in the face of deplorable provocation (ibid.).

As Young explains, advance justification for this suppression was achieved, not only by highlighting the subversive nature of the women's peculiar idealism and behaviour, but via a discourse revolving around a particular conception of womanhood:

> Once perceived as having left the sphere of perfect ladyhood, the women forfeited any chivalrous respect: it is in this light that the violence of 'Black Friday', the derogatory press reports, the insults and jeers, must be understood. For the police, the press and others, these were not 'good wives and mothers', but shocking, image-shattering inversions of an ideal.
>
> (Young, 1988:287)

A similar sustained process of denigration was applied more recently against women peace campaigners at Greenham Common (Johnson, 1989; Young, 1988), a contemporary example which we shall return to in Chapter 8.

The unemployment marches

Even more violent than the suffragette disorders were the clashes between police and hunger marchers in the early 1930s. Contrary to popular belief, the high levels of unemployment accompanying the economic slump of this period affected some regions more than others, and were outside the immediate experience of large areas of the country (Stevenson and Cook, 1979). The only organisation prepared to mount protests on behalf of the unemployed was the communist-dominated National Unemployed Workers' Movement (NUWM). The NUWM sought an end to the means test, an extension of work schemes, a restoration of cuts in wages and unemployment relief, and a reduction in council rents. They organised numerous marches for the jobless.

Peaceful though these marches were, they generated an obvious concern on the part of the authorities. The Labour Government of May 1929 to August 1931 maintained a policy of 'continuity' with the attitude of their Tory predecessors, involving the sanctioning of police repression against working-class organisations. Similarly, the right-wing dominated Trade Union Congress (TUC) was 'prepared to give more than tacit approval to police action against manifestations of working-class militancy and, not infrequently, to incite it' (Bowes, 1966:28).

By 1931, more than thirty different towns had witnessed clashes between the police and unemployed. In September 1932, there was rioting in Birkenhead when police broke up a demonstration by 8,000 outside the town's Public Assistance Committee office. Birkenhead Labour councillors denounced the rioters. It was in this climate of rising antipathy that the unemployed marches to London took place. On 19 October 1932, the Home Secretary stated that the NUWM, 'a Communist organisation, or in the main a Communist organisation, has been the root, and the instigator, of these difficulties' (quoted in Stevenson and Cook, 1979:173). Even as the minister was speaking, eighteen NUWM contingents were marching on London as part of the 'Great National Hunger March against the Means Test', their ultimate aim being to present a petition of one million signatures to the House of Commons.

The marches received little press publicity while making their way to London. 'Once they arrived in the capital, on the other hand, they met an almost blanket condemnation as a threat to public order, verging upon the hysterical in the case of some of the more conservative press' (ibid.:222). Information passed on to the police via NUWM informers and Special Branch infiltrators suggested that the organisers anticipated spectacular clashes, and were intent on using concealed weapons, if necessary, to counter any moves to prevent them from reaching Westminster.

From these and other signals, the police derived a very clear reading of their responsibility:

> Even if the intentions of the NUWM fell short of revolution, the police could hardly ignore the open exhortations of the movement for 'mass struggle on the streets', 'mass and stormy activity against the authorities', and the calls for 'day to day mass rallies, steadily mounting in force and intensity'. On the other hand, the Home Secretary's implicit acceptance of a tough line against the NUWM meant that little quarter was given by the police.
>
> (Stevenson and Cook, 1979:232)

When tens of thousands of marchers entered Hyde Park for a welcoming rally on 27 October, they were met by 5,000 police, many of them Special (volunteer) constables. The marchers were subjected to several police charges which caused fighting to spread onto the surrounding streets, as a result of which seventy-five people were reported injured. The Specials were involved again, 3 days later, when mounted police and officers on foot charged demonstrators in Trafalgar Square, making seventeen arrests.

On 1 November, the day the petition was due to be handed over, large numbers of police officers were out in force.

> Police cordons extended as far as Holborn and King's Cross. In Gray's Inn Road, Farringdon Road and Holborn, mounted and foot police charged marchers. Trams and buses were boarded and anyone who looked like a demonstrator was forcibly ejected. Flying-squad cars driven at high speeds scattered crowds in and around Parliament Square. At Charing Cross Station, police trapped the deputation which was to present the petition, seized the document, and by this flagrant inter-ference with civil liberties deliberately provoked fighting.
>
> (Bowes, 1966:31)

When word of the police action spread, there were confrontations throughout the city – in Parliament Square, Whitehall, Trafalgar Square, along the Embankment and on Westminster Bridge Road. The disturbance lasted way past midnight, by which time there had been over fifty arrests.

The fascist marches

In the mid-1930s, the British Union of Fascists (BUF) came to prominence under the leadership of Sir Oswald Mosley. The rise of British fascism was possibly due to the fact that 'many of the ingredients which were shortly to bring Hitler to power existed also in Britain. Here also there was mass unemployment and a paralysing economic depression; here also the middle class was insecure and looking for a saviour' (Branson and Heinemann, 1971:281). The scapegoating of the Jews as responsible for Britain's economic ills, and provocative marches through London's city centre and the East End by BUF members in full blackshirt uniform, led to clashes between the police and anti-fascist counter-demonstrators, including members of the NUWM, trade unions and Jewish organisations.

Some authors (cf. Bowes, 1966) argue that the police took a more lenient attitude towards the fascists – a reflection of their own ultra-conservatism. Stevenson and Cook take a different view of this relationship. They maintain that part of the reason for this police discrimination was that the fascists 'claimed to be a party of order, were disciplined, and usually co-operated fully with the police' (Stevenson and Cook, 1979:242). By contrast, the NUWM was demonstrably anti-police. Furthermore, 'The NUWM and the Communist Party were openly committed to a revolutionary creed and had connections with a foreign power. The BUF. could, until the rise of European fascism, be seen as less of a threat' (ibid.).

Peace campaigns

In the late 1950s and early 1960s, as middle-class concern grew over the deployment of nuclear weaponry, anti-war and nuclear-arms protesters were the victims of unprovoked police aggression. The first examples of this occurred in November 1956 when 30,000 people gathered in Trafalgar Square to protest against the British invasion of Suez. It was an orderly demonstration but, once it was over and the crowd started to stream through Whitehall, thirty or so mounted police officers charged, without warning, into the procession of men, women and children. According to the *Daily Herald* (5 November 1956),

> They formed a line across the road and rode stirrup to stirrup towards the crowd. Women screamed as they tried to retreat ... The police line kept moving on, determined not only to bar the entry to Downing Street, but to clear the whole of Whitehall. Men and women fell, trampled by the horses' hooves.

(quoted in Bowes, 1966:85)

On 'Battle of Britain Day', 17 September 1961, a demonstration was organised in Trafalgar Square by the Committee of 100, a splinter group from the Campaign for Nuclear Disarmament (CND), committed to non-violent civil disobedience. Twelve thousand people attended the demonstration in defiance of legal bans, Although the police made no attempt to prevent demonstrators from entering the square, it was not long before the first of a total of 1,314 arrests were made. In what seemed like a premeditated show of force, police officers dragged sit-down protesters by their arms, legs and clothing, depositing some into awaiting buses, dropping others into the icy-cold waters of the fountains (Bowes, 1966:88–95).

During the Hands Off Cuba rally in Trafalgar Square in October 1962, the police arrested 150 demonstrators. Many of these occurred when a sit-down protest was staged in Whitehall by people who had just been prevented from marching to Admiralty House. Many of the men, women and children present were dragged by the hair, kicked or punched in the process of being forcibly removed. Later, demonstrators who tried to march from Trafalgar Square to Grosvenor Square were driven into by police motorcyclists willing to mount pavements in quest of people to push, strike or kick (ibid.:95–6).

Almost a year later, in June 1963, the police dealt severely with demonstrators who defied a ban forbidding demonstrations over the assassination of a Greek peace campaigner, scheduled to coincide with a visit to Britain by Greek monarchs.

An important political factor was involved. News of planned demonstrations had caused a political crisis in Greece. The Greek Prime Minister, Mr. Karamanlis, who had wanted to call off the visit, had resigned when his view was not accepted by his Queen and King. Success of the visit had become of prime importance, both to the Greek Royalty and the British government who had invited them.

(Bowes, 1966:97)

The organisers of the march, the Committee of 100 and the Save Greece Now Committee, appealed for a non-violent protest, involving a march from Trafalgar Square to Buckingham Palace, where a silent vigil would be held. However, the police ignored the peaceful intentions of demonstrators to rigidly enforce the ban. Ninety-four arrests were made as the police 'employed brutality on a scale rarely exceeded in the post-war period' (ibid.:100). Even before the march reached Whitehall, participants were punched, kicked and randomly arrested. On reaching Whitehall, a section of the crowd sat down in the road and on adjoining pavements. Mounted police quickly moved in to discourage the squatters, arresting and injuring scores of them in the process.

The anti-Vietnam War marches

By the late 1960s, the focal point of political activism war America's was with the North Vietnamese. Here we concentrate on the activities involved in the largest of the British anti-war demonstrations, when 60,000 people marched from Charing Cross to Hyde Park on 27 October 1968. Previous demonstrations, organised by a group called the Vietnam Solidarity Campaign (VSC), had resulted in violence. In October 1967, for example, 5,000 people marched from Trafalgar Square to the US Embassy in Grosvenor Square, a police cordon was charged and missiles were thrown from the crowd. In March 1968, a similar march – though five times bigger – broke through police lines and 280 people were arrested (cf. Halloran *et al.*, 1970:73).

As part of their classic study of the 27 October march, Halloran and co-workers discuss whether the violence displayed at these earlier demonstrations reflected a growing disaffection from parliamentary politics and a corresponding preference for the violent expression of dissent. Their analysis is based on the premise that, by 1966, many radical British students and other political activists had become pessimistic about the prospect of political reform due to a gradual loss of faith in the Labour Party, which they had previously supported.

Above all, it was the socialist government's open support for America's bombing missions which caused an abandonment of constitutional methods in favour of 'extra parliamentary forms of direct action'. In September 1966, for example, demonstrators interrupted performances at several London theatres and addressed audiences from the stage; and, a month later, they heckled the Prime Minister, Harold Wilson, as he delivered the second lesson at the Labour Party's pre-conference church service in Brighton.

Demonstrators were now more likely than before to see disruption and non-co-operation with the police as legitimate tactics. Halloran and co-workers also speculate that, following the instances of police brutality on the peace demonstrations in the early 1960s, people were prepared collectively to resist arrest or defend themselves and others, where appropriate. They were less inclined, however, to embrace the direct confrontational approach advocated by the American academic, Herbert Marcuse, and adopted by some sections of the US anti-war movement.

Bugler (1968) noted that what distinguished the March 1968 protest from earlier CND protests was that 'The CND marches were highly organised, efficient and much staffed', designed to avoid interfering with people or traffic, whereas the VSC march was wilfully *dis*organised in order to create maximum disruption. A National Council for Civil Liberties (NCCL) report was equally critical of the police organisation: the seemingly arbitrary setting up of cordons prevented people from using certain exit routes and created unnecessary tension and frustration (Halloran *et al.*, 1970:72–3). However, the demonstrators' actions never regressed into unprovoked attacks on the police. Most violence was perpetrated 'either in self defence, or in order to avoid arrest' (ibid.:73).

The media focused in their build-up to the 27 October march on recent 'riots' which had occurred on similar marches in Paris and Chicago, and highlighted the potentially agitational role of French and American personalities who would undoubtedly be present (see Chapter 8 for further details). But, generally speaking, press and television exhorted demonstrators to avoid similar confrontations. The march organisers also eschewed violence, appealing in their pre-march publicity for a peaceful protest, and asking demonstrators not to go to Grosvenor Square.

The police attitude was also generally low-key: they raised no objections to the route and diverted traffic away from it.

> It is true that the police mostly behaved well: they seem to have learnt from the Grosvenor Square rally in March, when they infuriated the protestors by throwing cordons across the march. It is also true that the organisers of the demonstration mostly tried to keep things calm. (The loudspeaker constantly blared: 'Can we link arms; this will be a solid demonstration'; 'We can be proud of a demonstration in the best tradition of the labour movement.') But most important, I would suggest, was the spirit of the demonstrators themselves.
>
> (Barker *et al.*, 1968:633)

According to a study carried out by Barker and his colleagues, many of those present were seasoned demonstrators. Some 70 per cent of the crowd had demonstrated before. A high proportion of them were students, CND, and middle-class people with 'grammar school ideas of how to protest' (ibid.). Although many participants feared that violence might occur, most regarded it as detrimental to their interests.

Halloran and co-workers report that, as the march progressed, a particular 'tone' developed: 'as it soon became evident that neither the marchers nor the police intended to provoke a confrontation, the tension, so marked before the start, disappeared and was replaced by a general mood of good humour' (Halloran *et al.*, 1970:38).

A number of symbolic channels of protest were arranged on behalf of the marchers: a letter was delivered to the Prime Minister, Harold Wilson, signed by '70,000 socialists', a wreath laid and a bagpipe lament played for the Unknown Vietnamese. These gestures were followed by speeches by recognised leaders, after which there was an orderly withdrawal. Halloran and co-workers see these tactics as an indication 'that attempts to influence the policies of government through traditional channels of protest had not been completely abandoned' (ibid.:61).

There was practically no trouble on the main body of the march. Two subsections of protestors, mainly anarchists, broke away from the main march and went to the American Embassy at Grosvenor Square, where they tried (repeatedly and unsuccessfully) to break the police cordon. Only a small number of those who converged on the square were involved in this attempt (ibid.:45). The remainder stood and watched while the movement of traffic continued unhindered. At the end of the main march, police and demonstrators linked arms to sing 'Auld Lang Syne' (ibid.:46).

We can therefore point to several crucial cultural, contextual, situational and interactional variables as reasons for the overridingly peaceful nature of this protest. But perhaps the major reason why this march was characterised by less violence than any other protest so far considered in this chapter was that the police seemed determined not to let their attitudes be swayed by the vilificatory remarks levelled against the demonstrators, principally by the media.

On the following day, the *New York Times* drew an interesting comparison with events in the city of Chicago 2 months earlier, suggesting that: 'Americans who saw the Grosvenor Square events could not help drawing the contrast with the violence that erupted between the police and demonstrators at the Democratic Convention in August' (quoted in Skolnick, 1969:188). The violence of the Chicago protest, in which hundreds of participants were arrested, was, itself, in sharp contrast to the peaceful outcome of a similar protest in Washington, DC, in January 1969. The historical coincidence of these demonstrations, allied to their contrasting outcomes, makes them a natural basis of comparison. Before looking at our American examples in close detail, we briefly review the twentieth-century tradition of political violence in America preceding the period of student unrest.

TWENTIETH-CENTURY AMERICAN POLITICAL DISORDER

There have been two notable eras of political violence in America this century: the brief period of clashes between police and unemployed marchers in the early 1930s, and, of course, the violence accompanying the anti-Vietnam War protest.

Like their British counterparts, the marches by the American unemployed of the inter-war years of the depression were communist-organised. The earliest of these marches met variable responses from the authorities. This is illustrated by events on International Unemployment Day, 6 March 1930, when marches and rallies took place throughout the nation. In some major cities, like San Francisco, where the chief of police joined the march and the mayor sympathetically addressed a subsequent rally, peace prevailed. But in other cities, 'local officials grew alarmed and ordered police to disperse the crowds with tear gas. In Detroit, Cleveland, Milwaukee and Boston, the crowds resisted and fierce battles broke out between the demonstrators and the police' (Fox Piven and Cloward, 1977:50). The worst clashes took place in Detroit, where police ordered bus and street-car drivers to aim their vehicles at the crowds, and Milwaukee, where there was a 3-hour street battle. In each case, there were over forty arrests.

Some city authorities responded to the deprivation highlighted by these marches by forming committees to collect and distribute funds. Others were responsive to press scorn and castigation, and hardened their attitudes accordingly. When thousands of unemployed workers and their families marched on Washington in the spring of 1932 to request the early payment of their pension entitlements, Army tanks were ordered in to clear the streets (ibid.:52–3).

The anti-Vietnam War protest was 'a unique exception to the support which the American public habitually grants its leaders in matters of national security' (Skolnick, 1969:22). Brooks (1989:183) confirms that during the Korean War there was only 'one brief flash of opposition', when New York mounted police charged and badly beat up demonstrators in August 1950. As Skolnick explains, the Korean War broke suddenly, leaving the nation little time to reflect the relevant issues.

> The intellectual climate in 1950 was not conducive to detached thought concerning the war – there were hardly any Americans who questioned the Cold War policy of containment – except of course for those who favored 'rollback' and 'liberation' of Communist-occupied territories. The rise of Communist China abroad and of McCarthyism at home did not allow for the development of a respectable anti-war segment of opinion.
>
> (Skolnick, 1969:26)

By contrast, Vietnam was, to use Skolnick's term, 'A War With Time To Think'. As America's involvement intensified, there was growing evidence of the US government's mendacity and hypocrisy. Opponents of the war persistently argued that America's role was unconstitutional, in violation of the United Nations Charter and a series of separate treaties; they disputed the official 'body counts' of US and civilian casualties; and emphasised that conciliatory gestures by the North Vietnamese were being poorly publicised. In addition, President Johnson was voted into office with a landslide majority, largely by insisting that he was a 'candidate of peace'. Thus millions of Americans felt misled and betrayed by his decision to escalate the war.

College students were central to the expression of anti-war sentiment. According to Muncie, 1968 was the 'watershed year' when several radical student organisations became prominent in America.

> Their contemporary origins lay in the Free Speech Movement and campus protest at Berkeley, California, in September 1964, when the university authorities tried to ban all political activity on the campus. In the spring of 1965 the movement was fuelled by Lyndon Johnson's order for saturation bombing to start in North Vietnam. The three issues of American imperialism in Vietnam, black civil rights and educational control were at the centre of a spate of university sit-ins, marches and demonstrations of 1968 in which the strange agglomeration of black militants, students, drop-outs, draft dodgers, mystical hippies and women's liberationists seemed to be momentarily united.
>
> (Muncie, 1984:117)

Among the most visible of these were the 'Yippies' (Youth International Party), whose style of protest involved 'aesthetic rather than violent means, by mocking militarism, disturbing processions and interrupting court proceedings' (ibid.:118).

The two issues of Vietnam and alienation from campus authority were the most central components of the students' unrest. Such issues were more salient for them than civil rights matters because of the likelihood that they might be subjected to draft or conscription:

> From the beginning ... the war had been an on-campus reality by virtue of military and war-industry recruiters, the extensive cooperation of university institutes and departments with Pentagon-sponsored re-search, the tendency of universities to award honorary degrees to public officials who are also official spokesmen for the war, and of course the normal campus atmosphere of controversy and debate.
>
> (Skolnick, 1969:43)

Between 1965 and 1968, student and middle-class American opposition to the war intensified. In 1965, 20,000 people marched in Washington, and student activists blocked the paths of trains transporting American troops in Berkeley and Oakland. In October 1967, the first major *cause célèbre* took place when 100,000 protestors besieged Washington, scores of them being arrested and many beaten by local police.

This was only one of numerous protests to be violently suppressed by police officers. Stark (1972:22–3) sets out the details of a 'police riot' when a crowd of middle-class Los Angeles anti-war protesters gathered outside a hotel shortly to be visited by President Johnson were subjected to police attack. In forcing the demonstrators to move on, the police seemed intent on abusing or insulting every person in sight, turning on casual bystanders or passers-by and dragging innocent motorists from their cars. Stark argues that the police could justify their actions by seeing themselves as representing the 'silent majority', opposed to an unpatriotic, if more strident, minority.

> They seem to have felt that the march should not occur, and when they found that they had no choice but to permit it, essentially refused to condone it. Possibly they believed that the kinds of people they would be dealing with ought to be harassed for their affront to the president, to 'the boys over there', and to the civic reputation of Los Angeles.
>
> (Stark, 1972:31)

Intransigent government policy and police harassment helped escalate the forms of protest. On 23 April 1968, radical students led by the local Students for a Democratic Society chapter at Columbia University took a Dean hostage. Several university buildings were occupied and barricades drawn across. The students demanded the right to demonstrate inside the university, and insisted that the university detach itself from a research project which was assisting the war effort. The police eventually forced an entry and, in arresting the occupants, provoked further conflict on campus. In all, 692 people were arrested.

One upshot of this activity was that, by 1968, a small minority of student leaders had come to believe that violence was the only viable alternative to futile peaceful protest. It was against this growing radicalism that the Chicago demonstration at the Democratic National Convention of April 1968 and the protest at the Presidential inauguration in Washington in January 1969 each took place.

As Campbell and co-workers (1969:343) explain, the two demonstrations were organised and attended by the same group of radicals – representatives of the National Mobilization Committee to End the War in Vietnam (MOBE) – and their supporters. Both demonstrations were similar in size and focus, but one was peaceful and the other violent. Thus the protests can almost be regarded as field experiments in why disorder does or does not occur at mass demonstrations.

In Chicago, the police were accused by an official report of unleashing 'unrestrained and indiscriminate' violence against protesters and media personnel (Walker, 1968:xv); whereas in Washington, events were generally good-natured and the violence more sporadic. Based on official, government-sponsored reports, the 'Rights in Conflict' report on Chicago (ibid.), and the 'Rights in Concord' report on Washington (Sahid, 1969), we now examine the characteristics of each demonstration to establish the reasons for this contrast.

The Democratic National Convention demonstration, Chicago, 1968

The sinister motives which the authorities attributed to the thousands of protestors who were eventually to descend upon the city of Chicago was one of the main contributory factors to the disorder which occurred at the Democratic National Convention. Police intelligence agents reported that demonstration organisers had urged their followers to risk arrest, and even 'shed blood', if necessary. The slogan of the day exhorted 'War on the Streets' until there was peace in Vietnam. The list of malicious rumours was unending.

> Reports came in from all directions stating that the protestors would block the expressways, dose the city's water with LSD, storm the Amphitheater, set fires, vandalize buildings, invade the Loop hotels, jam key city streets, and pour into Loop department stores.
>
> (Farber, 1988:162)

MOBE was said to be training 2,500 marshals for a likely confrontation with the police; incendiary devices and *agents provocateurs* would be deployed to stir up incidents in the black ghetto; prostitutes would be used to discredit delegates; and there were plans to assassinate the Presidential candidates and the Mayor of Chicago, Richard Daley.

Such reports framed city officials' perceptions of the demonstrators and validated their eventual decision not to grant a permit for marches and rallies during convention week.

> Those who were convinced that Daley would ultimately give way on the permits had not calculated, however, on the mayor's loathing for young white radicals. They were outsiders, not constituents, and he offered them no courtesies. They were ingrates, punks, parasites. They

offended his sense of morality, they did not fight according to the rules, they publicly ridiculed him. Privately he shared their objections to the war, and had told Lyndon Johnson as much. But he would not let a bunch of brats create havoc within the Democratic party or the city of Chicago, institutions he loved.

(Viorst, 1979:450)

In addition, the organisers of the protest seemed confused about their objectives and there was a strong feeling that they 'would not be able to control their followers'. Hence city officials made it clear that 'the "law" would be enforced' (Walker, 1968:2).

Police attitudes were hardened by the general atmosphere and Daley's public criticism of their allegedly soft approach to policing the riots which followed the assassination of Dr Martin Luther King, Jnr in April (see Chapter 3). Thus when, during a 27 April peace march to the Civic Center in Chicago, some marchers broke through a restraining rope, 'The police officers on the scene then made it clear that they had heard the message the Mayor had given them after the King riots' (Farber, 1988:151). They used chemical Mace and clubs to scatter the crowd. Some police covered their identification numbers, whilst others confiscated cameras as a safe-guard against accusations of brutality (ibid.:152). Then,

Shortly before the convention, the rank and file were cheered by strong backing from the Mayor. Openly and loudly he came out foursquare against an [American Civil Liberties Union] ACLU-sponsored report that criticized police handling of the April 27 peace march. The Mayor blasted the report as 'not true' and announced that he was 'just sort of amazed (at) the constant efforts of these people (peace marchers) to confront the police department'.

(Farber, 1988:163)

Chicago itself was fertile ground for Daley's sentiments. It:

was not a city with a natural tolerance for nonconformists. Its huge white working class, only a generation away from Europe, extolled religion and hard work. Its blacks, however disaffected in their ghettos, saw hippies and radicals as just spoiled, overprivileged white kids. Its police, never seriously inhibited by libertarian niceties, dreamed of reprisals against the ne'er-do-wells who had the nerve to call them pigs. Only a few liberals, concerned about civil liberties and the war, worried about Daley's intentions, and their influence in the city was negligible.

(Viorst, 1979:450)

The police prepared themselves for violence. In the run-up to the convention, the city's 12,000-strong police force was placed on 12-hour shifts. Three hundred of them were armed with helmets, revolvers and shotguns. Six thousand Army troops and 5,000 National Guardsmen were placed on emergency standby, having rehearsed military manoeuvres.

The protest organisers and city authorities failed to liaise effectively. Roger Wilkins, head of the US Justice Department's Community Relations service, met with MOBE's Rennie Davis at the latter's request. Both parties agreed that continued liaison would be beneficial, but Mayor Daley rejected any outside involvement (Farber, 1988:156–7). The authorities thus remained ignorant of the organisers' intentions. On a practical level,

> Refusal to grant a permit meant that for most of the time they were present, the demonstrators would have no focal point to their activity. Random groups were thus forced to remain random. This complicated the police function greatly. Rather than being able to focus their surveillance on limited numbers of mass gatherings, they were forced to spread themselves thinly over a large geographical area without the ability to recognize leaders with whom they could communicate in the event of an emergency.
>
> (Campbell *et al.*, 1969:347)

The demonstrators and police were therefore polarised. The lack of a permit increased the demonstrators' determination to uphold their rights of dissent, but only increased the police's perception that the protest was unwelcome and illegitimate (ibid.:348). Many would-be protesters were deterred from attending by the absence of a permit. This was exactly what the authorities wanted but, as Campbell and co-workers point out, 'the plan backfired, for many members of the more staid and responsible groups were the ones who were thus intimidated. This meant that fewer responsible people were present to restrain their less rational (sic) compatriots when the escalation began to take place' (ibid.).

In such an atmosphere of latent hostility and an unwillingness to compromise, both protesters and police reacted angrily to what they saw as provocation by each other. There was a predictable escalation of violence. There were three major violent incidents. The first of these occurred when the police tried to enforce a curfew on the late-night occupation of Lincoln Park, where many protesters had gathered prior to the convention, intending to sleep out for the night. Trouble started when displaced protesters caused traffic jams by pouring onto the roads. Chants went up of 'The streets belong to the people!' and stones were hurled as the police moved into their midst.

But it was the police who forced them out of the park and into the neighborhood. And on the part of the police there was enough wild club swinging, enough cries of hatred, enough gratuitous beating to make the conclusion inescapable that individual policemen, and lots of them, committed violent acts far in excess of the requisite force for crowd dispersal or arrest. To read dispassionately the hundreds of statements describing at firsthand the events of Sunday and Monday nights is to become convinced of the presence of what can only be called a police riot.

(Walker, 1968:4–5)

A second violent incident occurred close to a band shell in the Grant Park area of the city where MOBE had been granted a permit to stage a rally (but not to march on the Amphitheatre where the convention was being staged). By 3 p.m., 10,000 to 15,000 people were gathered around the bandshell, many of them having already heard speeches exhorting them to march illegally. The protesters were surrounded on three sides by police officers and the National Guard. Half an hour later, a teenage boy who climbed a flagpole was quickly arrested by police who believed he intended to desecrate the flag. As they beat him, they were pelted with rocks, concrete and bags of urine. The police retaliated by attacking several demonstrators, including a well-known organiser.

Subsequently, hundreds of protesters ignored police warnings that it was illegal to head off towards the convention. The National Guard fired tear gas into the demonstrators, and soon the order was given for police officers to act.

Policemen came at the tightly packed crowd from all sides. Some officers attacked people watching from the sidewalks. Others pursued fleeing demonstrators for blocks. One of the first groups of police reinforcements, furious over reports of injured comrades, stormed off their bus chanting, 'Kill! Kill! Kill!' A police lieutenant sprayed Mace indiscriminately at a crowd watching the street battle. Policemen pushed a small group of bystanders and peaceful protestors through a large plate glass window and then attacked the bleeding and dazed victims as they lay among the glass shards. Policemen on three-wheeled motorcycles, one of them screaming, 'Wahoo!' ran people over. A group of officers cheered and protected a soldier (a deserter, as it turned out) as he beat up a white-coated Mobe medic; and when a photographer took pictures of the event the police beat him up.

(Farber, 1988:200)

On the following day, there were several attempted marches on the amphitheatre, all of which were put down by the police. Hundreds of people were gassed by the police, and similar numbers arrested. The total number of arrests during convention week was 668.

The counter-inaugural protest, Washington, DC, 1969

The second, largely peaceful demonstration in Washington was held in protest against Richard Nixon's Presidential inauguration ceremonies and festivities, in the US capital, Washington, DC, between 18 and 20 January 1969. Four violent incidents took place but, unlike many other demonstrations of this period, no tear gas or Mace was used. There were 119 arrests, most of them in street skirmishes occurring on the last day. However, contrary to expectations, there was no major riot of the magnitude of the Chicago showdown (Sahid, 1969).

The momentum for the march was provided when an MOBE Steering Committee met in Washington, DC, on 14 September 1968. Representatives of Students for a Democratic Society (SDS) and over one hundred other groups covering the 'entire spectrum of MOBE's membership' took part in the meeting (ibid.:79). A decision to mount a protest against the Vietnam War was consensually accepted, but MOBE officials emphasised their commitment to a peaceful protest. The chairperson placed a positive accent on a 'political, not a physical confrontation', to indicate to the President Elect the extent of America's opposition to the war. He warned that 'To get into a street fight with the police is simply to focus on the wrong issue' (ibid.). The organisers none the less emphasised that the peacefulness of the demonstration was contingent on the authorities recognising their legal right to stage a protest. It was their stated intention to converge on Washington regardless of whether a permit was officially sanctioned.

Intelligence provided by the Federal Bureau of Investigation (FBI), based on the monitoring of anti-war groups, suggested a potential for violence: MOBE militants were reported as saying there would be Chicago-type confrontations with police. However, Washington officials preferred to heed their own prognosis that, while disruption might occur, there was no serious evidence of a threat. Some Congressional members registered their opposition to the granting of a permit. A resident of Maryland tried, but failed, to obtain an injunction against granting permit. However,

Beginning with the negotiations for the permit, officials tried to deal in good faith with the spokesmen for the dissenting groups. Compromise and patience were the watchwords. Determined to grant full expression to Constitutional guarantees of freedom of speech and peaceable assembly, they acted to insure that unreasonable requests were not made of the demonstrators. Once reasonable rules were established, they insisted that the rules be obeyed.

(Sahid, 1969:115)

Organisers and officials operated according to a principle of give and take. Government authorities agreed to the use of Pennsylvania Avenue as a route for the march, even though it was a direct route through the seat of government. In return, the organisers agreed to pitch a tent (to host a 'Counter-Inaugural Ball' on 19 January and provide a focal point for speeches) at a location nominated by government officials.

This had an instantly beneficial effect. Once the permit negotiations were known to be progressing well, several of the more 'staid' anti-war groups enlisted their support: 'Their numbers did much to restore a more moderate balance to the roll of demonstrators that had been disrupted in Chicago, where the recalcitrance of city officials had discouraged many members of these more responsible groups from participating' (ibid.:85). The National Co-ordinator for MOBE expressed the sentiment that 'we have here the kind of cooperation we did not have in Chicago. For this reason I do not expect the physical confrontations and riots we had in Chicago' (ibid.).

Recent events played an important part in the authorities' calculations. There was a widespread belief that anti-war feeling had 'undergone a catharsis' in the wake of Chicago, and the controversy surrounding the events at the Democratic National Convention served as a clear warning to Washington authorities not to risk discrediting the city in a similar way.

The chief responsibility for the policing of the march lay with the Civil Disturbance Unit (comprising 340 full-time men, and a further 150 who were temporarily assigned). Several weeks before the event, this unit received special classes 'to acquaint them with the types of provocation they might encounter and to caution against overreaction'. On the eve of the inauguration, they were further cautioned 'not to use excessive force, to maintain their dignity, and to conduct themselves with restraint' (ibid.:90).

On the morning of 19 January, 10,000 marchers assembled by the specially erected tent, before marching on the counter-inaugural parade. Participants proceeded in an orderly fashion until some confusion occurred at a five-cornered intersection, causing some protesters to move off in an unauthorised direction. The Deputy Chief of Police feared that this was the prelude to serious disruption and ordered his men to move the crowd forward. A number of sticks and rocks were thrown out of resentment, and the police made fifteen arrests. However, the situation was defused when marshals intervened and persuaded the demonstrators to continue along the prescribed route.

Another skirmish occurred at the HEW building where protesters disagreed among themselves over whether to lower a US flag to half-mast in protest at American foreign policy. The marshals successfully intervened again, and the official report praises the police readiness at this point to avoid interfering or appearing to take sides.

Later in the afternoon, 5,000 demonstrators unexpectedly descended on the lightly guarded Smithsonian Building. As presidential guests started to arrive, there was some shouting and throwing of missiles. Most guests seemed unperturbed by this until a women panicked when a firecracker exploded near her arm. At this point, police made a number of arrests and started to clear the area.

> Those in the crowd sensed that the police could not tolerate the actions of the few people who were throwing objects and were therefore required to disperse the crowd from the area. The mood seemed to be that this was a necessary and legitimate action taken by the police.
>
> (Sahid, 1969:100)

A second, more aggressive attempt to move the demonstrators back involved one police officer swinging his baton wildly, and another losing control of his horse. Generally, though, the report congratulates the police on their overall attitude and emphasises that they carried the sympathy of the crowd. One measure of their commitment to a low-key approach was that eighty police officers who were parked up in squad cars one block away were never called upon.

Later that evening, the protesters were granted a permit to line the route of the presidential motorcade. However, the police grew concerned by rumours that SDS chapels were gathering sticks and bats to hurl at the President's car, and female demonstrators were reported to be piling stones into their bags and pockets.

The crowd assembled at the widest spot on Pennsylvania Avenue. As a precautionary measure, CDUs were placed directly in front of them. However, aside from arrests related to the odd instance of flag burning or occasional missile-throwing, little trouble occurred. Indeed, the crowd seemed generally unwilling to become involved in scuffles with police officers (as on the occasion when a sergeant moved in to enforce arrest).

This was also true of the authorities: a police officer who lost his hat in a mild scuffle was dissuaded from trying to retrieve it by a representative of the Mayor's office and subsequently removed from the front line.

Just before the presidential motorcade was due to pass by, units of the Regular Army 82nd Airborne were introduced to deter any attempted breaches of police lines. At this point, a police captain let the situation get the better of him, scuffling with demonstrators and a MOBE attorney who had tried to restrain his behaviour. He, also, was withdrawn in favour of a substitute commander.

The president's car was struck by a rock, but there was no attempt to break through the police lines; nor was there a riot, Afterwards, however, demonstrators began to disperse haphazardly. Fearing a possible convergence on the White House, the police moved in swiftly, with sirens wailing, and order broke down. All available police and National Guard units were brought in. Very soon, the police operation became disorganised and, as instructions became progressively more ambiguous, there were some local incidents of unrestrained and indiscriminate beatings. Calm was restored when MOBE officials impressed on city officials that the majority of demonstrators were preparing to leave. After discussions with the Deputy Mayor, the Assistant Chief of Police instructed all officers to return to normal duties and the disorder abated.

In the final analysis, there were few injuries to police or demonstrators. The Task Force report that the majority of arrests resulted from 'street skirmishes' or pedestrian violations. In its view, the Washington police and city officials:

> succeeded in allowing a full spectrum of constitutional freedoms to be exercised. At the same time they controlled the few potential trouble-makers in the crowd without antagonizing and radicalizing the bulk of the demonstrators who did not engage in disruptive forms of protest.
>
> (Sahid, 1969:129)

Table 2.1 sets out the distinctive characteristics of the Chicago and Washington demonstrations. It can be seen at a glance that variations in the political and communication contexts encouraged highly contrasting policing responses. The contrast is neatly encapsulated by the comments of a MOBE official quoted by Campbell and co-workers.

> The difference between Chicago and Washington was a permit and a tent. The police react as the officials react. In Washington the officials

Table 2.1 A comparative profile of the Chicago and Washington demonstrations

Level of analysis	Evidence of predisposing factor	
	Chicago	Washington
Structural		
Ideological alienation (Vietnam War)	Yes	Yes
Political/ideological		
Protesters marginalised (government = unresponsive)	Yes	Yes
Political delegitimation	Yes	Ambiguous
Ideological vilification	Yes	Yes
Opposition from local community	Yes	Ambiguous
Permit refused	Yes	No
Cultural		
(a) Police		
Special units	Yes	Yes
Outsiders	Mainly	Few
Tough reputation	Yes	No
(b) Protesters		
Militants present (e.g. SDS, Yippies)	Yes	Yes
Moderates discouraged from attending	Yes	No
Contextual		
(a) Police		
Prepared for/anticipating disorder	Yes	No
Saw organisers as incapable of controlling members	Yes	No
Took rumours of planned atrocities seriously	Yes	No
(b) Protesters		
Disunity re objectives	Yes	No
Organisers advocate violence	Yes	No
(c) Both sides		
Lack of liaison/co-operation	Yes	No
Situational		
(a) Police		
High profile	Yes	No
Unclear lines of command	Yes	No
Poor communication with crowd	Yes	No
(b) Protesters		
Absence of focal point	Yes	No
Absence of stewards	Yes	No
Absence of moderates	Yes	No
Interactional		
(a) Police		
Heavy-handed	Yes	No
Indiscriminate aggression	Yes	No
Intolerant of symbolic dissent	Yes	No
Unwilling to negotiate improvised remedies	Yes	No
Unwilling to restrain officers	Yes	No
(b) Protesters		
Rude and offensive	Yes	No
Unwilling to obey instructions	Yes	No
Unwilling to restrain other demonstrators	Yes	No
Ready to retaliate	Yes	No

reacted well and the police reacted well. As a result, the demonstrators acted well towards the police and the officials.

(Campbell *et al.*, 1969:351)

There is clearly a two-way interaction between variables at the political and contextual levels. For example, opposition by Chicago authorities was reinforced by perceptions that MOBE officials were disunited in their objectives (some openly advocated violence) and incapable of guaranteeing the peaceable behaviour of their followers. This affected their decision not to grant a permit which, in turn, influenced the attitudes of the police and discouraged moderate protesters from attending.

Ironically, the clashes in Chicago were one factor which persuaded the Washington authorities to adopt a conciliatory approach. MOBE leaders were also more agreed about the tactical need to avoid violence, and publicly declared their commitment to a peaceful demonstration. Thus there was reciprocal co-operation and negotiation on both sides. This contrast with Chicago was reflected in the differing crowd management arrangements at the two demonstrations and, resulting from this, in the sharply discrepant quality of police–citizen interaction characterising the two marches.

DISCUSSION

The comparative case study of the Chicago and Washington demonstrations provides further proof of the flashpoints model's capacity to explain orderly or disorderly episodes of political protest. This comparison was featured, partly because the pair of examples are so well-documented, and partly because, despite their basic similarities the two demonstrations were so contrasting in their outcomes. Lack of space and access to detailed information has prevented a similar, in-depth analysis of other cases. However, even a relatively cursory review of other British and American examples provides strong support for the model.

The sequence of historical examples highlights the significance of conjunctural factors. Without obvious exception, they show how the police tactics towards demonstrators are most commonly informed by the attitudes of national and local political elites. Skolnick goes so far as to maintain that, 'when police are encouraged by public officials to regard free assembly as subversive, they do not need provocation to attack even innocent bystanders' (Skolnick, 1969:47). The suffragettes, the unemployed, the anti-fascists and student peace campaigners referred to in this chapter would undoubtedly endorse this statement.

The way that the police choose to supervise or intervene in demonstrations appears to be the most crucial determinant of the outcome. As Bowes explains,

The post-1829 history of political movements shows clearly that when the police co-operate, or at least do not interfere with political demonstrations, these remain almost without exception disciplined and peaceful; but when the police seek to enforce bans, discipline is often violently destroyed and sometimes police violence is returned in kind.

(Bowes, 1966:77)

The contrasting outcomes of demonstrations in London, in March and October 1968, and in Chicago and Washington, in April 1968 and January 1969, respectively, show that where the police hold the preservation of public order as their uppermost priority, public disorder is likely to be avoided. The police's ability to create and maintain a 'contract with the crowd' (something which they achieved in London and Washington) is the key to ensuring non-violent political protest.

Chapter 3

The American urban riots

The next two chapters focus on arguably the most destructive forms of public disorder seen in Britain and America this century. The present chapter examines the American ghetto riots of the 1960s, while Chapter 4 deals with the British inner-city riots of the 1980s. The American riots were much larger in scale than their British counterparts – not surprisingly, given the unequal sizes of their ethnic minority populations. Nevertheless, important similarities have been acknowledged between them (Benyon and Solomos, 1987; Field and Southgate, 1982), and the reasons why they occurred are to be found at the six levels of analysis referred to in Chapter 1.

The historical patterns of rioting in Britain and America this century have been roughly comparable. The migratory movements of ethnic minorities in both countries help to explain why there have been two distinct phases in their respective histories: an earlier period dominated by inter-racial clashes between whites and ethnic minorities; and a subsequent, contemporary period characterised by confrontations between ethnic minorities and the agents of social control (Janowitz, 1969; Joshua *et al.*, 1983).

Rioting tends to involve the most deprived and discriminated against sections of society. This is why black people (easily the most dispossessed social groups in Britain and America) have been over-represented in the major urban disorders of this century. By focusing on the summer riots of 1919 (in Chapter 4) and the recent disorders of 1991 (in Chapter 10), both of which involved mainly white participants, we shall see how it is not the 'race' of urban rioters, but their location in the social structure which contributes to our understanding of their behaviour.

This chapter and the next are similar in structure. The present chapter begins with an overview of the twentieth-century pattern of rioting in America. The analysis of this pattern commences with a brief discussion of the migratory movements of relevant sections of the American population.

Particular attention is devoted to explaining the Watts (Los Angeles) disorder of 1965, seen as an 'ideal type' contemporary American riot. The next chapter comprises a similar approach to the British disorders, concentrating especially on the Brixton (London) disorders of 1981. In addition to these central case studies, each chapter contains a general analysis of other major recent riots. The final section of Chapter 4 summarises the similarities and differences between the American and British disorders, and uses the events of 1919 as the basis of a general discussion of urban rioting.

The choice of the Watts and Brixton riots as exemplary case studies is not purely arbitrary. Their selection is justified according to the following criteria:

1 they each occurred after other disorders originally viewed as isolated incidents;
2 each riot was followed by a series of similar riots in other parts of the country;
3 they each involved destruction, looting and disorder not witnessed in their societies for several generations, and were described as landmark or watershed events in their countries' race relations; and finally,
4 each riot was the subject of a major official inquiry into its underlying causes (McCone, 1965; Scarman, 1981).

With that justification, we now begin our analysis of the riots by examining the historical pattern of American disorders from 1900 to the present.

AN OVERVIEW OF TWENTIETH-CENTURY AMERICAN URBAN RIOTS

Two contrasting forms of racial violence have occurred in twentieth-century America. Some American academics have distinguished between them as 'commodity' and 'communal' riots (Janowitz, 1969). Communal riots are defined as struggles over contested areas of territory between black and white residents. The major examples of these occurred in East St Louis, Chicago and Washington, DC, between 1915 and 1919, and in Harlem and Detroit in the 1940s. By contrast, commodity riots are defined as involving the destruction and looting by black residents of property owned by white merchants and traders, located in the ghettos. Such riots seldom involved aggression towards white people *per se*, though they tended to be precipitated by the actions of white police officers in the context of tense police–black relations. Examples of this type of rioting occurred in Harlem in 1935 and 1943, but most notably of all in the period between 1964 and

1968 when there were some 500 such riots across the USA (Button, 1989:298) in which nearly 250 people died (Gurr, 1989b:109).

Some riots during and since the sixties do not slot simply into these categories. In April 1968, for example, the nation was struck by a wave of riots precipitated, not by a police–black encounter, but by the political assassination of the black civil rights leader, Dr Martin Luther King, Jnr. A subsequent riot, in Miami in 1980, was sparked off by the acquittal of four police officers accused of killing a black motorist. The riot was 'preceded by an unusually long succession of alleged police abuses and failures of the criminal justice system' (Horowitz, 1983:208). Unusually for post-war American riots, there were direct attacks (some fatal) on white and Hispanic citizens.

Since 1980, American disorders have, with one exception, been more typical of commodity riots. Between 1980 and 1989, there were four other major riots in Miami, and a small series of riots, between February and May 1987, in nearby Tampa. Each of these was triggered by the fatal shooting of a black person by an Anglo or Hispanic police officer. The Washington, DC, riot of May 1991 was also of this type, although the main protagonists were police officers (many of them black) and a section of the city's Hispanic population. The most recent riot of all – in the Crown Heights area of Brooklyn, New York, in August 1991 – was a latterday example of a community riot, though this time it involved a confrontation between blacks and Hasidic Jews.

It is impossible to explain the changing character of American racial relations without taking note of the underlying pattern of migration which has occurred during the twentieth century. The next section reveals this changing character.

Patterns of migration

At the turn of this century, 91 per cent of the 9.8 million American negroes lived in the south (Kerner, 1968:116). Significant northward migration first began around 1910, stimulated by 'the push of deprivation and the pull of opportunity'. A key factor was the decline of the cotton industry, accelerated by the development of synthetic fibres, flood and crop devastation by an epidemic of boll weevils. This coincided with the imposition of restrictions on white immigration into the USA which left thousands of vacancies in low-paid, unskilled jobs in the north.

The demand for labour during the First World War further encouraged the northward migration of blacks, a trend which continued into the relatively prosperous 1920s. The migration slowed temporarily in the

1930s as a consequence of the depression, but was reinvigorated by the demand created by the Second World War. After the war, blacks were displaced from the south rather than attracted to the north. The mechanisation of cotton and corn and the general expansion of soybean farming, which uses little labour, meant that the use of agricultural labour fell by 72 per cent between 1949 and 1952.

The growth of the automobile industry and the Korean War meant that some, though by no means all, of the displaced labour was absorbed. However, blacks came under increasing competition from white migrants (e.g. Appalachian miners who had been made redundant due to the mechanisation of the mines) and found themselves handicapped by their poor education and a lack of relevant skills (Fusfield, 1973). Another economic factor added to the growing unemployment and poverty levels of black Americans in the 1950s and early 1960s. Prior to 1933, northern employers had taken advantage of black people's lack of economic power to encourage their role as substitute labour in disputes with recalcitrant white workers. According to Bonacich (1976:43), the growth of formal and informal organisations opposed to black migration and their exclusion from 'white only' trade unions meant that 'black workers had no alternative but to turn to strike-breaking as the only means of entering white-dominated lines of work'.

The National Industrial Recovery Act 1933 stymied strikebreaking in many categories of dispute, and outlawed the sweatshops and cheap labour practices which had enabled employers to use black labour to undercut the wages of white workers. The rising labour costs of the 1950s, which indirectly resulted from this legislative change, gave American capitalists three possible strategies:

> First, they could relocate part of the industrial process overseas to make use of cheaper foreign labor. Second, they could relocate internally to those sectors of the economy where organized labor and/or protection had not yet penetrated. And third, they could mechanize, displacing jobs which had previously been performed by 'cheap labor.' These processes all had a negative effect on black employment.
>
> (Bonacich, 1976:47)

The overall effect of these migratory and economic trends was that, between 1910 and 1966, the number of black people living outside the south increased eleven-fold, from 900,000 to almost 10 million. The number of blacks living in cities as opposed to rural areas was up 500 per cent, from 2.7 million to 14.8 million (Kerner, 1968:116). Low wages, high unemployment, discriminatory housing policies and the support offered to new migrants by established communities tended to concentrate the black populations in the older, more dilapidated urban areas.

Simultaneously, there occurred the reverse migration of white, middle-class families moving out of these areas. New factories were built outside of the black residential areas, creating 'lily white' suburbs. The urban tax base withered with the absence of middle-class whites and a preponderance of low-income blacks. Welfare, health and public services, including education, were seriously depleted, just when most needed.

Just as these migratory and demographic trends are fundamental to our understanding of urban riots involving black Americans, so recent disturbances in Miami and Washington among Hispanic communities relate to their migratory experiences over the last 30 years. Miami is a special case: the influx of successive waves of refugees fleeing the Cuban revolution in 1959 led to the 'Latinisation' of large tracts of the city, with blacks and Hispanics competing for housing and employment (Ladner et al., 1981). Nationally, 9 million immigrants entered the USA between 1960 and 1980 at the rate of 450,000 to 600,000 per year, two-thirds of whom were from Asia or Latin America. It is estimated that Hispanic people comprise 33 per cent of the nation's legal and 72 per cent of its illegal immigrants (Massey, 1985; Massey and Denton, 1987).

Though Hispanic immigrants tend, at least initially, to settle in particular enclaves, they are apt to be less concentrated in the city areas than black people and show less segregation from white society. They are more socially mobile and there is a tendency for second-generation immigrants to become more spatially and culturally assimilated (Massey and Denton, 1988), though black Hispanics tend to remain segregated and confined to inner-city areas (Darden, 1989).

The American disorders of the 1990s reflect local migratory patterns. The Washington, DC, riot of March 1991, involved a particular area of the city populated by recently arrived and as yet poorly assimilated Salvadoreans who fled the civil war in the mid-1980s. Such people were badly affected by immigration laws which displaced them from their jobs and led, as will become apparent, to confrontations with the police (The Economist, 11 May 1991). The Hasidic Jews who engaged in clashes with blacks in Brooklyn in May 1991 were members of the Lubavicher sect who settled in the Crown Heights area in the 1940s and 1950s, having escaped from the threat of fascism (cf. The Guardian, 23 August 1991).

With this understanding of how migratory patterns have affected the ethnic structure of American society at different points of this century, we are now in a position to see why different types of rioting were synonymous with particular historical periods. We begin by looking at the community riots of 1900–43.

Community riots (1900–43)

Community riots were a feature of American racial relations from the start of the century to the Second World War. Most occurred between 1915 and 1919 when there were twenty-two major riots involving white aggressors and black victims. These chiefly resulted from perceived challenges to the status quo (in terms of jobs, housing and political power) accompanying large migration. The 1917 East St Louis riot was the bloodiest riot of the twentieth century. Blacks were waylaid and beaten by white gangs angered by the use of black migrants as strikebreakers. The rioting was sparked when a trade-union delegation leaving a meeting at which they had appealed to the mayor to stop the immigration of blacks heard that a negro had accidentally shot a white person during a hold-up. Whites burned houses and shot the blacks as they fled. Thirty-nine people were killed and hundreds injured (Wade, 1978).

Two years later, there were major riots in Washington, DC, and Chicago. In Washington, hundreds of sailors rampaged throughout the black southwest district of the city to avenge an insult to a sailor's wife. In Chicago, where the number of blacks had risen from 44,000 to over 100,000 since 1910, putting a severe strain on housing and recreational facilities, blacks complained about their exclusion from a white-only beach. A black teenager was drowned in the latest of a series of similar assaults. A police officer refused to arrest the white man held responsible and chose, instead, to arrest the black complainants. The blacks attacked the arresting police officers, provoking a massive white backlash (ibid.).

A similar development took place in Detroit in 1943, where rioting was responsible for the deaths of nine whites and twenty-five Negroes. As in Chicago, there had been a large increase in the black population. Contested spaces, like recreational areas, became the scene of flashpoints. The precipitating incident for the riot was an attack on whites by Negro teenagers who had been ejected from the Belle Isle Amusement Park a few days earlier. Amidst the mounting tension, a rumour emerged in the ghetto that a bunch of whites had killed a black woman and her baby at Belle Isle. This provoked the stoning of passing cars driven by whites and the smashing and looting of white-owned businesses in the main street (ibid.).

The riots of this period had several distinctive features. They tended to occur in highly charged environments, stoked up by media scare-mongering:

The classic example was the Washington DC fray of mid-July 1919 when the *Washington Post*, with its vastly exaggerated tales of Negro rapists, played a major role in provoking the disturbance. The press of East St. Louis is supposed to have played a similar role in provoking the riots that occurred in that city in the same month.

(Paletz and Dunn, 1969:239)

Paletz and Dunn also refer to the findings of the Chicago Commission on Race Relations (1922) that blacks and whites throughout the country blamed the media for making inter-racial relations more difficult, 'fostering new antagonism and enmities and even precipitating riots by inflaming the public against Negroes' (ibid.).

Against a background of intense competition for jobs and housing, actual or rumoured atrocities in contested areas of the city acted as the precipitant for inter-ethnic rioting (Lieberson and Silverman, 1965). Further antagonism was sometimes aroused via press allegations of Negro brutality (e.g. the beating of a helpless Caucasian child). These invariably provoked acts of white vigilantism: 'Symbolically, the riot was an expression of the white community's impulse to 'kick the Negro back into his place' (Janowitz, 1969:320). Even where rioting continued for several days, newspaper editorials were slow to press for legal intervention, while police officers were themselves 'deficient in their duties and occasionally assisted the white rioters' (ibid.).

A key difference between the pre- and post-First World War riots was that the latter involved greater retaliation by black citizens. Meier and Rudwick attribute this difference to two related factors: changes in black people's perception of the situation and in their capacity to organise:

> The agitation of the recently founded NAACP [National Association for the Advancement of Coloured People], whose membership doubled in 1918–19, the propaganda of fighting a war to make the world safe for democracy, and especially the great Negro migration to the Northern cities which Southern peasants and workers viewed as a promised land, all created new hopes for the fulfillment of age-old dreams, while Negro soldiers who had served in France returned with new expectations. But the Negro's new hopes collided with increasing white hostility... In the northern cities like East St. Louis and Chicago, Negroes found not a promised land, but overcrowded ghettos and hostile white workers who feared Negro competition for their jobs.

(Meier and Rudwick, 1969:312–13)

Prior to this period, blacks subscribed to a 'sentiment of accommodation to white superiority' (ibid.:313). This was temporarily displaced by the determination to fight back. But, once overpowered by the superior might of white society, blacks reverted to their previous attitude. A second upsurge of black militancy, around the Second World War, may have influenced the Detroit riot. None the less, this was 'a period in which the expectations of the masses did not quickly outrun the actual improvements being made' (ibid.:314). It would be two more decades before the level of discontent was high enough to spill over into violence.

Commodity riots (1935–68)

The Harlem riots of 1935 and 1943 were exceptional for their period, being 'spontaneous, unorganized and precipitated by police actions' (Fogelson, 1971:19). The former was sparked off by false rumours that a black youth caught shoplifting in a department store had been killed; the latter when a black woman was arrested for disorderly conduct in a Harlem hotel, and a black soldier who intervened on her behalf was shot by a policeman, prompting false rumours of his death.

Fogelson speculates that one reason why these riots prefigured the later riots was that Harlem 'matured' as a black ghetto some 20 years earlier than those of other American cities. Social problems were apparent in Harlem long before they surfaced in other ghetto areas. By the 1960s, most American northern black ghettos were 'a full generation old, about as old as Harlem was in the 1930s and 1940s' (ibid.:22). The time was ripe for confrontation. Once again, Harlem was the location of the first major riot.

On 16 July 1964, a black youngster was shot dead by a police officer in Harlem. Two days later, police dispersed a crowd which was demonstrating against police brutality. That evening, rioting erupted. As in the previous Harlem riots, whites were assaulted and neighbourhood stores looted and burned. Order was restored on 21 July, but not before rioting had engulfed Brooklyn's vast Bedford-Stuyvesant ghetto. By this time, one person was dead, over 100 injured, 500 arrested and millions of dollars' worth of property devastated.

The next major riot, the Watts riot of 1965, was easily the country's worst racial disorder since 1917:

So vast, so awesome, so devastating and so widely reported were the Los Angeles riots – for a full week they received front-page coverage nationally and internationally – that henceforth there could be no doubt that a distinct pattern of summer violence was emerging in the black ghettos.

(Fogelson, 1971: 3)

Watts heralded the start of a 3-year pattern. According to one estimate, there were no fewer than 1,893 disturbances of varying sizes in America in the 1960s (Porter and Dunn, 1984:175). The three most serious of these were the Watts riot itself, in which thirty-five people died, the Newark riot of July 1967, which involved twenty-three deaths, and the Detroit riot of the same month, in which forty-three were killed. We shall briefly return to the Newark and Detroit riots in a later section. In the meantime, we concentrate on the Watts riot of 1965, an ideal type from this period.

THE WATTS RIOT

The following account of the riot begins with an overview of the main sequence of activities, based largely on the descriptions provided by Cohen (1970), Fogelson (1971), McCone (1965), Oberschall (1971) Sears and McConahay (1973) and Viorst (1979). The riot is then analysed, in terms of the six levels of the flashpoints model (Waddington *et al.*, 1989).

An overview of Watts

The incident which acted as the immediate precipitant, or 'flashpoint', of the Watts riot of 11 to 17 August 1965 was the arrest of a 21-year-old black man called Marquette Frye. Frye was out driving with his brother in their mother's car, when they were stopped by a Californian Highway Patrol officer for failing to observe a red light. The officer conducted a series of sobriety tests before deciding to arrest Frye for speeding and drunk driving. This exchange remained good-humoured, despite the presence of a small crowd of observers.

Several more officers eventually arrived, one of them driving a tow-truck. Soon, they were joined by Frye's mother, who lived nearby and had recently heard of the incident. Frye suddenly grew more belligerent and provoked a confrontation in which he and the other two members of his family were forcibly subdued: one police officer batoned Frye's brother in the stomach and ribs and hit Frye on the head. Though angered by this spectacle, onlookers were initially responsive to the officers' attempts to disperse them. However, just as the prisoners were being led away, a police officer felt someone spit on him. He and several colleagues entered the crowd to seize the miscreant.

They dragged a young woman in a barber's smock, which resembled a maternity dress, from the crowd and threw her into a police car. Upon seeing this, the crowd became an outraged mob. Someone threw a bottle at the departing police vehicles and then a stream of rocks, bottles, bricks and other missiles burst from the mob. The Watts riot had begun.

(Sears and McConahay, 1973:5)

This relatively minor incident developed into 6 days of the worst rioting in America's history. The police's first reaction to the disorder was to withdraw from the area in order to avoid any further provocation. For the remainder of the evening, the police held off, allowing angry Watts residents to throw stones, rocks and bottles at police officers and passing motorists. There was no evidence of arson or looting at this stage.

On the following afternoon, the police implemented a special contingency arrangement for dealing with outbreaks of this nature, returning to the area in a calculated show of force. A large crowd occupying this part of town resisted this strategy. Looting began and, soon afterwards, 'a large portion of Los Angeles was in flames and thousands of people were in open revolt against the agents of law and order' (ibid.:6).

Rioting spread across a 46-square-mile section of the city. A curfew zone was established which people were prevented from leaving or entering. Once it became evident that the local police were incapable of containing the rioting, the National Guard was brought in. This marked a new phase in the confrontation, characterised by shooting on both sides. By Tuesday, 17 August, the riot had been quelled, but it left a bitter legacy. Thirty-four people were killed during the hostilities and a further 1,032 treated for injuries. Nearly all of these were blacks. No fewer than 3,952 people were arrested and 1,000 buildings looted, damaged or destroyed.

Explaining the Watts riot

The 6-day Watts riot may be usefully explored in terms of the six levels of analysis comprising the flashpoints model of public disorder, commencing with the structural level.

The black population of Watts increased around the two World Wars. During the First World War, many blacks moved north to occupy jobs in the war industries. In the Second World War, blacks migrated from the south to fill jobs in the automobile and shipbuilding industries.

Watts and the entire South Central Area became the port-of-entry for this new multi-problem population, partly because of low-cost public housing in the area and partly because deed restrictions and social and job discrimination made it difficult for Negroes to settle in other sections of the County. As Negroes moved in, there was a steady exodus of the white population to the suburbs and the Mexican-Americans gradually resettled in other sections of the City ... Between 1940 and 1960 there was an eightfold increase in the Negro population of Watts. By 1965, the community had become a full-fledged ghetto, with Negroes comprising 87 per cent of the total 34,000 residents.

(Cohen, 1970:43)

Living conditions within the Watts ghetto were lamentable. Surveys like those undertaken by the McCone Commission, or as part of the 1965 Special Census, documented that Watts 'was a deprived area, high on all the indicators of depressed social conditions – unemployment, poor housing, inadequate transportation, poor medical and social services, and so forth' (Rossi, 1971:410).

Another significant characteristic of the South Central community was its lack of political power. Cohen (1970:76) remarks upon the: 'Growing frustration and sense of hopelessness within the community; it lacked an organizational structure through which the growing protest could be channelled within the Negro community. It lacked access to the community establishment which could redress the grievances.'

Factors at the political/ideological level were clearly relevant here. Black communities like Watts were politically disadvantaged and unable to register their grievances, much less remedy them. In addition, peaceful black protesters found themselves kicking against a locked door of political unresponsiveness and media apathy or denigration and were soon forced to resort to other, more disruptive means of expressing their grievances (Monti, 1964:65).

Indifference by white society was compounded by the white-dominated media. The local press rendered their culture and interests 'invisible' for several years leading up to the riot (Johnson et al., 1971). In any case, the equally white-dominated local polity was reluctant to make any concessions which might ruffle the sensibilities of white supporters growing anxious at the rate of black progress (McAdam and Moore, 1989). Though the surrounding white population displayed few signs of overt racism, there was widespread evidence of 'symbolic racism' on their part (Sears and McConahay, 1973). Symbolic racism:

represents a form of resistance to change in the racial status quo based on moral feelings that blacks violate such traditional American values as individualism and self-reliance, the work ethic, obedience and discipline. Whites may feel that people should be rewarded on their merits, which in turn should be based on hard work and diligent service. Hence symbolic racism should find its most vociferous expression on political issues that involve 'unfair' government assistance to blacks.

(Kinder and Sears, 1981:416)

These attitudes were reflected in the political institutions of the Watts area: 250 black protest demonstrations in South Central Los Angeles in the 2 years preceding the Watts riot yielded no political response (Horowitz, 1983:197). On the contrary, there was an increasing trend for the police and local political elite to denigrate and confront such political activity, especially as it became more disruptive of community life (ibid.).

This growing sense of political marginalisation lessened customary restraints on violence, as indicated by Ransford's findings on the attitudes of working-class Watts ghetto residents shortly after the riot:

These Negroes have lost faith in the leaders and institutions of the community and presumably have little hope for improvement through organized protest. For them, violence is a means of communicating with white society; anger can be expressed, control exerted – if only for a brief period.

(Ransford, 1968:591)

Political and ideological processes can also affect the way the law is enforced. American police policies seem to reflect the preferences of prominent local politicians, notably the mayor (Rossi et al., 1974:179–84). This has important implications, not only for the way the police respond to political protests or outbreaks of public disorder, but also for the quality of their day-to-day interactions with culturally dissenting sections of society. The Los Angeles Police Department's (LAPD) policy in Watts prior to the riot was based on 'standard institutional procedures' favoured by the Police Chief (Parker) and the mayor (Yorty) and endorsed by the wider 'old Angelenos' community. This highly bureaucratised method of policing allowed little room for the use of police discretion and made no concessions to the contrasting values, attitudes and norms of behaviour embodied in the ghetto subculture (Sears and McConahay, 1973).

As several authors (e.g. Hannerz, 1974; St Claire Drake, 1969) point out, black ghettos contain vibrant, street-based societies. They have their own distinctive atmosphere in which 'gambling, excessive drinking, the use of narcotics and sexual promiscuity are prevalent forms of behaviour, and violent interpersonal relations reflect an ethos of suspicion and resentment'. The Watts ghetto was no different: 'It was a high crime area, tortured by violence, prostitution, drugs, petty gambling' (Viorst, 1979:314).

Cohen (1970:64) maintains that: 'The police make no attempt to gain an understanding of the forces of poverty and discrimination which are feeding the problem.' Cultural responses to poverty and discrimination collide with the crude, and often racist, typifications used by police officers to make their role more manageable. Such devices are often counter-productive: as one LAPD officer admitted to the McCone Commission, most police 'cannot differentiate between ordinary blacks and black criminals; to them few blacks are worthy of respect and even fewer are free of suspicion' (quoted in Fogelson, 1971:64).

Prior to Chief Parker's arrival, police–community relations had settled into a pattern of accommodation. However, the chief's earliest reforms involved taking foot patrol officers off the beat, putting them in cars, and insisting on standard operating procedures for dealing with all clients, thus breaking the fragile 'contract with the community'.

> In a matter of months police lost the special knowledge and contacts with neighborhoods which alone makes law enforcement bearable, especially in lower-class neighborhoods. When police enforced the law strictly and without exception, it was violating previous practices that had become part of the social structure, and hence caused hostility and resentment. These, in turn, led to resistance to arrests, with local groups helping the victim evade arrest, which in turn led the police to intensify its law-enforcement practices in this 'lawless' community.
>
> (Oberschall, 1971:90)

Sears and McConahay (1973:44) further hypothesise that recent changes in the way the 'New Urban Blacks' were socialised, compared with their southern rural counterparts, help to explain their greater readiness to engage in confronting the police. The childhood socialisation of the New Urban Blacks emphasised 'equality, basic democratic rights and trust of the political system' (ibid.). Northern blacks were allowed more freedom to 'express hostility against whites, particularly against whites in positions of power and authority' than black people in the south (ibid.:44–5). Thus,

> Blacks were more conscious of their deprivations – indeed, deprivation had a whole new meaning for them; they were dissatisfied with conditions that their fathers and grandfathers would have found tolerable (or at any rate inevitable). The blacks were also less concerned about

social constraints, more militant and aggressive, at the least impatient
and, when frustrated time and time again, dangerously desperate.

(Fogelson, 1971:23)

Not surprisingly, it was the younger ghetto blacks, aged between 15
and 24, who were most active in the Watts and other American riots. It
was their 'political consciousness' and black pride which marked them off
from the non-rioters (Field and Southgate, 1982). Thus we can identify a
confluence of ideas involving the growing cultural assertiveness of black
people and the realisation that justice was unobtainable via conventional
democratic channels. By the time of the Watts riot, young blacks were
'already gravitating towards the ideology which would be called Black
Power' (Viorst, 1979:323). The role model was not Martin Luther King,
but Malcolm X, whose speeches resonated most powerfully among the
ranks of the disaffected: 'Malcolm had gone beyond justifying outrage, as
other civil rights leaders had done, to sanctioning conflict. "I remember
people out there during the Watts riot," (one participant) said, "crying
'Long live Malcolm X' " (ibid.). By the summer of 1965, cultural and
political developments had ensured that some sort of backlash was high on
the agenda: 'submission among blacks had gone out of style' (ibid.:321).

This lack of accommodation helped foster a communications context
with a high potential for disorder. Police–community relations in Watts
had steadily deteriorated just before the riot:

> The Los Angeles cops read Parker's message to mean that, within the
> wide limits of professionalism, they were free to conduct themselves as
> they chose. To Watts, this meant that a policeman could, with impunity,
> vent whatever racist animosities suited his fancy, and Watts replied with
> an equal degree of hate. The result was warfare, normally low-level, but
> unrelenting, between citizens and police on the ghetto streets.
>
> (Viorst, 1979:314–15)

The events of August 1965 conformed to the general pattern noted by
the Kerner Commission (Kerner, 1968) whereby riots tended to be
preceded by a series of smaller incidents which gradually contributed to
the growing atmosphere of tension and frustration. As Viorst explains, 'In
Watts itself, several tense encounters over the previous two or three years
between police and small crowds would, in retrospect, have to be classified
as near misses' (Viorst, 1979:310–11).

Rumour transmission surrounding the rough handling of the pregnant
woman further ensured that the moral indignation over the Frye arrest was
soon widely shared:

Word spread quickly through the community that police had brutalized a pregnant black woman. She was not pregnant, as it turned out, but the hundreds who were now standing around grumbled that the police would never have treated a white woman like that.

(Viorst, 1979:331)

As Oberschall (1971) points out, it is because this perception of the police behaviour was consistent with their expectations that black people did not question its validity.

Once the initial stage of the riot was under way, advance planning and preparation by the police came into effect, albeit counter-productively. The police contingency plan demanding that officers 'display their superior strength by returning in force' (Sears and McConahay, 1973:6) had the inadvertent effect of escalating the disorder.

Certain characteristics of the situation in which the precipitating incident occurred also encouraged the likelihood of disorder. The car that Marquette Frye was driving was stopped by the highway patrol officer on the busy corner of 116th and Avalon, right in the heart of the Watts ghetto, and, as Oberschall (1971:91) explains, 'The evening this occurred was one of the hottest so far of the summer; a lot of people were simply hanging about on the sidewalks outside their homes.' Further, the Watts residents were:

> communicating their hatred of policemen, firemen and other representatives of white society who operate in the black community 'like an army of occupation'. They were asserting a claim to territoriality, making an unorganized and rather inchoate attempt to gain control over their community, their 'turf'.
>
> (Blauner, 1973:253)

We know that, at the interactional level, flashpoints often signal a breakdown or lack of accommodation, especially if 'intensifiers' are also present. The rough treatment of the Frye brothers and, in particular, the arrest of the 'pregnant' woman both come into this category. The latter is an example, *par excellence*, of what we mean by an intensifier for, as Oberschall emphasises, 'such action is one of the clearest violations of a basic norm of human conduct and arouses everywhere condemnation and revulsion' (Oberschall, 1971:92).

There were several points in the riot when 'pacifiers' may have been used to placate the rioters. On the second day, the Los Angeles police were presented with an ideal opportunity to make a negotiated withdrawal. The Los Angeles County Human Relations Commissioner, John Buggs, worked out an agreement with youth gang leaders and other community representatives that, if they were willing to spread rumours that the riot was over and urge participants to 'cool it', the police would withdraw from the ghetto. When Buggs outlined this agreement, the Deputy Chief of Police 'berated him for dealing with criminals, telling him that the police knew how to put down a riot and that the police department would demonstrate who ran the town' (Sears and McConahay, 1973:6). This refusal to countenance anything less than a surrender had disastrous consequences for the city.

Active rioters in the Watts community appeared to experience intense feelings of elation, cameraderie and pride.

> The riot was a collective celebration in the manner of a carnival, during which about forty liquor stores were broken into and much liquor consumed. It was also a collective contest similar to that between two high school or college athletic teams ... Both sides in this tragic and deadly contest had a high emotional stake in the outcome. While the riot was put down eventually, many Negroes saw it as a victory for their side and derived a sense of pride and accomplishment from this public demonstration of their collective power.
>
> (Oberschall, 1971:98–9)

The sense of exhilaration stemming from participation in the riot cannot be separated from meanings residing at earlier levels of analysis, principally the political/ideological. The riot was a 'singularly successful attempt at communication ... This time white society did pay attention (even if many of its leaders did nothing but denounce the rioters and suppress the rioting)' (Fogelson, 1970:146).

According to Oberschall, 'There is considerable evidence that the (Watts) rioters observed certain *bounds*, that they directed their aggression at *specific* targets, and that they selected *appropriate means* for the ends they intended to obtain' (1971:95, emphasis in original).

White motorists were occasionally dragged from their cars and assaulted, but none were actually beaten to death. Los Angeles police officers were the principal targets of black aggression while National Guardsmen were not. Property was selectively targeted: private houses and civic buildings (post offices, churches, schools and libraries) were spared, though white business establishments were systematically destroyed. Firemen were prevented from extinguishing blazing business premises in one minute, and then beseeched to put out a fire to a home which had accidentally caught fire in the next (ibid.). These forms of interaction are also explicable in terms of variables residing at the structural, political/ideological and contextual levels of analysis. The main factors affecting the outbreak of disorder at Watts are summarised in Table 3.1.

OTHER CONTEMPORARY AMERICAN URBAN RIOTS

Oberschall points out that the Watts riot was the prototype for other American riots.

> It is the magnitude of the Los Angeles riot, both in duration, participation, amount of damage and casualties, and the forces needed to control it, which led many to characterize it as more than just a riot. But aside from magnitude, (it) was structurally and behaviourally similar to the Negro riots in other cities during the summers of 1964, 1965 and 1966.
> (Oberschall, 1971:100)

This statement equally applies to later disorders, too, like the major Newark and Detroit riots of July 1967. Both of these riots occurred in sprawling black neighbourhoods blighted by deprivation and decay. Local residents were severely under-represented in local political institutions and incensed by media double standards in highlighting crimes perpetrated by black people while suppressing news of those committed against them.

The flashpoint for the Newark riot of 12 July 1967 was the arrest of a black taxi driver and the resulting attack on a police station (Kerner, 1968:30–8). However, the precipitant was merely one of a catalogue of such incidents, including the shooting of an 18-year-old black youth, which had produced a deterioration in police–community relations. Eleven days later, the Detroit riot broke out (ibid.:47–61). It was triggered by an early morning police raid on an after-hours drinking and gambling club called a 'blind pig'. The club had been subjected to earlier police raids, resulting in a total of thirty-eight arrests. Black patrons regarded the latest raid, which interrupted a party being held in honour of two servicemen home from Vietnam, as especially over-zealous. As the last of eighty-two prisoners was being led away, a local youth threw a bottle at a police car, touching off the riot. As in the Newark example, the incident occurred in the context of tense relations between Detroit's blacks and local police.

Not every American riot since 1964 has followed a similar dynamic to Watts, Newark and Detroit. Whilst it is indisputable that the majority of American riots were sparked off by routine confrontations between black people and police officers, others were instigated in the absence of any triggering incident. The wave of rioting which followed the assassination of Martin Luther King, Jnr in April 1968 fits this paradigm. These riots were the result of moral outrage and despair. Of the 200 riots which flared

Table 3.1 A profile of the Watts riot

Level of analysis	Evidence of predisposing factor
Structural	
Material inequality/ inferior life chances	Relative deprivation re whites; racial discrimination
Political powerlessness	Poor political representation; poor organisation
Relationship to state	State viewed as unresponsive, unsympathetic
Political/ ideological Marginality/ vilification	Conventional forms of violence ignored and vilified; Civil Rights movement viewed as ineffectual; black 'invisibility' in press; evidence of anxiety and symbolic racism among whites; black disaffection and acceptance of Black Power ideology
Police policy	Traditionally bureaucratic form of policing strengthened by white concern/symbolic racism
Cultural Contrasting notions of 'rights'	Conflict between ghetto subculture (gambling, drugs) and police law-enforcement orientation; New Urban Blacks less deferential than southern blacks ('fully paid-up citizens')
Accommodation	Breakdown of accommodation due to new police regime
Norms of behaviour	Police/blacks share emphasis on machismo and solidarity
Contextual Police–community relations	Deteriorating relations; spate of incidents over previous 2 years
Rumour/expectation of conflict	Rumours re arrest of 'pregnant' woman; police contingency planning for riot
Situational Critical mass	Popular meeting place: corner of 116th and Avalon
Symbolic territory	Symbolic turf to be defended (by blacks)/seized (by police)

Table 3.1 (continued)

Level of analysis	Evidence of predisposing factor
Interactional	
Flashpoint/ intensifiers	Arrest of motorist; arrest of 'pregnant' woman
Negotiation/ escalation	Police refusal to negotiate withdrawal with co-operation of street gangs
Dominant activities	Selective, purposive, limited attacks/arson/looting
Dominant emotions	Feelings of release, celebration and pride

up across the nation, the one in Washington, DC, was the most serious. Twelve people were killed, 7,600 people were arrested, and 1,200 buildings were affected by property damage estimated at $12 million (Gurr, 1989b:109).

The Miami riot of 1980 had superficial similarities with the 1960s riots.

As in the 1960s riots, there was a great deal of looting and property destruction, some $100m. of it. But, in addition, there were brutal killings: three young whites dragged from a car and stomped to death, a Cuban man pulled from a car and mutilated, an elderly Cuban burned alive. In all, eighteen people died. The Miami riot had elements of both the 1960s riots and the anti-black riots of the earlier part of the century, except that the ethnic identity of the victims was reversed.

(Horowitz, 1983:207)

The riot was provoked by the acquittal of five white police officers widely held responsible by the black community for the manslaughter of a black insurance officer. Two factors helped transform the incident into a riot. First, the killing of the black man was the most recent of a series of police transgressions against local blacks (Porter and Dunn, 1984:xiii–xiv). Second, Cuban immigrants were increasingly usurping the economic standing of Miami's black population and aggravating the competition for jobs, houses and welfare amenities. Given the advantage of skin colour and ability to speak Spanish in a popular tourist region, Cuban refugees were leapfrogging black residents in the chase for unskilled jobs. A massive influx of 125,000 Cubans just before the police acquittal heightened anti-Cuban resentment and was a major ingredient in the riot (Ladner *et al.*, 1981).

Subsequent riots in south Florida between 1980 and 1989 were more representative of the commodity riots of the 1960s, but reflected antagonism between local black and Hispanic communities. The Miami riot of January 1989 is typical of this series. Three nights of rioting broke out when a black motorcyclist was shot dead by a Hispanic patrolman. 'Black leaders blamed the violence on outrage over police tactics, neglect of the black community's problems by the Cuban-dominated power structure and a belief that new waves of Hispanic immigrants were receiving preferential treatment in jobs and housing' (*The Guardian*, 20 January 1989).

The Washington, DC, riot of 1991 was precipitated when a black policewoman shot a young Hispanic male in the chest as he pulled a knife on her while resisting arrest for being drunk and disorderly. This was the prelude to 2 nights of rioting in a small sector of Washington called Mount Pleasant which resulted in the burning of nineteen police cars and a bus, the looting and/or burning of some thirty shops and restaurants and eighty arrests.

Central to the explanation of this riot is the plight of the Salvadorean refugees who populated the Mount Pleasant area. In May 1988, new legislation was passed which penalised employers for taking on illegal immigrants, but which provided an amnesty for anyone employed before 1982. Since most Salvadoreans had arrived after this date, many of them were forced out of jobs in the construction and tertiary sectors. There may be a link here between the resulting unemployment and a tendency to hang around on the streets which provoked complaints of drunkenness and anti-social behaviour.

> At the same time, Mount Pleasant was being yuppified and the new arrivals put pressure on the police to 'clean up' the area. Already driven from newly fashionable Adams-Morgan (just down the road) by yuppification, the Hispanics began to feel they were being pushed from Mount Pleasant too. The shooting lit the fuse.
>
> (*The Economist*, 11 May 1991:44)

The inter-ethnic clashes between blacks and Hasidic Jews during the Brooklyn riot of August 1991 were a throwback to the first half of the century. During 3 nights of rioting, blacks threw stones and bottles at Jewish people and property, and engaged in running battles with police. In the later stages of the confrontation hundreds of blacks and Jews threw similar missiles at each other as riot police endeavoured to keep them apart. Some of the most serious clashes occurred in front of the Lubavitcher sect's headquarters on Eastern Parkway, one of Crown Heights' major through roads (cf. *The Times*, 23 August 1991).

The trigger for the riot was an incident in which a car from a motorcade accompanying a Chief Rabbi suddenly mounted a kerb, killing a 7-year-old black boy. A rumour quickly spread that a Hasidic-owned ambulance which arrived on the scene only administered aid to the car driver and his passengers, leaving the boy and his injured cousin to wait for a city ambulance. Afterwards, a visiting Australian rabbinacal student was stabbed to death, apparently in reprisal.

Blacks saw the subsequent police decision not to arrest the driver as symptomatic of the preferential treatment given to the Jews by local police and politicians. There had been a long history of tension between the 30,000-strong Hasidic community and the surrounding black population of 250,000, primarily concerning the allocation of housing and over-stretched emergency services. Just prior to the disorder, the head of the African–American department at New York's City College had accused Jews and the Mafia of devising 'a system of destruction of black people' (*The Independent*, 23 August 1991). There was speculation that such comments may have contributed to growing resentment among blacks.

DISCUSSION

There have been two dominant phases of rioting in America this century: an early period (from 1900 to 1943) of inter-ethnic conflict between whites and blacks, involving competition over employment and housing opportunities; and a later period (from the mid- to late 1960s) involving confrontations between black people and the agents of social control, against a background of grievances over police practices and relative deprivation.

Despite obvious dissimilarities, the two phases have important things in common:

> In both periods retaliatory violence accompanied a heightened militancy among American Negroes – a militancy described as the 'New Negro' in the years after World War I, and described in the sixties with the phrase, 'the Negro Revolt.' In neither case was retaliatory violence the major tactic, or the central thrust, but in both periods it was a significant subordinate theme. However, in both periods a major factor leading Negroes to advocate or adopt such a tactic was the gap between Negro aspirations and objective status.
>
> (Meier and Rudwick, 1969:312)

In the earlier period, it was agitation by the National Association for the Advancement of Colored People – which advocated retaliatory violence – and the thwarted expectations of black migrants and returning servicemen which heightened black resentment. In the 1960s, it was the lack of social reform following the civil rights protests which created a similar sense of grievance.

Other important similarities are also revealed by the above analysis. For example, the precipitating incidents (the flashpoints) which sparked the riots tended to involve encounters between representatives of rival groups (blacks versus white citizens or police in the earlier phase, and police–black incidents in the 1960s) which somehow went 'beyond the pale' of acceptable behaviour. Such incidents were apt to occur on 'symbolic' or contested cultural space, and within an atmosphere of worsening inter-group relations. Mutual antagonism was exacerbated by media indifference towards, or denigration of, black people and their political objectives, and by the opposing sentiments of the more powerful white society. Our analysis of the ideal-type Watts riot of 1965 emphasises the value of the flashpoints model as a coherent analytic framework.

The post-1960s riots have been sporadic and more varied than those of previous eras, confounding the straightforward distinction between communal and commodity riots. However, they, too, reflect the apparently helpless plight of ethnic minorities (whether Florida's or New York's blacks, or Washington's Salvadoreans) who feel that their social opportunities have been blocked or their quality of life is diminishing relative to other sections of society. These fears – allied to indignant perceptions that rival groups hold unfair cultural advantages or receive preferential treatment from the legal or political authorities – contribute to highly combustible feelings of resentment which may only require the spark of a single flashpoint to transform them into a riot.

Chapter 4

The British urban riots

AN OVERVIEW OF TWENTIETH-CENTURY BRITISH URBAN RIOTS

The history of twentieth-century urban rioting in Britain also occupies two distinct phases: a period, from 1900 to 1962, where violence was inter-racial in form, corresponding to Janowitz's (1969) community riots; and a period, lasting from the 1970s to the present day, where violence has taken the form of confrontations between black youths and the police, approximating to Janowitz's commodity riots. As with the American disorders, it is impossible to fully understand the British riots without first considering twentieth-century patterns of migration.

Patterns of immigration

At the turn of the twentieth century, Britain's black population consisted mainly of colonial seafarers. A population growth had taken place around 1880, involving West Indians, Arabs, Somalis, Indians and Chinese, responding to capital's need for cheap, exploitable labour prepared to occupy undesirable jobs aboard steamships which were shunned by whites, or embark upon long journeys aboard tramp steamers which white employees were not prepared to make (Joshua *et al.*, 1983). However, the inferior rates of pay afforded to colonial seafarers, their ostracism by white society and segregationist policies by the local polity created immigrant colonies in the poorer housing areas of major British seaports (e.g. London, Cardiff, South Shields, Liverpool and Glasgow).

Further impetus was given to colonial immigration by the two World Wars, when many West Indian and Indian troops decided to settle in Britain after serving in the nation's armed forces. By 1945, there were 10,000 blacks in Britain. In the next few years, there was a sustained surge in immigration. Full employment, economic expansion and improved living standards led to active encouragement by prospective employers of New Commonwealth immigrant workers. Coincidentally, the passing of the McCarren Walter Act in the USA limited migration by West Indians to America to only 800 per annum, increasing the incentive to migrate to Britain. The prospect of a 'new life' overseas was potentially more satisfying than the one presently being experienced by many residents of the West Indies and Indian sub-continent, where unemployment and miserable poverty were endemic (Fryer, 1984:373).

Thus attracted to Britain, New Commonwealth citizens started to occupy jobs in those sectors of industry which were rejected by white workers (e.g. health, transport, textiles, clothing and foundry work), and in newer industries (e.g. motor-car manufacture and chemical processing) where the jobs were considered monotonous and soul-destroying. Thus immigrants settled in the industrial heartlands and growth areas, like the South East, the major conurbations of the Midlands, Yorkshire and Greater Manchester, or ports like Liverpool, Bristol and Glasgow.

The first significant group of post-war immigrants were the West Indians, followed by people from the Asian sub-continent (firstly male 'pioneers', then their dependants and extended kinship networks). Later, there were the displaced Kenyan and Ugandan Asians, who tended, on the whole, to be better educated and more prosperous than their predecessors.

Discrimination in the housing and employment markets segregated immigrant families into the poorer housing areas, where large Victorian houses were multi-occupied. In many of the large cities of Britain, quasi-ghettos were formed, resembling – albeit on a smaller scale – the American black neighbourhoods.

Inter-racial clashes (1900–62)

These immigration trends help to explain the twentieth-century pattern of rioting, which is now summarised in close detail. One of the most famous of the early disorders was the 1911 anti-Chinese riot in Cardiff, South Wales during a General Strike by the National Seamen and Firemen's Union. The owners threatened to use non-union Chinese labour to break the strike. Whites were hostile, disapproving of relationships between Chinese men and white women. Rumours were deliberately spread by the trade union that the Chinese were doping white children and using them as unpaid labour. Tensions rose and spilled over into conflict. Members of the Chinese community were assaulted and their laundries set ablaze.

Sexual relationships between white women and black men were also a central theme in the British seaport riots of 1919. White describes how:

> First in Limehouse, then in Liverpool, Newport, Cardiff, Tyneside and Glasgow; then in east London again (Poplar and Canning Town), black sailors were attacked by large crowds. The whites' grievances were said to centre round fears of blacks taking work and consorting with white women. The black sailors' lodging houses were besieged, stormed and emptied of furniture, which was then burnt in street bonfires.
>
> (White, 1982:13)

The media and police responded unsympathetically, accusing the blacks of bringing the violence on themselves (Fryer, 1984:310). The police arrested more blacks than whites, supposedly for 'their own safety'.

Few race riots occurred in the 1920s and 1930s. However, there were sporadic disturbances in Cardiff (in 1923 and 1929) and in South Shields in 1930: 'All were the direct product of industrial dispute and as such, were more akin to the 1911 disturbances than to the major rioting of 1919 and that which was to follow in Liverpool after the war' (Joshua *et al.*, 1983:28).

The 1948 Liverpool riot took place in the South End of the City where 8,000 immigrants had settled in order to help with the war effort. Thirty per cent were seafarers, 10 per cent were employed on shore, and the rest unemployed. Determined to exclude blacks from jobs aboard ship, the National Union of Seamen pressured employers not to take on colonial labour.

This was the social background to three nights of rioting. The first night's hostilities were precipitated by a fight outside a blacks-only club. A crowd gathered which attacked the club and then moved in on a nearby hostel and other premises frequented or owned by blacks. On the second night there were street battles and another attack on the black hostel. The police arrived and arrested many blacks who had barricaded themselves in. On the third night, plans by groups of white men to attack a club were thwarted because the blacks had armed themselves with swords, daggers and coshes. Instead, the police advanced on the club:

> A volley of hundreds of bottles and stones thrown from the windows halted their advance for a time. But when the defenders ran out of ammunition the police burst their way in, breaking down doors, hitting out right and left with their truncheons, and throwing people down the stairs.
>
> (Fryer, 1984:369)

The police went on the rampage, breaking into houses and beating up the occupants. Sixty blacks and ten whites were arrested.

The Nottingham riots of late-August 1958 began on 30 August when hundreds of local white men and women congregated in the St Ann's Well Road of the city centre, chanting 'Let's get the blacks!' One week earlier, there had been a 90-minute confrontation between whites and blacks at a pub along the same road. In the intervening period, two Nottinghamshire MPs (one Labour and one Tory) had called for restrictive controls on immigration and the deportation of black people, while a large influx of news reporters had acted as a magnet for would-be rioters (ibid.:371). The rioting of 30 August was precipitated when whites attacked and tried to overturn a car containing three black men. Police intervened, enabling the driver to accelerate away. A few days later, a smaller crowd gathered and besieged black people's homes with volleys of bricks before police vans arrived (Ramdin, 1987: 205).

The London riots of August and September of the same year were the culmination of a series of attacks by gangs of white youths – notably members of a notoriously violent and racist subculture, known as 'Teddy Boys' (cf. Muncie, 1984) – on isolated black individuals. On 23 August, several black homes were attacked and, in the small hours of the next morning, black persons walking alone or in pairs were picked off and assaulted by a small gang of white youths combing the area on 'nigger hunting' expeditions. A few days later, hordes of white people, sometimes several hundred strong, took to the streets in numerous areas of London to stone (and, in some cases, petrol-bomb) black people's homes, prompting retaliatory and even pre-emptive fighting by blacks.

The Dudley (West Midlands) riot of August 1962 stands apart from the Nottingham and London disorders. Here, rioting occupied 4 nights, but largely involved crowds of white, working-class men confronting police officers who were preventing them from attacking the small black enclaves of the area (Joshua et al., 1983:46).

Joshua and co-workers emphasise that, in order to understand the riots of 1900–48, we must 'look to the nature of race, class and power in the seaport city'. Colonial labour is central to this formula.

This labour significantly structured power relations between capital and organised labour, it limited the ability of the union to pursue better wages and conditions for its members, and enabled capital to resist union demands. In the eyes of organised white labour resident colonial seamen not only represented a threat to jobs and wage levels, they were also perceived as an unwitting tool in the hands of capital through which the union could be contained, even undermined. Thus there were sufficient reasons to oppose colonial labour in its own right, but additionally, to oppose colonial labour was also to oppose capital.

(Joshua *et al.*, 1983:36)

Given the value attached to colonial labour, maritime capital was prepared to locate colonial seafarers in their own settlements. City councils, equally aware of its importance, but conscious of the opposition of the white community, sought to segregate it within restricted areas. This lack of integration helped foster and amplify racial and imperialist ideologies. These ideologies were vigorously propagated by the media, senior police officers and members of the local polity: 'The actions of the police were ... shaped and structured by local white concerns' (ibid.:39). As in America, the police often looked on impassively, assisted white aggressors or, at best, removed blacks 'for their own safety'; and, as in America, black resistance proved strongest during the post-war periods of 1919 and 1948 when black people's right to a proper stake in society – their reward for helping the war effort – was either denied or revoked by the combined efforts of employers and trade unions.

The late-period riots – of 1958 and 1962 – have much in common with their predecessors of 1900–48, notably the evidence of 'structured antagonism' over housing and jobs in the context of economic recession and rising unemployment (Joshua *et al.*, 1983:47). As Ramdin remarks, working-class attitudes carried the hallmark of a familiar xenophobia:

They feared that black workers would cut overtime earnings and weaken agreements, that employers would use them as a pool of cheap, sweated labour and in the event of strike, use them as 'blacklegs' ... This time-worn traditional prejudice towards the foreigner was real; it was rooted in the fear of economic competition and the racist legacy of imperialism and colonialism.

(Ramdin, 1987:200)

Such resentment towards blacks was compounded by suspicion about their reluctance to join trade unions, and the 'folklore of the black man's sexual prowess' (ibid.:202).

Economic competition was most clearly manifested in the Dudley riots where resentment focused on the fact that blacks were supposedly holding down secure jobs while white workers were working short time or experiencing unemployment (Joshua *et al.*, 1983:46). What differentiated the Dudley riot from the Nottingham and London disorders was that the earlier riots reflected a a degree of preliminary agitation and organisation by fascist groups, and were notable for the involvement of the Teddy Boys (Fryer, 1984:376–81; Ramdin, 1987:204–10). These riots predate the racial attacks on Pakistanis (Paki-bashing) and political struggles involving fascists and anti-racist organisations in the 1970s. The inter-racial element was still apparent in the Southall disturbance of 1981, involving fighting between skinheads and Asian youths, which was sparked off by attacks on Asian shops (Kettle and Hodges, 1982).

Black people versus the police (1970–90)

The transformation from inter-racial conflict to confrontations between black people and the police is related to the economic and political crisis of the 1960s and 1970s (Hall *et al.*, 1978). This was a period of high unemployment, soaring inflation and low profitability. State intervention emphasised the need to curb immigration, hence the Immigration Acts of 1962, 1968 and 1971. Anti-immigrant sentiments were encouraged by the media. As Hartmann and Husband (1974) point out, the media concentrated on the high numbers of immigrants allegedly 'swamping' the country, the 'illegality' of their entry, their potential burden on the state and arguments in favour of their repatriation. Police and immigration officials were given sweeping powers to stop and search blacks or their premises on suspicion of illegal entry, and the authority to impose surveillance over 'ghettos', and prosecute raids on social centres. This activity ostracised and alienated Britain's blacks, a condition exacerbated in the 1970s when higher unemployment had a demoralising effect, especially on black youth.

These developments provided the context for a series of police–black confrontations in the 1970s. Though minor in scale compared to the subsequent riots, these confrontations were precipitated by police raids on black-only clubs or the heavy-handed policing of demonstrations and processions. Disorder broke out at the 1976 and 1977 Notting Hill Carnivals. On both occasions, the formidable police presence was regarded as oppressive by blacks who reacted to arrests they perceived as wrongful by smashing the windows of vehicles and throwing missiles at the police. Sixty people were arrested in connection with the troubles, fifty of them black; but, of ninety charges brought to court, all but eight were rejected by jurors (Joshua *et al.*, 1983).

The first of Britain's major 1980s riots took place on 2 April 1980 in the seaport city of Bristol: 'At the time many commentators and politicians seemed to regard the Bristol eruption as a one-off event – a strange aberration in social behaviour' (Benyon and Solomos, 1987:3). However, such 'complacent interpretations' were rudely undermined by a devastating riot in Brixton (10–12 April 1981). Three months later, while a Royal Commission of Inquiry under Lord Scarman was conducting its investigations, the Toxteth (Liverpool) riot of 3–6 July broke out. One day later, Manchester's Moss Side erupted and there were disturbances in Handsworth, Birmingham and dozens of other British towns and cities.

Benyon and Solomos (1987) maintain that instances of unrest in places like Liverpool and London between 1982 and 1984 were under-reported. The police–black conflict forced its way back onto the agenda in September and October 1985. On 9 September 1985, there was a massive disturbance in the Handsworth Lozells Road area of Birmingham. Two Asian men died of asphyxiation when their post office was one of the scores of local buildings set ablaze.

Then, from 28 to 29 September, there was rioting in Brixton following the near-fatal shooting of a black woman, Cherry Groce, by armed police officers who searched her home. A freelance photographer injured during the riot died 3 weeks afterwards. Two days after the Groce shooting, there was more rioting in Toxteth, Liverpool. Finally, on 6 October 1985, there was the most serious rioting of all, on the Broadwater Farm Estate in Tottenham, North London. Disorder was triggered by the death of Cynthia Jarrett who fatally collapsed while police were searching her home. During the resulting riot, PC Keith Blakelock was stabbed to death and, in a new departure, guns were fired at police, causing several injuries. CS gas and plastic bullets were available, but not used. As one of the most turbulent decades in British history moved to a close, there were minor police–black confrontations in Wolverhampton (May 1989) and Notting Hill (August 1989).

THE BRIXTON RIOT

We now move on to describe and analyse in much closer detail our ideal-type example of the 1980s British disorders, the Brixton riot of 1981. The following case study is based on material drawn from chapters in Benyon and Solomos (1987), Kettle and Hodges (1982) and, of course, the official report of inquiry (Scarman, 1981).

An overview of the Brixton riot

The 1981 Brixton riot was the culmination of a series of events, commencing on Friday, 10 April, when a police officer patrolling the Brixton area saw a black youth running across the street towards him, evidently being chased by two or three other black youths. The constable, PC Stephen Margiotta, was uncertain what was happening but, sensing that an offence may have been committed, grabbed hold of the youth, 19-year-old Michael Bailey, and managed to overpower him.

Bailey was found to be badly bleeding. Before the constable was able to establish why, the youth broke away, only to be recaptured on a streetcorner where Margiotta and another freshly arrived police officer had caught up with him. Soon, they discovered that Bailey was carrying a four-inch stab wound but, before they had time to question him about it, they were joined by three other black youths who excitedly yelled 'Leave him alone!' The officers tried to explain that they were only trying to help, but were jostled into allowing him to escape.

The youth fled to a nearby block of flats where he was taken in by a sympathetic white family. They called a mini cab which eventually arrived to take him to hospital. In the meantime, Margiotta had informed the local police station of Bailey's condition and of the urgent need to help. Thus alerted, a police transit van spotted the minicab and ordered it to stop. A police officer then administered first aid while a second called for an ambulance. However, a crowd of thirty to forty people, mainly black youths, surrounded the officer and began shouting, 'What are you doing to him?', 'Look, they are killing him', and 'We will look after our own.'

The crowd was unresponsive to police explanations. They hailed down a passing car and whisked Bailey away. The youths were pursued, in turn, by officers responding to a call for assistance. This resulted in a skirmish in which some forty police officers, including two dog handlers and several in riot gear, were confronted by one hundred black youths. Four vehicles were damaged, six people were arrested and six police officers injured.

This disorder lasted approximately 80 minutes. Once it was over, the police drafted ninety-six officers into the Brixton area. Foot patrols were stepped up so that twenty-eight officers were permanently patrolling the area in pairs. Five community representatives were contacted and asked to dispel rumours that the youth had been attacked by police and prevented from receiving treatment. Nevertheless, the police decided that the recently implemented 'Swamp 81' – an ongoing plain-clothed operation involving the widespread use of stop-and-search powers – should continue as planned.

A second significant incident happened on the following day, Saturday 11 April, when two plain-clothed policemen decided to question a minicab driver outside the S & M Car Hire premises at the top of Railton Road. The police suspected that the driver had pushed a small quantity of drugs down his right ankle sock. It was, in fact, a wad of pound notes. Nevertheless, the officers continued to search the car.

A crowd of thirty people quickly grew to around 150. A few uniformed police officers were also drawn to the incident. A section of the crowd angrily accused the police of planting something incriminating on the driver. As one of the officers tried to placate them, an altercation took place in which a black youth was arrested and taken away in a police van.

Members of the crowd started to rock the van before it could pull away. While this was happening, a policeman emerged from the crowd, clutching his stomach. Wrongly believing he had been stabbed, a colleague immediately called for reinforcements. Police poured in from the surrounding area and tried to force the crowd back onto the pavement. The crowd stood its ground and proceeded to complain to a Chief Superintendent about the long history of police harassment in the area, and accused officers of possessing iron bars and National Front badges. But suddenly, the police were bombarded with missiles; a police van was hit, turned onto its side and set alight. The police drew their truncheons and charged. Sections of the crowd dispersed, then set about looting and damaging property.

As the disorder escalated, petrol bombs were thrown at the police, and a barricade, consisting of an upturned car and sheets of corrugated iron, was assembled across Railton Road. The police drew up their own cordon, and there was a temporary stand-off. While this was going on, looting and destruction took place in the town's commercial centre. Emergency service vehicles, including ambulances and fire engines responding to arson attacks, were themselves attacked by rioters. The police, finding themselves outnumbered and suffering heavy bombardment, turned the fire hoses on to the rioters. Eventually, as more reinforcements arrived, the crowd fled.

On Sunday, there were more isolated attacks on the police; some also occurred on Monday, but the riot fizzled out. In total, 145 buildings were damaged, 207 vehicles were damaged or destroyed, 450 people were reported injured and 354 arrests were made. It had been necessary to deploy 7,300 officers in order to put down the riots.

Explaining the Brixton riot

Like the Watts case study, the following analysis is based on the six levels outlined in the flashpoints model of public disorder. We therefore begin by looking at the structural factors relevant to the riot.

The black people of Britain experience social and political deprivation similar to their American counterparts. They, too, suffer poor housing conditions, high unemployment (especially among young adults) and political under-representation (Review Panel, 1986:13). The social conditions experienced by the black community of Brixton exemplify this reality.

Brixton's black population is tightly concentrated. At the time of the riot, unemployment for Brixton as a whole was 13 per cent; for blacks it was 25.4 per cent, and for blacks under nineteen it was 55 per cent. Scarman (1981) reports that around 20 per cent of Brixton's housing stock was substandard and 12 per cent of it in need of major renovation. Lambeth Borough Council further estimated that 12,000 households were overcrowded.

According to Scarman, the sense of rejection experienced by black Britons 'is not eased by the low level of black representation in our elective political institutions' (1981, para. 2.35). Greaves also points out that:

> Black people are hardly ever in a position to influence decisions made about them – decisions which sometimes alter the course of their lives in fundamental ways. They are hardly ever consulted about matters which affect them, and on the rare occasions when they are consulted they feel their advice goes unheeded. If they protest they are then accused of 'having chips on their shoulders'.
>
> (Greaves, 1984:71)

There is an obvious parallel between the attitudes of the New Urban Black referred to by Sears and McConahay (1973) and the second-generation British black youths who were prominent in the Brixton and other 1980s disorders.

> The first generation of immigrants entering this country in the 1950s and 1960s more often than not had *lower* expectations of living standards than the indigenous population because comparisons were still being made with conditions in the country of emigration... It is the second generation, born in this country of immigrant parents, educated to be equal in job expectations by the school, and in consumer demands by the mass media, that begins to see itself, when compared with the native population of the same age, as manifestly unequal.
>
> (Lea and Young, 1982:7)

Here we delay discussing key factors at the political/ideological level to concentrate next on significant cultural factors, for it was in response to this inequality and sense of rejection that black youths formulated a subcultural response, based on a synthesis of elements of the Rastafarian and Rude Boy ('rudie') cultures, imported from the Caribbean (Brake, 1985; Cashmore, 1981; Dodd, 1978; Hebdige, 1979). This synthesis placed a positive accent on negritude and involved a rejection of 'shit work' in preference for a more assertive streetcorner lifestyle, carrying a potential for disorder.

The 'rudie' hints at petty crime as an acceptable cultural solution to the life situation of young blacks, embodying as it does coolness and defiance of authority. The use of marijuana (ganja) as a sacred drug has also driven black youths into situations where they will encounter the police. The organizing of 'blues' parties with 'sound systems' and the use of the streets as meeting places have in turn raised the visibility of their cultural 'deviance'. Throughout the 1970s relations between Rastas and the police noticeably deteriorated. A stereotype, that all youths wearing dreadlocks and tams in the Ethiopian colours of red, green and gold, were criminal and violent was constructed by the agencies of white authority.

(Muncie, 1984:123)

The importance of particular political/ideological factors becomes apparent here. The hard policing style which gradually evolved in response to the activities of black youth was influenced by an ideological process, in which a 'muggings' moral panic in the early and mid-1970s was central. During the early 1970s, there had been small increase in the crime rate without any corresponding development of a police policy. It was:

a *combination* of rising street crime statistics, the construction of public opinion as 'anxious and concerned' on the matter, and the tough, uncompromising attitude of the courts to offenders unlucky enough to be labelled as part of the street crime problem, which has to be understood as the essential backcloth for the development of a distinctive police strategy.

(Jefferson and Grimshaw, 1984:89)

The media played a crucial role in generating this moral panic by importing the 'muggings' term (with all its connotations of vulgar force) from America and stereotypically defining it as a violent 'black' crime. This was followed by dire warnings of what would happen without urgent legal intervention.

These factors are likely to have had an invigorating effect on crime figures. As Jefferson and Grimshaw explain, most crimes are initially reported by the public. The police then take a decision on whether they are serious enough to be entered. Public 'sensitisation' and anxiety generated by the media encourages more reports to the police; meanwhile, because of their own heightened concern, the police are more sympathetic and receptive to such complaints and more willingly record them. Thus the crime figures escalate, provoking a demand for a tougher policing policy. Equally important was the absence of any ideological counterweight to the muggings moral panic. Allegations of police harassment had been raised by black spokespersons as early as 1972, but dismissed as the exaggerated complaints of an unrepresentative minority (ibid.:98).

As more police personnel were devoted to the 'growing muggings problem', the black community became increasingly alienated from the law. Finding themselves deprived of the co-operation of the Brixton community, and conscious that street crime is typically 'unplanned, random, (and) casual' in nature, the police had to rely on pro-active clear-up strategies. These strategies were 'sus' (Section 4 of 1824 Vagrancy Act) – loitering with intent to commit an arrestable offence – and 'stop and search' on suspicion of robbery (Section 66 of 1839 Metropolitan Police Act).

Evidence to the Home Office in 1975 showed that pro-active policy, including the use of the Special Patrol Group (SPG) – a specially trained, mobile unit of Metropolitan police officers with a reputation for their uncompromising use of force (cf. Rollo, 1980) – was backfiring: the crime rate had actually tripled in the space of 5 years.

> What seemed to have happened was that the police campaign like a crude blunderbuss had directed its fire against general illegality and delinquency in Brixton, catching many with its blast and threatening innocents, without restraining the growth of the central problem. More than that, the hostility of black people to the police was a direct consequence of the police campaign, and was arguably increasing the difficulty of the police task.
>
> (Jefferson and Grimshaw, 1984:99–100)

There were six SPG visits to Lambeth up to 1979. These visits were endorsed by the Police Federation magazine as 'the only practical means' at their disposal (ibid.:101).

Deteriorating police–community relations thus became the most salient feature of the communications context in which the Brixton riot occurred. These relations worsened considerably in 1978, shortly after a liaison committee had been set up by the police and the Council for Community Relations in Lambeth (CCRL) to study the area's policing problems. Three days after their first meeting, the SPG were brought in without any prior warning to the committee. Liaison immediately collapsed. Then, in February 1979, three members of CCRL were arrested at their office and taken to Brixton police station in connection with an incident at a local club where two plain-clothed police officers and a bar staff member were stabbed. The only obvious link between them and the person suspected of the stabbing was that they wore sheepskin coats.

A report carried out (without police co-operation) by the Lambeth County Working Party on Police Relations, published in January 1981, was strongly critical of the police. The report described recent police tactics as 'attacks by the SPG on the people of Lambeth'. It further highlighted the extent of police harassment and intimidation and expressed a complete lack of confidence in the complaints procedure.

Then, 1 week prior to the riot, Swamp '81 took place. This operation was scheduled to be carried out from Monday, 6 April, to Saturday, 11 April. However, on Friday, 3 April, a number of premises on the so-called front-line, Railton Road, were searched for drugs. Twenty-two people were arrested. This pre-emptive strike contributed to a heightened atmosphere of tension which Swamp '81 further exacerbated. The operation consisted of 112 plain-clothed officers circulating the area on the lookout for muggers and robbers; 943 people were stopped (over half of them black and two-thirds of them under 21) and 118 arrested. Seventy-five charges were made, but only one for robbery, another for attempted burglary and twenty more for theft or attempted theft.

The profound distrust engendered by the collapse of police–community relations, was evident in the interpretations placed of police behaviour surrounding their treatment of Bailey. Rumour also played a part. Among the more insidious rumours were allegations that the hospital authorities had been warned to expect trouble *before the riot occurred*; and that Bailey had been prevented by police officers from going to the hospital, or had even died in police custody. Each successive incident created an even more highly charged communication context for the next encounter.

At the situational level, the area of Brixton where the rioting occurred was clearly of spatial and symbolic significance.

> As the front-line (the term is variously used to describe a battle front or a meeting place) Railton Road was the centre of the rioting. On most days it is a focus like Grosvenor Road in Bristol's St Paul area. Although it is not a red-light district, it does contain the familiar social activities – shebeens, gambling dens and cannabis dealing – of black working-class life. The street is rarely empty, especially in the evening. The presence of street crowds often appears deliberately aggressive to whites. Black youths flock to the front-line for want of anything better to do.
>
> (Kettle and Hodges, 1982:101)

Finally, we come on to the interactional level of analysis. In Kettle's and Hodges' view (1982:108), the incident which provided the 'final spark' for Saturday's disorder (the police intervention outside the S & M Car Hire) was needlessly prolonged by the police: 'A very ugly situation had developed, but instead of beating a quiet and hasty retreat the officers dragged out the incident further.' They quote Robin Auld QC, counsel to Lord Scarman's inquiry, who referred to the incident as follows: 'It was a needless display of authority, just another of the many examples of needless police harassment to add to many' (ibid.).

As in the Watts riot, the Brixton police displayed an unwillingness to negotiate or compromise, even when opportunities were presented. The attempt to continue the controversial Swamp '81 in a climate of mounting tension was criticised by Lord Scarman. At the height of Saturday's disorder, two local councillors, a local vicar and one other person approached the senior police officer to propose a negotiated withdrawal. But 'Commander Fairbairn replied that, in view of the seriousness of the disorder, he was not willing to withdraw and risk the possibility of the disturbances spreading' (ibid.:31). The four intermediaries then offered to talk to the crowd. Eventually, they returned to tell the commander of the crowd's terms for ceasing hostilities. These were: a full police withdrawal, the release of all prisoners, and an end to police harassment. These terms were rejected because Commander Fairbairn 'did not believe that those who had said they would disperse if the police withdrew could, even if they wished, enforce their view on others in the crowd' (ibid.:32).

The destruction, arson and looting followed a logical pattern. The rioters were condemned for obstructing the work of the emergency ambulance and fire brigade services. However, as Greaves explains,

> It was believed that ambulances were ferrying in police reinforcements, and the belief that the fire brigade might be actively assisting the police was reinforced when (the police) commandeered fire hoses from the firemen and turned them on the crowd in a desperate attempt to prevent themselves from being over-run.
>
> (Greaves, 1984:66)

Those businesses with a reputation for exploiting black people or treating them with incivility were the principal targets of attack.

As in the Watts riot (and, indeed, the anti-poll tax disorder of 1990), the Brixton disorder took on a carnival atmosphere:

> There must have been a feeling of *release*, as they could now give vent to the anger which they had suppressed for so long. Mingled in with the other emotions must have been the feeling of *power*: did they not put the police, who until then were inviolable, on the defensive? There

was also *fear*, as they entered into a pursuit fraught with many dangers
in its execution.

(Greaves, 1984:69)

OTHER MODERN BRITISH RIOTS

The above profile of the Brixton riot is summarised in Table 4.1. Many of
its characteristic features were reproduced in the other British riots of the
1980s. As we saw in Chapter 1, the 1980 Bristol riot was provoked by a
police raid by officers looking for drugs and illegal supplies of drink on the
'Black and White Cafe' in the St Paul's area of the city (cf. Joshua *et al.*,
1983; Reicher, 1984). The immediate trigger for the hostilities was the

Table 4.1 A profile of the Brixton riot

Level of analysis	Evidence of predisposing factor
Structural	
Material inequality/ inferior life chances	Relative deprivation re whites; racial discrimination
Political powerlessness	Poor political representation; poor organisation
Relationship to state	State viewed as unresponsive/unsympathetic
Political/ ideological	
Marginality/ vilification	Moral panic re 'muggings': public anxiety and police vigilance producing rise in reported street crime; black youths viewed as threatening; black youths increasingly alienated and disaffected
Police policy	Saturation policing influenced by moral panic
Cultural	
Contrasting notions of 'rights'	Conflict between Afro-Caribbean youth subculture (Rastafarian and Rude Boy elements) and police law-enforcement orientation; British-born blacks less tolerant of racism than parents ('fully paid-up citizens')
Accommodation	Absence of accommodation since early 1970s
Norms of behaviour	Police/blacks share emphasis on machismo and solidarity

Table 4.1 (continued)

Level of analysis	Evidence of predisposing factor
Contextual	
Police–community relations	Permanent state of police–community tension; high-profile policing culminating in Swamp '81
Rumour/ expectation of conflict	Rumour that police had told hospitals to expect casualties; rumours of police atrocities re stabbed youth
Situational	
Critical mass	Popular meeting place: 'front-line' of Railton Road
Symbolic territory	Symbolic turf to be defended (by blacks)/seized (by police)
Interactional	
Flashpoint/ intensifiers	Over-zealous search and arrest of taxi driver
Negotiation/ escalation	Police refusal to negotiate withdrawal with co-operation of councillors; continuation of Swamp '81
Dominant activities	Selective purposive, limited attacks/arson/looting
Dominant emotions	Feelings of release, celebration and pride

arrest of the popular café owner and another man whose trouser leg was torn while he resisted.

According to Kettle and Hodges,

> the riot was racial in that it began as a clash between black people and white policemen on a piece of black territory. It was a clash of cultures: a West Indian life-style of cannabis smoking and illicit drinking versus a white British view that condemns such behaviour.
>
> (Kettle and Hodges, 1982:30)

Participants in the disorder were predominantly, but not exclusively, black. According to Reicher (1984:15), even for the white people involved, the 'black experience provided a potent framework for understanding their own problems: lack of a job, poverty, problems with the police. As one witness observed of the crowd, "politically they were all black" ' (ibid.).

In the days preceding the riot, 'There was much talk about a St Paul's youth who had been arrested on "sus" in London and was appearing in court on the following day. Young blacks were angry about the "police harassment" and talked of going to London to protest' (Kettle and Hodges, 1982:26). The police raid was carried out without any consultation with the community liaison officer, and without involving the regular beat officer.

Though police reinforcements were brought in once the riot started, their attempts to restore order were fragmented and greatly disorganised and, at certain points, their command structure appeared to break down. Though subsequently described by the police as a tactical withdrawal, the police were actually driven out of St Paul's (Reicher, 1984). As noted earlier, the crowd behaviour was extremely selective and purposive. Here, as in the Watts and Brixton riots, the mood of the rioters was euphoric: '"It was really joyful", said one white male, while a black counterpart claimed, "We took on the police and beat them. They will never again treat us with contempt ... They will respect us now"' (ibid.:16).

In the wake of the 1981 Brixton riot, there were subsequent outbreaks of disorder at Toxteth (Merseyside), Moss Side (Manchester) and Handsworth (Birmingham), each a severely deprived area (Scarman, 1981:13–14; Vogler, 1991). All were set against a background of intense and arbitrary stop-and-search operations.

The Toxteth riot was triggered when a 20-year-old black man tried to prevent the arrest of a motorcyclist whom police had been chasing for a traffic offence. Reinforcements were called in and the police presence soon attracted a large, angry crowd. This was the prelude to a riot which spread throughout Toxteth and other parts of Merseyside: 214 police vehicles were damaged, and a civilian run over and killed by a police van. CS gas was used for the first time on mainland Britain, resulting in serious injuries to four civilians (Scraton, 1985a:71–2).

The Handsworth (Birmingham) and Moss Side (Manchester) disorders were defined as 'copycat' riots (Hytner, 1981; Scarman, 1981). This is an oversimplification. At Moss Side, the trigger for the riot was a skirmish between police and local youths at closing time in the small hours of 8 July (Parry et al., 1987:215). Nally (1984:55) remarks that both the police and local residents strongly anticipated trouble before the riot occurred. The Brixton riot may have been partly responsible for this, but care should be taken not to overlook the negative history of police–community relations, including the 'capricious use of "stop-and-search" powers, illegal detentions and racial abuse of young people' (Venner, 1981:275).

The flashpoint for 3 nights of rioting in Handsworth was an attack on a locally known police Superintendent who was trying to dispel rumours of an impending National Front march (Southgate, 1982a). Handsworth was regarded as an important vindication of the community-policing philosophy. However, black youths disputed that police–black relations were amicable before the riot (Review Panel, 1986:64). Southgate's (1982a) Home Office survey reported that 38 per cent of Afro-Caribbeans interviewed had been stopped and searched by police in the 12 months preceding the riots; this was even higher (41 per cent) for West Indians in the 16–24 age group.

The Handsworth disorder of 4 years later occurred in the context of severe industrial decline which disproportionately affected Afro-Caribbean youths (Review Panel, 1986:15). In addition, a previous emphasis on community policing was discarded when a new superintendent moved regular beat officers to other duties. This was part of a policy to clamp down on previously tolerated minor traffic and drug-dealing offences in response to local and national pressures to tackle the 'heroin epidemic' (Rex, 1987:109). The riot was sparked off when a black youth became involved in an argument with a police officer over a parking ticket. A crowd developed and more police arrived. A black woman was allegedly assaulted by one of the officers and, within 3 hours, forty buildings were burning down (Benyon and Solomos, 1987:6).

The involvement in this incident of a black woman provides an obvious link with the disturbance in the Tottenham Broadwater Farm area of North London in 1985, which revolved around the death of Cynthia Jarrett. The episode began when police stopped a car, driven by her son, Floyd, a Broadwater Farm youth worker, on the grounds that his tax disc was out of date. Floyd Jarrett explained that he had just returned from a youth exchange trip to Jamaica. Officers were unimpressed and decided to arrest him for the suspected theft of the car. Jarrett is alleged to have assaulted a police officer while resisting arrest.

Members of Jarrett's family subsequently complained that police used his door key to enter his mother's home. Police insisted that the door was already open. During a search of the house, Mrs Jarrett collapsed and died. Allegations that her death was caused when a police officer pushed her to the floor were refuted by the police. Nevertheless, news of her death circulated the estate that evening and disorder broke out at 7 p.m. on the following day.

Broadwater Farm had long been regarded a 'problem estate' by the police. Police–community relations had rapidly deteriorated in the preceding 12 months and, a week before the riot, police had implemented a stop-and-search operation at the entrance to the estate. The local black population had complained of its arbitrary nature and made allegations of abusive and rough treatment by police officers (The Women of Broadwater Farm, 1989:126).

DISCUSSION

The twentieth-century pattern of British rioting shows compelling similarities with the corresponding American pattern. It, too, falls into two clearly differentiated phases: an earlier period of inter-ethnic clashes, followed by a more recent era of police–black confrontations. As in America, the resistance mounted by ethnic minorities against racist attacks was most pronounced in the post-war years of 1919 and 1948 when they were appalled by society's unfair treatment, given their contribution to the war effort.

Comparisons between the American riots of the 1960s and the British disorders of the 1980s reveal important similarities. Field and Southgate (1982:6) confirm that, among the most significant common features were: shared sets of underlying grievances (notably concerning police practices, unemployment and housing conditions); almost identical dynamics, including a similar degree of spontaneity and absence of preliminary organisation; a tendency to be compressed into a given period of time (i.e. to occur in 'waves'); and a resemblance between the American black migration patterns from the rural south to the urban north, and the immigration of West Indians to Britain, where they settled in the major ports and conurbation areas.

Other factors indicated by the present study could also be included here; notably, the fact that the riots tended to occur at 'symbolic locations' in the heart of black neighbourhoods, and within political climates which denigrated political or culturally dissenting activity by black people and encouraged coercive policing policies against them.

Race is an important explanatory variable in this analysis – but only to the extent that black people have suffered, disproportionately, the effects of deprivation and discrimination. Rioting is not a 'black phenomenon', as a cursory examination of the exceptional events of a single year of the present century will illustrate. Between May and August 1919, four different types of rioting occurred (White, 1982). In addition to the inter-racial clashes in seaport districts, referred to above, there were running battles between white youths and the police, riots by soldiers who had recently been discharged or were awaiting demobilisation and mass looting in Liverpool during a police strike.

As White points out, '1919 was a very troubled year', marked by unprecedented inflation, a 'house famine' and intense competition for manual jobs caused by a demobilisation rate of 10,000 personnel per day (ibid.:13). Also,

> There was the mental tension that followed the release from four and a half years of forced discipline and social turmoil. And there were the disappointments of servicemen returning from a war which had achieved little or nothing for the great majority of people who had suffered so much.
>
> (White, 1982:13)

The London youth riots of July and August 1919 have a great deal in common with the inner-city riots of the 1980s (Muncie, 1984). They were sparked off when police officers attempted to break up or move on young men engaging in 'rowdiness' or over-boisterous behaviour. This was a young generation aggrieved that they, like black workers, were systematically passed over by employers eager to privilege returning soldiers and sailors. Working-class youths were increasingly forced onto the streets as wartime entertainment restrictions and high inflation curtailed their leisure opportunities. There:

> They came up against a police force hardened by military duties, and embittered by its own failed strikes in 1918 and 1919. The right to use the streets in the way they wanted – particularly in weekend evenings – was the cultural background over which youth fought the police.
>
> (White, 1982:14)

Despite the advantages afforded to them by prospective employers, demobilised soldiers were badly affected by unemployment and housing shortages. They felt resentful that sections of the capitalist class had 'grown fat' out of their misery and sacrifice. These grievances lay at the root of their riots, the most serious of which was the Luton disorder of 19 July 1919. There, a crowd attacked the local town hall and set it on fire after borough councillors decided to lay on a Peace Day banquet for local dignitaries, but refused permission for ex-servicemen to hold a memorial service in a public park.

Finally, when the Liverpool police went on strike on 1 August, the city's dockside residents systematically looted local shops. Afterwards, children sold off barrels of beer and stout while pianos were dragged out of music shops to become the focal point of street parties. According to Critchley (1970:181), the 'half starved crowds' who looted in Liverpool 'were out to get their own back after years of squalor and misery'. White confirms this was more than sheer greed:

The causes were buried deep in the structure of inequality, which means that social ills always fall hardest on some sections of the population; in the economic and cultural adaptations which working people (especially the rougher sort) devised to ease their predicament; and in the class which, when it seems most vulnerable, invites attack by those who usually have no power.

(White, 1982:13–14)

Analysis of twentieth-century riots in Britain and America suggests that disorder most typically occurs in those periods where relatively powerless sections of society experience a shattering denial of something they feel legitimately entitled to. Under these circumstances and the added weight of state repression, rioting has been a way of expressing indignation, a form of redressive action, or a means of temporary liberation; a method of making society sit up and listen, if only for a while.

Chapter 5

Strike violence

The 1984–5 coal dispute was one of the most bitterly contested strikes in British industrial relations history, involving violent industrial confrontation on picket lines in the North of England, the Midlands, Scotland and South Wales. The most notorious confrontation took place around a coking plant at Orgreave, near Sheffield.

> From 23 May, when the first brick smashed through a lorry windscreen, to the final cataclysmic encounter almost four weeks later on 18 June, the violence rose in a series of tidal waves. Thanks to television ... the nation had an armchair view of the violence: uprooted telegraph poles, rolling down the hill towards the police cordon; a workmen's hut dragged into the road and going up in petrol-fed flames; a lone policeman with his truncheon repeatedly laying into a recumbent miner; the wall of riot shields parting like the Red Sea as groups of police, in black one-piece suits and NATO helmets, dashed into the crowded pickets while a senior officer, with loud-hailer, encouraged them to 'take prisoners'.
>
> (Wilsher *et al.*, 1985:88)

Mounted police officers, long, wooden batons in hand, cantered off to join in the chase. Many pickets fled; others stayed to fight.

> Men with blood streaming from their head wounds stood defiantly hurling stones. A police rider fell from a horse stunned by a half-brick. Constables with small, round, Perspex shields, like latter-day gladiators, engaged in hand-to-hand combat with miners. Helmeted ambulancemen loaded casualties into an armoured Land Rover, bought for the purpose from the army. Smoke from a burning barricade further up the hill hung in the air. Often only the absence of sabres and bullets differentiated it from full-scale war.
>
> (Wilsher *et al.*, 1985:89)

One year beforehand at Warrington in Cheshire, and 3 years after at Wapping in North London, violent clashes occurred on picket lines involving print workers. Why had such disputes reverted to a pattern of disorder more reminiscent of the nineteenth than twentieth century?

Geary (1985) has examined the historical pattern of industrial confrontation in Great Britain, looking for the distinctive features of periods marked by high or low levels of disorder. We begin this chapter with a discussion and critique of his model of the changing nature of industrial confrontation from 1893 to 1985. In the second and third sections, we concentrate on our contemporary example, an extended case study of public disorder during the 1984–5 coal dispute. We set out the political context of the strike (second section), before analysing the most notorious mass picket of the dispute, the 'Battle of Orgreave'.

American labour–management relations have shown similar patterns. From the 1870s to the 1930s, violence was 'pervasive and intense' (Graham and Gurr, 1969), but has been less common since the Second World War, with notable exceptions, such as the major coal-mining strikes of 1977 and 1981. The fourth section is devoted to an overview of American 'labor violence' from the 1870s to the 1980s (Taft and Ross, 1969; Thieblot and Haggard, 1983). A final section evaluates a recent Canadian explanation of 'Why strikes turn violent' (Grant and Wallace, 1991), discussing its relationship to the flashpoints model.

STRIKE VIOLENCE IN GREAT BRITAIN, 1883–1985

Between the late-nineteenth century and the 1980s, there was a progressive decline in the occurrence of industrial confrontation only for it to dramatically reappear between 1983 and 1985. According to Geary (1985) this history went through five distinct phases, each characterised by its own dominant form of disorder by strikers and preferred type of control tactic by the police or military.

The first of these periods (from the late nineteenth to early twentieth century) usually involved confrontations between stone-throwing strikers and armed troops, who would sometimes resort to gunfire to restore order. This period is exemplified by the Featherstone shootings of 1893, where troops opened fire on a group of miners involved in a lock-out, leaving two dead and fourteen wounded.

In the second phase (1910–14), baton-wielding police sought to protect strikebreakers from the wrath of pickets. This was, in Geary's terminology, a pivotal period, in which the responsibility for controlling public-order situations passed, backwards and forward, between central government and local employer–magistrates. Although the military were used more sparingly than in period one – the government intervened to prevent their use in the South Wales coal dispute of 1910, for example – they *were* despatched to South Wales during the national railway strike of 1911, when fears of imminent revolution were rife.

Between 1915 and 1945 (period three), picketing was largely non-violent. Any disorder that occurred, as in the General Strike of 1926, was directly due to provocation by the police and Specials (volunteer constables), involving repressive baton charges. Such tactics were carried out and sanctioned in a 'political atmosphere of panic'.

During period four (1946 to 1980), violence between pickets and police was quite rare. Geary points out that, by this stage, picket-line behaviour had evolved into a ritualised pushing and shoving. Perhaps the most famous cases of this period were the confrontations at the Saltley coal depot in Birmingham during the 1972 national coal dispute, at the Grunwick film processing laboratory in London in 1977 and outside the Hadfields private steel works during the 1980 national steel dispute.

According to Geary,

> the picketing at Saltley – often presented as a extreme example of industrial violence – consisted of large numbers of strikers pushing against smaller numbers of police. Such behaviour is hardly the ultimate manifestation of anarchy that it is often depicted to be.
>
> (Geary, 1985:78)

At Grunwick, elbows and boots were used, especially when snatch squads entered the crowd to make arrests, but 'the general pattern of picketing was one of relatively non-violent pushing and shoving' (ibid.:86). Although the media coverage of Hadfields suggested a violent encounter between police and pickets, even on the most serious day of violence, 12 March when seventy-five arrests were made, the confrontation was relatively tame (ibid.:90–1).

The last of the five periods identified by Geary is the 1980s, when industrial confrontation reverted to a more violent form. The first indication of this change occurred in 1983 during the closed-shop dispute between the National Graphical Association (NGA) and the Messenger Group of Newspapers, owned by Mr Eddie Shah. The largest mass picket of the dispute, 4,000 people, assembled outside the company's Warrington print works on 30 November to make its ritual attempt to block the route of newspaper delivery vans. Previously, picketing had taken the form of pushing and shoving on both sides, but the confiscation of union banners and the pickets' public address system by the police led to the throwing of stones and bottles by strikers. This was the prelude to an aggressive baton charge by police in full riot gear which resulted in seventy-three arrests (Geary, 1985:135). This willingness by police and pickets to engage in violent confrontation was dramatically revealed during the 1984–5 coal dispute.

Geary attempts to explain both the long-term trend away from violence and the sudden return to it in terms of three socio-political developments: the increasing constitutionalisation of trade unions and the police, the growing impact of the media and the progressive democratisation of civil liberties. The constitutionalisation of the trade unions and the police refers to the former's growing commitment to procedural settlements and closer political alliance to the Labour Party, and to the latter's growing independence from local political control.

Unions are more wary of the need to avoid jeopardising the Labour Party's (and their own) interests by engaging in violence, and therefore are more apt to exert control over their members. Correspondingly, the police have become gradually more independent of local capitalist interests. The Home Office directs the police, rather than (as used to be the case before the First World War) local magistrates, many of whom were owners of local industries, with a vested interest in the breaking of strikes.

Geary maintains that both the police and trade unions are committed to carrying public opinion. A second factor, the growth of the media, is said to have made both sides wary of possible bad publicity resulting from violence. The media are held to have played a key educational and civilising role – by keeping people better informed of the issues involved in industrial disputes and of the 'proper' way to conduct them. The third factor has been the democratisation of civil liberties. The monitoring and criticism of police conduct on picket lines by such independent organisations as the National Council for Civil Liberties has served to highlight, and therefore moderate, misbehaviour, especially by the police.

Geary explains the return to tactical violence in the 1980s partly in terms of the police's tougher and more sophisticated approach to public disorder induced by the inner-city disturbances of 1981, though he attributes much of the unusually high level of violence in the miners' strike to certain exceptional characteristics of the dispute:

It seems that several unique features – the lack of wholehearted support from other unions, the marked absence of internal unity, the militant leadership, the sheer length of the stoppage – prevented the constraints on violence which had proved so effective in the past from being fully operative.

(Geary, 1985:147)

The success of the police strategy – involving roadblocks and the central co-ordination of riot-trained support units – caused the pickets to rely increasingly on stoning tactics. This was the prelude to a spiral of conflict. Picket-line disorder eventually spilled over into mining communities, which became the sites of major disturbances.

Though impressively coherent, Geary's model is open to three important criticisms. First, as will be demonstrated below, he tends to underplay the severity of the violence which occurred at places like Grunwick and Hadfields during a period supposedly devoid of such conflict. Second, he clearly misunderstands the media's role in relation to industrial disorder. Typically, media coverage refers only superficially (and usually disparagingly) to the issues involved in a dispute and, far from moderating police aggression, tends to justify hostility towards the pickets.

Ultimately, Geary's general argument is politically superficial (Jefferson, 1990). His explanation should have been more sensitive to the interplay between local and national democratic influences on the policing of industrial disputes. Greater emphasis should also have been placed on the economic context in which disputes occur and on the state of political consensus – primarily, whether the trade unions are accepted in a 'partnership' role with the state, or are defined as problematic to its objectives (Ragin *et al.*, 1982:243).

By briefly reconsidering the major industrial disputes covered by Geary's final two periods, it will be shown how it is more advisable to explain the characteristics of the key industrial confrontations of the period in terms of the specific audiences influencing police behaviour. This overview will serve the related function of showing the gradual development during the 1970s and early 1980s of a climate of opinion, antithetical to trade unions in general and mass picketing in particular, which was conducive to the repressive police tactics deployed during the coal dispute.

THE CONTEXT OF THE COAL DISPUTE

Political antecedents

Geary is undoubtedly correct to highlight the mutual restraint shown by the police and pickets at Saltley. At the peak moment of the 6-day picket of the coke works, 800 police officers found themselves containing 15,000 pickets. The depot was closed by the police in the interests of public safety. However, as Scraton points out,

> That one incident was taken as the moment when the predicted breakdown in law and order, the full-blown crisis in industrial relations, had arrived. It symbolized the potential power and solidarity of the unions and demonstrated that collective action on a large scale could close workplaces. It was also clear from the Saltley Gates confrontation that the police, regardless of their offensive tactics, were not capable of handling well-organized mass pickets.
>
> (Scraton, 1985a:143)

This panic stimulated a reconstruction of government mechanisms for responding to mass picketing. First, central government set up the Civil Contingencies Unit (CCU), a formal institution based in the cabinet office whose brief was to monitor and respond to industrial disputes in key industries. Second, a greater emphasis was placed on the provision of mutual aid between police forces, an operation to be co-ordinated from the National Reporting Centre (NRC) at Scotland Yard.

In February 1974, there was a second national miners' strike. The Prime Minister, Ted Heath, called a general election, based on the slogan, 'Who runs the country?'. The Tories lost the election, misjudging the mood of the electorate. The spectre of Saltley haunted the right of the Conservative Party for another decade. The Tories' period of opposition was partly spent contemplating a future showdown with the miners. The Ridley Report (cf. *The Economist*, 27 May 1978) was the blueprint for a possible strategy. It advised a future Conservative cabinet to: (i) build up stocks of coal at power stations; (ii) plan contingency coal imports; (iii) introduce dual oil- and coal-fired burning in power stations; (iv) cut the social security entitlements of strikers; and finally, (v) set up mobile police squads to deal with flying pickets and obtain sufficient numbers of 'reliable' non-union drivers to cross picket lines.

The next major episode of industrial conflict took place at the Grunwick film-processing factory in London, where workers – a high proportion of them Asian women – were demanding the right to unionise. If anything, Geary underestimates the ferocity of the encounters between pickets and the police. According to Dromey and Taylor, it was clear from first day that the police:

> intended to interpret the law rigidly and arrest *en masse* those who did not instantly obey their dictates, however unlawful ... Forty pickets were arrested within minutes as the police emptied out of their coaches

and were ordered to pile into the pickets, hem them in either side of the factory gate and arrest anyone who stepped off the pavement.

(Dromey and Taylor, 1978:110)

Jefferson and Grimshaw show how the police control of the mass picket reflected the relative influence of several 'audiences':

On this occasion.. the police saw their legal-democratic duty quite clearly: in their terms, it was to maintain the rights of all parties to the dispute – those of Grunwick's boss to continue production with his remaining labour force, of pedestrians and road-users to 'perambulate freely', of the pickets to peacefully make their protest, and of the community as a whole to be protected from scenes of public disorder. Their occupational duty, as they saw it, was equally clear – sufficient numbers and mobile reserves for the trouble spots. But given the lengthiness of the dispute, the demands of other policework, and the regularity of 'trouble', the 'permanent' mobile reserve, the SPG, became a routine feature of the policing of Grunwick, and especially the confrontational aspects.

(Jefferson and Grimshaw, 1984:108)

The media projected a view that the pickets were primarily responsible for the violence at Grunwick, adding to the clamour to curb mass picketing. The so-called Winter of Discontent (1978–9) generated even more anti-trade-union sentiment, especially as Labour's attempt to establish a 5 per cent pay norm led to strikes by lorry drivers and the low paid and produced television scenes of 'mountains' of uncollected refuse (Scraton, 1985b).

Partly as a consequence, the Tories were returned to power under Margaret Thatcher in 1979. Their first real test by the unions was the 12-week national steel strike, commencing January 1980. Mass picketing was focused on the Hadfields private steel works in Sheffield. Regarded as a routine industrial dispute, without sinister political connotations (Kahn et al., 1983), the picketing was seldom violent, very much conforming to Geary's push-and-shove model. Moreover, the policing of the picket line was organised and controlled by local police officers according to a 'hearts and minds' philosophy: the Chief Constable of South Yorkshire sensibly recognised that almost every family in Sheffield had connections with the steelworkers and was keen to ensure that the police did not alienate themselves from the wider community. The police therefore adopted a highly discretionary approach, often choosing to overlook technical infringements in the interest of public order. Such tactics pre-empted violent resistance even when occasional arrests had to be made (Waddington *et al.*, 1989:76–7).

During a 4-week lull in activity outside Hadfields, there was a mass picket on 22 February on the Isle of Sheppey in Kent. Events at this picket were to shape the character of the next major mass picket of Hadfields on 12 March. The pickets travelling to Kent were met by unbridled hostility from local people, orchestrated by local newspapers. Handbills appeared, depicting Lord Kitchener admonishing local people, 'Your Island Needs You!' and signs in shop windows declared: 'No pickets served' (Docherty, 1983:198). Pickets' coaches were stopped en route and searched by the police. On the picket line itself, the conduct of Metropolitan police officers prompted accusations of brutality (ibid.:199).

This was a different experience of picketing. Support for the strike was also waning. Pickets turned up at Hadfields on 12 March seeking a confrontation. The police anticipated trouble and had drafted in reinforcements from neighbouring forces. Pickets charged them and there was hand-to-hand fighting. Clearly all basis of accommodation had collapsed and seventy-five arrests were made.

Hadfields was largely peaceful but attitudes had hardened on both sides. The mass picket helped justify such subsequent developments as more mobile squads of police, greater mutual aid between forces and the introduction of the Employment Act 1980 which outlawed secondary picketing and allowed the police to determine the maximum size of the picket.

The 1980–1 riots also suggested a need for improvements in police training and equipment, which were first evident in the Warrington Messenger dispute of 1983. Ostensibly a dispute concerning the protection of a closed-shop arrangement and an attempt to resist the introduction of new technology, it is clear that the strike was symptomatic of Eddie Shah's (the newspaper proprietor's) intention to strike a blow against trade-union power. Government ministers portrayed him 'not only as a champion of the law but a defender of the rights of workers not to unionise' (Scraton, 1985b:158).

In anticipation of two large mass pickets on 29 and 30 of November, designed to block the distribution of the newspaper, the Home Secretary is said to have personally intervened to make sure that the police had sufficient personnel to guarantee normal distribution (Gennard, 1984:16). Specialist police squads were brought in from outside constabularies, and their containment tactics included the deployment of 'snatch squads' and the indiscriminate batoning of pickets (Scraton, 1985b:158). Hain (1986:131) is convinced that: 'The police, publicly urged on by the Prime

Minister and Home Secretary, were determined to break the strike by preventing the mass picketing.' The speed of the Home Secretary's intervention and the rapid deployment of riot-trained officers between forces 'announced the arrival of a national police response to "civil disorder"' (Scraton, 1985a:149). This was to be seen with more telling effect in the coal dispute which started some 6 months later.

The immediate context

The immediate political context was framed by the central issue of the strike itself: the National Union of Mineworkers' (NUM's) opposition to pit closures and their implications for the loss of jobs and the demise of mining communities. The trigger for the strike was the closure of the Cortonwood mine in South Yorkshire. The NUM responded with an 'area by area' strategy, obviating the need for a national ballot. When moderate areas, principally Nottinghamshire, failed to comply, Yorkshire miners tried to bring them into line by picketing their pits. The year-long strike eventually resulted in defeat for the NUM, due, not least, to the police success in enabling working miners to continue to enter pits and strikebreakers to return to work.

Police tactics deployed during the strike included roadblocks designed to prevent miners from reaching picket lines. On one occasion, 'action likely to cause a breach of the peace' was invoked by Kent police successfully to turn miners back at the Dartford tunnel, over 100 miles from their intended destination. On the picket lines themselves, the police made uncompromising use of the discretion available to them under public-order law. Minor offences, e.g. stepping off a pavement or shouting 'scab' – activities generally tolerated in industrial disputes – were sometimes used as the pretext for an arrest. In addition, long-forgotten statutes, e.g. 'watching and besetting', were conveniently resurrected; bail conditions were used to deter picketing; and there were widespread allegations of the use of covert surveillance and police *agents provocateurs*.

The Association of Chief Police Officers (ACPO) claimed that the NRC was merely a convenient device for guaranteeing effective mutual aid for overstretched forces. An alternative view was expressed that the NRC were under the direct influence of the Home Office, thus undermining any form of independence previously enjoyed by Chief Constables (Scraton, 1985a).

The notion of police audiences provides a useful basis on which to explain why this policy was adopted. Taking the influence of occupational audiences first, it is reasonable to assume that rank-and-file preference would be to avoid 'another Saltley'. Senior ACPO members, notably its president Charles McLachlan, the Chief Constable of the Nottinghamshire Constabulary, also prioritised the right to work over the right to picket. Therefore, there was strong pressure on chief constables to adopt a hard-line approach from within their own institution.

The legal influences on police policy were formidable. The Home Secretary wrote to and held regular briefing sessions with Chief Constables, leaving them in no doubt as to what he expected of them (Uglow, 1988). Once the police roadblock strategy had been implemented, it received the immediate endorsement of the Attorney General, whilst their hard-line approach to picket-line misconduct was sanctioned by severe court sentencing of offenders.

Democratic audiences had to consent to this approach. A virulent ideological onslaught was waged against the miners by an unsympathetic media and a large cross-section of politicians. For the whole of its duration, the strike, which was instigated without a ballot, was condemned as illegitimate and unconstitutional. The NUM's leaders were branded as subversive and the 'right to work' held as absolute.

Violent conduct by miners was condemned; that by police justified as defensive or reactive. Any opponents of the policing strategy (e.g. pro-NUM police committees) were dismissed as partisan. The creation of an ideological climate conducive to the harshest possible policing of the strike culminated in the Prime Minister, Margaret Thatcher's, 'enemy within' speech, which equated the pickets with IRA terrorism and 'subversive' local governments (Scraton, 1985a). The net result was a political atmosphere 'in which it became impossible for the police as a whole to avoid a distortion of priorities and for individual police officers it became more and more difficult to disentangle fact from prejudice in assessing those whom they were sent to police' (McCabe and Wallington, 1988:134–5).

PUBLIC DISORDER DURING THE COAL DISPUTE: THE 'BATTLE OF ORGREAVE'

We are now in a position to examine the implications of the prevailing ideological climate for the policing of public-order situations during the coal dispute. This process is achieved by looking at our principal case study, the Battle of Orgreave. The mass picketing of Orgreave – a tactic used to discourage the British Steel Corporation (BSC) from increasing its daily supplies of coke to its Scunthorpe steel works above a quota already agreed with the miners' and steel workers' unions – was initially characterised by good-humoured pushing and shoving on both sides.

The first major flashpoint occurred when Arthur Scargill entered the premises on Sunday 27 May, to invoke the solidarity of steel union officials. When he re-emerged, a crowd gathered round him. The police chose this moment to charge at and disperse the pickets from the entrance to the plant and the NUM President was bundled to the floor. Outraged by the police action, Scargill appeared on news bulletins later that day, calling for reinforcements to turn up and emulate the closure of Saltley.

There was no delivery of coke on the following day but, on Tuesday 29 May, thousands of pickets plus police from eleven forces descended on the plant. From the outset, the police demonstrated a consistently uncompromising attitude. One crowd of pickets was prevented from getting within half a mile of the gates by lines of police officers, while a second group, who had managed to assemble earlier opposite the gates, was charged by police horses and dog handlers. When the convoys of coke lorries arrived, any attempt at picketing was rendered ineffectual: whenever serious pushing was exerted against police lines, snatch squads were instantly deployed. Sensing the futility of their actions, some miners threw stones. This was answered by the production of full-length riot shields and, as the throwing intensified, mounted horses with baton-wielding riders were sent in. On the following day, Arthur Scargill was arrested for obstructing the highway. Up until then, the number of pickets present had been small. Predictably, however, Scargill's arrest brought scores more miners into the area. Disorder escalated as on the previous day.

From 7 to 17 June, the NUM kept only a token picket on Orgreave. However, on 18 June, a secretly organised mass picket caught the police momentarily off guard. Scores of pickets brushed past the greatly reduced police presence to enter the coking plant, which had to be cleared by police. Later, on the picket line, there was a minor confrontation accompanying the arrival of morning convoy during which a police riot shield was captured and symbolically set alight. No further hostilities occurred until the late afternoon. Then, a group of youths rolled a tractor tyre towards the police line. Some officers broke ranks and were met with a volley of stones. At this point, police on horseback and riot officers carrying riot shields chased pickets across fields and railway lines into the village and through gardens. When the police regrouped with the intention of holding a railway bridge, pickets constructed blazing barricades out of the remnants of scrapped cars, telegraph poles and a portakabin to prevent a second advance.

The relevant explanatory variables are listed in Table 5.1. The patent absence of police–picket accommodation at all times may be partially explained in terms of a communication context characterised by a steady

Table 5.1 Factors affecting the 'Battle of Orgreave'

Structural
Confrontation between NUM and state (government rationalisation of
  coal industry versus defence of jobs, communities and union)

Political/ideological
Strike defined as 'threat to democracy'
Strike defined as 'illegitimate' (no ballot)
NUM leadership defined as subversive
'Right to work' prioritised over 'right to picket'
Government/police seek 'revenge' re Saltley
Antipathy to strike in places like Notts

Cultural
Masculine cultures (miners/police)
Most militant sections of NUM (Yorkshire, South Wales, Scotland,
  Kent)
Police/pickets from nationwide

Contextual
Roadblocks/picket lines build animosity
No liaison between police and NUM
NUM leaders tacitly approve of violence

Situational
High-profile policing
Uncertain lines of police command
No situational adjustment for police reinforcements
Poor picketing organisation
Symbolic targets of derision (lorries, strikebreakers)
Police seen as denying legitimate 'right to picket'
Pickets seen as obstructing 'right to work'

Interactional
No agreed set of norms limiting aggression
Ill-tempered pushing/shoving/stoning by pickets
Uncompromising arrests/charges/batoning by police on horses, in
  riot gear

accumulation of negative encounters between the police and NUM, a
complete lack of liaison between South Yorkshire police and the organisers
of the mass picket, frequent resort to tactics of surprise and NUM leaders
steadfastly resisting media pressure to disavow picket-line violence involving their own rank and file. Key situational factors were also important.
Prominent amongst these were a rapid turnover of police and strikers,

leaving them little time for situational adjustment, and a corresponding lack of discipline, organisation and effective command structure on both sides.

The miners and the police share occupational cultures in which solidarity and toughness were highly valued. Each side was therefore unwilling to give ground and ready to support or go to the aid of their colleagues. At the interactional level, the immediate precipitants of the conflict were a succession of undisciplined, uncompromising actions. However, it would be misleading to divorce such activities from the prevailing structural relationship between the state and NUM, and the political context of the strike:

> Orgreave was not seen as a local picket during an industrial dispute but a trial of strength in a politically charged struggle. The way it was policed and who policed it was similarly defined by national rather than local considerations. The conflict between the South Yorkshire police and the area NUM had been transformed into a confrontation between the state and the 'enemy within'.
>
> (Waddington et al., 1989:92)

STRIKE VIOLENCE IN AMERICA, 1870–1984

A general overview

It is common for serious disorder associated with British trade disputes to be referred to as 'American-style violence'. This is not without good reason. Taft and Ross (1969:221) point out that 'The United States has had the bloodiest and most violent labor history of any industrial nation in the world.' According to their analysis of American industrial confrontations from the 1870s to the 1960s, violence has been most severe on those occasions when employers have tried to 'break' existing unions, or deny recognition to newly forming ones.

> With few exceptions, labor violence was the result of isolated and usually unplanned acts on a picket line, or occurred on a prohibited parade or demonstration protesting employer obduracy or police brutality. It might also start by attempts to prevent the transportation of strikebreakers or goods, and a clash would follow police intervention. Where the employer refused to deal with the union, the possibility of eventual violence was always high. The desire of the American worker for union representation took place in the teeth of employer opposition that was able to impose heavy sanctions for union activity.
>
> (Taft and Ross, 1969:291–2)

As with the changing character of British industrial conflict, American 'labor violence' has undergone a series of transitions since the late-nine-teenth century. Between 1873 and 1878, for example, the hesitant growth of American trade unionism was dramatically set back by a 5-year economic depression. During this time, trade-union membership declined by five-sixths to 50,000. The employers saw this as an opportunity to ensure the complete destruction of trade unionism and, between 1877 and 1922, set out to achieve this aim.

> Acting both singly and through employer associations, they engaged in frequent lockouts, hired spies to ferret out union sympathizers, circulated the names of such sympathizers to fellow employers through so-called black-lists, summarily discharged labor 'agitators', and engaged the services of strikebreakers on a widespread scale.
>
> (Sloane and Witney, 1985:62)

Griffin *et al.* (1986:148) emphasise how the employers' tactics varied in their subtlety. Sometimes they resorted to 'divide and conquer' strategies (e.g. hiring immigrant labour to undercut white wages), they deskilled workers to reduce their craft monopoly, used sympathetic newspapers and journals to disseminate anti-union propaganda and successfully lobbied politicians. Some 200,000 *agents provocateurs* were used in 1928 alone, and the militia was called in to break strikes on 500 occasions between 1875 and 1910.

> Despite the controversy it often provoked, military intervention in labor conflicts was common from 1875 to 1925. Military forces, usually state militia, were frequently called upon during that period to preserve law and order in violent strike situations. In theory the militia's role was to keep peace, but in fact the military often used force, sometimes wantonly, to break strikes. During the great railroad strike of 1877, for example, 45,000 militiamen were called up in eleven states and more than 100 strikers were killed and several hundred were wounded. In fact, between 1877 and 1892, at least 30 percent of the militia's active duty assignments involved strikes.
>
> (Jacobs, 1982:163–4)

This situation was due to an imbalance in the law which permitted employers to reject union recognition and employ strikebreakers (Taft and Ross, 1969:230). The 1890s and early 1900s saw a series of bitter conflicts associated with drives for union recognition. Between 1902 and 1904, some 200 people were killed and over 2,000 injured as a result of industrial conflict (Thieblot and Haggard, 1983:15). This was perhaps the most violent 2-year period in American industrial-relations history. However, the most infamous of all confrontations occurred in 1914, the year of the 'Ludlow Massacre', when thirty-five militia opened fire on a tent colony of 8,000–10,000 members of mining families recently evicted from their homes during a union-recognition strike. Three men and a boy were shot dead and, when tents were set ablaze, two women and eleven children who had hidden in an underground cellar, were suffocated by smoke. Later, three prisoners, including a strike leader, were shot dead 'while attempting to escape'.

Outraged by this action, the miners, supported by the Colorado labour movement, took up arms and raided local mines. After 10 days of gun battles, Federal troops were called out to quell the violence. Including the twenty-one killed at Ludlow, the episode accounted for over fifty deaths. The union was unsuccessful in gaining recognition: 'The Ludlow war, one of the more tragic episodes in labor's history, failed to dissolve the adamantine opposition to unionism, which had become a fixed and immovable article of faith among many of the great industries of the United States' (Taft and Ross, 1969:256).

The war years (1914–18) were marked by attitudes of mutual restraint and government intervention on behalf of the military effort. These attitudes were soon lifted as peacetime dawned. There were protracted coal disputes (1919–21) as the United Mineworkers of America (UMW) sought to organise non-union counties in West Virginia. In May 1920, there was a gun battle between miners and company guards in Mingo County, caused by the eviction of workers from company houses. Ten people were shot dead (seven of them guards).

In the post-war depression years of 1923–32 there was a 25 per cent loss of union membership and a corresponding decline in industrial violence. The presidential election of Franklin Roosevelt in November 1932 coincided with the promise of a New Deal for the American working class. This was the stimulus for a new wave of conflict primarily concerned with union recognition and the right to belong to a union.

Between 1933 and 1937, a body of sympathetic legislation was enacted, notably, the National Industrial Recovery Act 1933 and the National Labor Relations Act 1935, giving trade unions the right to organise and bargain collectively, and compelling employers to bargain in good faith. The latter piece of legislation, the so-called Wagner Act, further established penalties for employers seeking to prevent unions from organising freely and set up a new federal agency, the National Labor Relations Board (NLRB) to ensure its provisions were enforced (Wallace et al., 1988).

None the less, the employers were intent on fierce resistance. Half of the 4,650 strikes in 1937 (involving two million workers) were over union recognition. The newly formed NLRB was successful in spotlighting a variety of anti-union methods encouraged by well-known corporations. These were the years of the infamous 'American Plan', which advocated the use of blacklists, spies, injunctions and propaganda, and the 'Mohawk Valley Formula' which urged employers to use the police to break up meetings and organise vigilante groups to protect strikebreakers (Fox Piven and Cloward, 1977:120). The work of the NLRB and the publicity generated by civil liberties groups helped to turn the tide against industrial violence:

> By 1940, the period of violence was over and unionism had won acceptance. There were several reasons: most immediate, perhaps, was the need for uninterrupted production as war orders from Europe mounted; secondly, the large size of the corporations and the new degree of union strength made it difficult to recruit the many thousands of strikebreakers for full-scale industrial warfare; third, government pressures put the corporations on the defensive; and finally, the entry of the United States into the war created a need for national unity.
>
> (Bell, 1954:246)

High inflation in 1946 heralded a strike wave of unprecedented proportions: over 4.5 million workers went on strike and more working days were lost than at any time since 1927 (Wallace *et al.*, 1988:8). This was the backdrop to a rising tide of anti-trade-union sentiment and pressure by the media and employers culminating in the passing of the Labor-Management Relations Act 1947 (the Taft–Hartley Act), which purported to recreate a more equitable balance of power between unions and management by prohibiting certain unfair practices by the former and providing specific rules for handling large strikes which, in the president's view, constituted national emergencies.

Section 8(b)(1)(A) of the 1947 Act gave the National Labor Relations Board the necessary power to proceed against union tactics involving 'violence, intimidation and reprisal or threats'. The Board's overriding concern was to deprive employees found guilty of such acts of their reinstatement rights. The Labor–Management Reporting and Disclosure Act 1959 (the Landrum–Griffin Act) imposed added restrictions on picketing, strikes and boycotts and limited the union leaders' control over union funds and other administrative matters.

According to Taft and Ross, the object of this legislation was the 'substitution of orderly procedures for trials of combat' (Taft and Ross, 1969:287). The cumulative effect of successive legislative acts has been, on the one hand to provide a platform for asserting labor's right to contend on an equal footing with capital but, on the other hand, to limit the very capacity to engage in militant confrontation. The price of legitimate access to the political arena is tactical moderation.

(Wallace *et al.*, 1988:23)

Many American academics now look upon strike violence as an occasional, rather than endemic, feature of American industry (Rubenstein, 1989:322). This view is not shared by Thieblot and Haggard. They maintain that,

Far from being an interesting but irrelevant aspect of collective labor relations, such violence and bloodshed continue to the present day. In many industries, a strike in 1984 is almost as likely to result in fatalities, injuries, or destruction of property as it would have been in 1934 or even 1904.

(Thieblot and Haggard, 1983:3)

Their study, based on newspaper accounts across the 6-year period, 1975–81, refers to 2,598 incidents of violence; 49 deaths; 2,732 instances of damage to vehicles (including tyre damage); the use of 20 tons of TNT explosive; 182 attacks on buildings or property; and finally,133 cases where homes were shot at, firebombed or vandalised. Obviously, these authors are including the threat or application of violence by, or against individuals, whereas this book refers to collective confrontations of a distinctively public nature.

Nevertheless, several of their assertions provide useful talking points. According to their data, the United Mineworkers of America is the 'most violent' of the larger American trade unions, with 7.36 incidents per 10,000 members during the period studied, compared with an average of 1.2 for twenty major unions with memberships of over 100,000. The authors also devote a chapter to describing the UMW's violent conduct during strikes in 1977 and 1981. Given its comparative relevance to the British coal dispute, it is essential that we examine this conduct in more detail.

Strike violence involving the UMW

In order to understand the UMW's tactics, one must first realise that the coal industry has a centralised bargaining structure. Since 1950, contracts have been negotiated at 3-yearly intervals between the Bituminous Coal Operators Association (BCOA) and the UMW. There has been a ritualised tendency, in the event of a failure to agree a contract, for union mines to close until settlement is achieved. Non-union mines are then persuaded by pickets to close down (technically illegally) to improve the strike's effectiveness. Every negotiation from 1968 to 1981 resulted in strikes (Navarro, 1983:214). The sticking point in the national strike of 1977 was the union's right to stage wildcat strikes between contracts, which had reached a very high level in 1975 and 1976.

The strike started in December 1977. It was called under very unfavourable conditions for the UMW. There was a low US energy dependence on coal (only 18–20 per cent); several months' stockpiles of coal were held by key consumers; UMW-dominated mines held a low share of the total number of national contracts (around 52 per cent, compared with 67 per cent in 1974); there was a growing influence on the markets of western strip mines (which tended to be non-union or organised by the International Union of Operating Engineers) who would not be sympathetic; and finally, the petroleum crisis of the early 1970s had prompted the re-opening of many smaller mines (6,100 operating units in 1969 to 7,000 in 1977) which were non-union. Thus,

> To win the strike on their terms, the unionists would have to shut down not only the union mines, but also the non-union ones – at least in the East where the manpower was available to do it. But their efforts were likely to be resisted by an increasingly strong non-union segment.
>
> (Thieblot and Haggard, 1983:99–100)

The UMW's primary targets of attention were some 1,800 non-union mines and a host of independent transportation companies. Within 2 days of the start, an explosion had wrecked a drilling machine at a small non-union mine.

> By the time the Taft–Hartley Act was invoked ninety-five days later, there would be a total of two killings, two assaults, thirty-five bombings, the taking of one hostage, and seventy-one other 'disruptions' involving such things as sabotage of railroads, gunfire directed against people, trains, and motor vehicles, property damage, and other incidents of violence serious enough to be noted by the Department of Justice.
>
> (Thieblot and Haggard, 1983:101)

In 1981, the union's position was even weaker: UMW mines accounted for only 44 per cent of national coal production; again, there were large stockpiles of coal; and generally, there was a more conservative, anti-union climate:

> The political winds had also been blowing from a different and more

conservative direction. In the event of trouble, many of the nonunion operators now would have easier access – in some cases for the first time – to the political system and its protective police arm.

(Thieblot and Haggard, 1983:112)

In Virginia, for example, large patrols of state police were deployed, restraining collective violence, but encouraging cat-and-mouse tactics by the UMW, whereby

Groups of strikers assembled and disbanded, led their trooper escorts on pointless all-night drives in caravans, painted broom handles to resemble gun barrels and pointed them out of windows, and generally tried to confuse the authorities with multiple feints and parries.

(Thieblot and Haggard, 1983:117)

Thieblot and Haggard do not provide a systematic analysis of the reasons for the supposedly violence-prone nature of the UMW, or indeed, for the differing characteristics of the 1977 and 1981 disputes. They present a general argument which sees violence as resulting from a widespread reluctance by the legal authorities to invoke potentially effective legislation, and tacitly to endorse such misbehaviour by passing it off as 'picket-line horseplay' or exuberance.

Nevertheless, these authors do list those characteristics of the 'strike setting' which they consider most conducive to violence (Thieblot and Haggard, 1983:10–11). Thus the probability of violence is high where: the industry is fragmented into a large number of firms; workers of the strike-hit firm are well-paid, but easily replaced (notably under conditions of high unemployment); union leaders condone the use of violence; the strike issues relate to matters of 'union security' rather than pay; and institutions like the police and media implicitly condone violence.

Thieblot and Haggard emphasise that these observations are made only on the basis of 'preliminary analysis' and do not offer any empirical validation. Notably absent from this taxonomy is any reference to the socio-political context – somewhat of a surprise given their reference to the changing direction of the 'political winds' in the 1981 coal strike. This variable, and others approximating to those listed by Thieblot and Haggard, are included in a recently formulated model by Canadian researchers. Certain of the variables included in this model augment the flashpoints approach to industrial confrontation. It is therefore essential that we study it in close detail.

A CANADIAN MODEL OF STRIKE VIOLENCE

Using official strike data from Ontario for the period 1958–1967, Grant and Wallace (1991) conclude that strike violence is a function of the following variables: (i) the legislative environment, (ii) the sociopolitical context, (iii) the distribution of skills among the workforce (and its corresponding degree of participation in the strike), and (iv) the strategies employed by the strikers and their employers.

Referring to variations in the legislative environment, Grant and Wallace explain that, under the Canadian industrial relations system, strikes may only legally occur after a compulsory waiting period has expired and a conciliation board has met to discuss the differences between workers and employers. According to Grant and Wallace, this technicality helps determine whether strikes turn violent. There tends to be more division between workers where the strike may be defined as 'illegal'; employers are likewise more apt to continue production and employ strikebreakers; and trade unions are more likely to elicit more public condemnation and encounter 'more vigorous state repression' when they deliberately flout the law (ibid.:1125).

In emphasising the significance of the 'socio-political context', Grant and Wallace point out that the existence of a pro-labour climate is likely to encourage high levels of violence. This is because a 'friendly' government is less likely to suppress violent conduct by its voters. Alternatively, violence is likely to decline during election years, when trade unionists are careful to protect 'their' party's image. High unemployment is singled out as a second, key socio-political variable: depressed labour markets mean that replacement workers are available, and this could lead to confrontations as they try to cross picket lines. The issues over which strikes are fought also fall into the category of relevant political variables. Strikes over ideological issues (e.g. union recognition and conditions of work) are liable to be more violent than bread-and-butter issues like wages and hours of work. The latter tend to be less emotive and are more amenable to compromise.

The 'skill mix' of the workforce may have a bearing on the conduct of the strike, since skilled workers tend to have a more harmonious relationship with the employer, and their relatively favoured position in the labour market usually enables them to achieve their demands without having to resort to violence. By contrast, semi-skilled and unskilled workers may have to employ more militant (i.e. potentially violent) tactics. Since they are more easily replaced, the employer is more likely to use strikebreakers against them. Differences of value-orientation may be manifested in contrasting levels of commitment and readiness to cross picket lines. The prospect of violence is greatest where there is a roughly equal division of support for and against the strike.

Finally, the strike strategies adopted by employers and workers will influence whether or not violence occurs. An employer's determination to maintain plant operations (possibly via the use of strikebreakers) and stare down the opposition through a protracted strike carries a high risk of violence. While the mobilisation of large numbers of pickets may be advantageous to the union's cause, it also invites problems of disorganisation and indiscipline.

DISCUSSION

The studies of Thieblot and Haggard and Grant and Wallace provide a useful checklist of those features of a 'strike setting' which make it particularly conducive to disorder. This checklist encompasses a range of relevant variables, such as the influence of particular forms of legislation, the condition of the economy, the principal features of the industry, its product and employees, and the central issues of the strike itself. Such variables are too specific to industrial relations to be included in the flashpoints model of public disorder. As such, they help to complement and enhance our understanding of strike violence; though, as the Orgreave case study demonstrates, the flashpoints model provides an adequate general basis for analysing picket-line disorder.

Certain key variables highlighted by Grant and Wallace correspond to those factors considered especially crucial by the flashpoints model. For example, each model sees the amount of legitimacy conferred upon a dispute as influencing the way it is handled by the police; and there is similar agreement that deep-seated 'ideological issues' are more commonly associated with disorder than more mundane 'material issues'.

There is more room for disagreement with Grant and Wallace's assertion that a pro-labour climate is most conducive to strike violence, principally because workers may feel that such behaviour will be tolerated under a supportive regime. The British experience of the past two decades suggests a positive correlation between the anti-union sentiments and activities of government and picket-line disorder. There may be a methodological basis for this disagreement. Grant and Wallace establish the relationship between strike violence and pro-labour climates on the oversimplified basis of a correlation between the incidence and severity of disorder and the percentage of Liberal seats in the Canadian parliament. As the all-party condemnation of mass picketing in Britain in the 1980s demonstrated, few politicians will express public support for militant trade-union tactics, and even those supporters of the labour movement may be reserved or critical in their attitudes.

Taken together, the historical and contemporary British and American examples reviewed above suggest that the way trade unions are perceived by society and responded to by the state are key factors in the genesis of industrial confrontation. Picket-line relations have been most tranquil in those periods of British and American history characterised by 'consensus politics' – where trade unions have been accepted into the polity (the government and those who are able to influence its policies) as legitimate 'members', rather than excluded as 'challengers' (cf. Ragin *et al.*, 1982:241).

By contrast, collective violence has been most prevalent and virulent during historical periods when trade unionism has been stigmatised as threatening or inimical to the interests and well-being of society. Under such circumstances, permissive legal structures have enabled governments or private employers to resort to strike-breaking tactics involving the police or military to prevent or undermine trade union organisation. Thus violence was sustained at a high level by American capital's 'first great offensive against labor' from the late-nineteenth century to the 1920s. In Britain, conflict was most severe prior to the First World War, when the power to call out the police and troops lay in the hands of local em- ployer/magistrates, and occasions like the General Strike of 1926 when fears of a worker revolution were aroused.

Since the mid-1960s, the post-war consensus politics of British society have virtually been abandoned: trade unions can no longer presume to have a partnership role and have increasingly been perceived as problematic to the national interest. The primacy of the individual's 'right to work' has been upheld as sacrosanct, to be defended at all cost against the 'tyranny of the mass picket'. Such was the message which right-wing politicians and the British press delivered to the police from 1983 and beyond. The 'space' which once existed for police and pickets to negotiate a mutually accept- able code of picket-line conduct has been closed off, as the miners and striking print workers disovered to their cost. The British coal dispute of 1984–5 had more in common with the American 'labor struggles' of the early twentieth century than the post-reform era UMW strikes of 1977 and 1981. Force, not compromise, was the key political watchword, and disorder the inevitable result.

Chapter 6

Football hooliganism

THE HEYSEL TRAGEDY

The summer of 1985 was described by one prominent football historian as 'the lowest ebb in the fortunes of British football' (Walvin, 1986:6). Two major disasters, costing ninety-four lives, provoked an unprecedented public outcry and led to a series of punitive measures against British clubs and their supporters. First there was the Bradford City fire. This occurred at an end-of-season game where a large crowd was gathered to celebrate the team's promotion to the second division. Fire broke out in an old, litter-strewn stand which soon became a death trap in which fifty-six people perished.

Within a few weeks of this tragedy, on 29 May 1985, further disaster struck at the European Cup Final between Italy's Juventus and England's Liverpool at Brussels' Heysel Stadium. This happened when Juventus fans were chased out of an enclosure dominated by English supporters and, in the ensuing panic and rush to escape, a stadium wall collapsed, producing an appalling crush of bodies in which thirty-eight people (mostly Italian) died and 400 more were injured.

The resulting Committee of Inquiry (Popplewell, 1986), highlighted the problematic nature of crowd-control arrangements for the final (notably the failure to ensure the effective segregation of rival supporters and the inadequate numbers of gendarmerie), and weaknesses in the physical structure of the stadium. The Committeee refuted suggestions that the British National Front had deliberately provoked the disorder, but indicated that large numbers of spectators had consumed too much alcohol. They emphasised as their 'final and most important lesson...that if hooligans did not behave like hooligans at football matches there would be no such risk of injury' (ibid.:8).

Following massive international condemnation, an indefinite ban was imposed on all English clubs playing in Europe. As Walvin (1986:9) explains, 'The country which had developed and then exported the game found itself ostracised and reviled in the world's footballing fraternity.' The Heysel tragedy was but the latest incident in a catalogue of infamy which had dogged the British game, both home and abroad, for as long as people could remember (ibid.).

In April 1989, hundreds of Liverpool fans were crushed to death on the terraces of Sheffield's Hillsborough Stadium before the FA Cup semi-final between Liverpool and Nottingham Forest. There was initial speculation that hooligan behaviour had contributed to the disaster, but an official inquiry by Lord Justice Taylor (Taylor, 1989) blamed police crowd-management tactics.

The Hillsborough disaster seemed to encourage a period of self-reflection and greater public sympathy for the beleaguered game of soccer. The ban on British clubs was lifted (except for Liverpool). There were hopeful indications of a possible decline in hooliganism both inside and outside the ground. However, 'riots' before and after the Leeds United match at Bournemouth in May 1990, which resulted in 120 arrests, suggested that football hooliganism had far from disappeared and that there was still no basis for complacency.

This chapter describes and analyses soccer spectator violence, both domestically and when British teams play abroad. The chapter begins by characterising the different forms of football hooliganism, and makes broad generalisations about the type of people who are most commonly involved. Preliminary insights are then developed by studying explanations of disorder (or the lack of it) at American soccer and baseball matches, and of sports riots in general. Particular emphasis is placed at this point on the distinction between *issue-oriented* and *issueless* riots, the latter tending to occur in the absence of any justificatory rationale (Marx, 1972). This distinction provides a useful basis for a review and evaluation of specific theoretical approaches to football hooliganism.

THE NATURE OF FOOTBALL HOOLIGANISM

Before discussing possible explanations of football hooliganism, it is necessary to clarify the different forms of behaviour incorporated within this term, where these activities typically occur, and what kinds of people most commonly engage in them. According to Melnick (1986:1–2), 'The forms of misbehaviour commonly associated with football hooliganism include physical assaults on opposing fans and police, pitch invasions, throwing missiles, verbal abuse, vandalism, drunkenness, theft and possession of an offensive weapon.' Such activities can vary in severity. For example, 'assaults on opposing fans' could refer to a fist fight between two rival supporters or a massive chase involving hundreds of people. Similarly, 'throwing missiles' embraces a number of possible behaviours ranging from the hurling of an orange to the lobbing of petrol bombs (Dunning *et al.*, 1986).

The nature and prevalence of soccer spectator disorder has undergone a number of historical transformations. The incidence of crowd misbehaviour reached a high point before the First World War, fell between the two World Wars, and continued to fall until the late-1950s, since when it continued to increase quite rapidly (Dunning *et al.*, 1982; 1984). Most contemporary forms of disorder have been evident since the inception of professional soccer in the 1870s. 'However, the balance between the different forms has tended to vary. More particularly, attacks on players and match officials were predominant before the First World War, whilst fights between opposing fan groups are predominant today' (Dunning, 1990:76).

There is clear evidence that both the pervasiveness and seriousness of soccer violence have been exaggerated: 'The plain fact is, the great majority of spectators who attend football matches are unlikely to ever witness an instance of personal assault let alone be the victim of one' (Melnick, 1986:9). This is chiefly because the hard-core hooligan element attached to one soccer club is only likely to be interested in a confrontation with the opposition's elite hooligan crew.

It is misleading to imagine that soccer violence most frequently occurs inside the football ground. This may once have been the case. As recently as the 1970s, for example, great kudos was attached to 'infiltrating' the section of end terracing behind the goals where opposing fans were gathered. However, this tactic has been abandoned due to improved police surveillance and the greater likelihood of being caught. Consequently, football hooliganism is more likely to occur wherever rival fans meet – i.e. in shopping centres, public houses, inside railway stations, on roads and rail, and motorway service stations (Dunning *et al.*, 1986).

The hooligan fans are mostly white, working-class males aged 17–20. (Though there are substantial deviations from this profile which we shall refer to below.) Often, the groups of fans most dedicated to hooligan behaviour are organised into hard-core 'fighting crews' (e.g. the Leeds United 'Service Crew', Manchester United's 'Red Devils', West Ham's 'Inter City Crew', Chelsea's 'Anti-Personnel Firm', Arsenal's 'Gooners', Millwall's 'Bushwackers', Tottenham's 'The Spurs Yids' and, in Scotland, Aberdeen's 'Soccer Casuals').

Several studies emphasise that, far from being marginally interested in the game, hooligan supporters tend to be among the most committed and knowledgeable of fans (Dunning *et al.*, 1986). It is equally undeniable that they derive great pleasure from physical confrontations with rival groups of supporters and go to great lengths to evade the authorities and make such confrontations possible. Such fans tend not to travel on the regular 'soccer special' bus coaches and trains, preferring to use scheduled public transport. Contrary to the popular stereotype, they take care to dress smartly, according to current youth fashions. Each of these devices improves the chances of escaping police surveillance (cf. *Observer*, 2 June 1985).

Other popular myths also fail to withstand close scrutiny. While there is no doubt that fascist organisations like the National Front have attempted to recruit members from the ranks of football hooligans, there is little to connect them with violence in the game (Popplewell, 1986:59). Dunning and co-workers (1986) further point out that there is little proof that soccer violence is caused by the excessive drinking of alcohol: many hooligans seldom drink prior to the match to keep a 'clear head' for any aggression which might take place. Common sense also suggests that there are many people who drink before attending sporting contests but do not become involved in fighting. While violence on the field of play may generate tension and even trigger violence, one must probe a little deeper to discover the underlying *social* roots of the problem.

AMERICAN SPECTATOR VIOLENCE

It is possible that some basis for explaining British football hooliganism may be found in appropriate studies of American sports-related disorder. Though violence sometimes occurs at American sporting contests, it is seldom of a comparable scale and intensity to the football hooliganism which so often takes place in Britain, West Germany, the Netherlands and Latin America (Guttmann, 1986; Smith, 1983). Lewis (1982) calculates that there were 312 sports-related 'riots' in the USA between 1962 and 1970. The seriousness of these riots varied in range, from object throwing and fist fights involving a handful of fans, to pitch invasions and damage to property involving several hundred participants. Nevertheless, the figures indicate that 97 (31 per cent) of the riots occurred at baseball matches and 66 (21 per cent) at American football games, with basketball (17 per cent) and hockey (12.5 per cent) recording the next highest frequencies.

Overall, the figures offer qualified support for Guttmann's assertion that spectator violence is class-related (1986:164). In contrast to the British game, American soccer is watched by a more middle-class audience of both sexes, and is practically devoid of violence. Against this, the largely 'blue-collar' sport of baseball is often affected by crowd disorder. It is worth pausing to look at the degree of crowd disorder associated with these sports and the possible reasons for such profiles.

British and American soccer violence compared

Football spectator violence is virtually absent from American society. The contrast with the British situation seems largely explicable in terms of the differing degrees of fan involvement in the sport, the class and gender composition of the crowd and the way the sport is packaged and approached as a form of entertainment. Roadburg (1980) provides a checklist of the key historical, ecological and social factors distinguishing British soccer as a spectator sport from its American counterpart. One important distinction is that British soccer fans tend to have a much greater sense of commitment to, and identification with, both the game itself and their favoured soccer team than American soccer spectators.

As Roadburg points out, 'the average British soccer fan is more able than his (sic) North American counterpart to identify with the game as a product of his heritage and culture' (Roadburg, 1980:269). There is a partisanship and collective involvement, heightened by the segregation of opposing fans (most notably behind each goal) which is absent from the American game. In the USA, loyalty is more likely to be spread across a variety of different sports and support for any one team is liable to be tenuous. Away supporters are seldom, if ever, present and the crowd has less solidarity: the match-day involvement is more privatised, starting off with a family 'tailgate party' (an informal car-park meal) before each spectator strolls to his or her seat. By contrast, most British supporters walk the last part of the way to the stadium and derive a greater sense of excitement, anticipation and being part of a crowd.

Guttmann (1986:10) reports that 74 per cent of North American Soccer League spectators are college-educated, and 45 per cent are women. Whilst Roadburg may underestimate the size of the middle-class and female components of the British soccer crowd, he is correct to emphasise that the terraces are chiefly made up of working-class males and that, of this group, it is the youth segment which most often engages in violence. Roadburg surmises that adolescent gang violence against persons and property is common to both societies, but that soccer acts as a vehicle of expression for deprived or disaffected youth in Britain in a way which is not possible in America.

Roadburg seems to be suggesting that certain characteristics of the

British fans' involvement in the game (partisanship, segregation, collective identity and pre-match build-up) give rise to a greater degree of passionate commitment (and enhanced potential for disorder) than in the American equivalent. He gives equal emphasis to the possibility that such characteristics make the game an ideal vehicle for aggressive confrontations between rival groups of young males. As we shall see in a later section, these views are consistent with the current thinking of several British theorists on soccer spectator violence.

Violence at baseball matches

As Fimrite points out, the popular, working-class sport of baseball has a disorderly tradition.

> The baseball fan at the beginning of the century – free of the possibly inhibiting influence of women spectators and close enough to the playing field in those tiny ball parks to take immediate action against erring players or umpires – was, by all accounts, an abysmal churl.
>
> (Fimrite, 1976:204)

In the intervening decades, there was 'a general trend toward spectator civility' (Talamini, 1987:66), only for aspects of disorder to creep back into the sport by the 1970s. A catalogue of disorderly incidents have occurred at baseball matches in the last two decades. Players, umpires and rival fans have found themselves being physically attacked by objects as varied as flashlight batteries and souvenir baseball bats (Edwards and Rackages, 1977; Fimrite, 1976; Talamini, 1987).

During the past two decades there have also been a number of disorderly sequels to championship victories. For example, when Detroit triumphed over the San Diego Padres in the 1984 World Series,

> A riot reigned for two and a half hours after the last game ended. The crowds burned one police car, destroyed five others, threw bottles at helmeted police, torched an overturned taxi, and ripped sod from the playing field at Tiger Stadium.
>
> (Talamini, 1987:67)

Popular wisdom suggests that baseball crowd violence is due to a combination of the macho tendencies of 20- to 30-year-old males, fuelled by the heavy consumption of beer. The growth of baseball 'rowdyism' in the late-nineteenth century has been an inverse function of diminishing female attendance at the game (Guttmann, 1986:114–15). Crowd-control measures have focused on the limitation or prohibition of alcohol, and the installation of special family enclosures, usually patrolled by extra security personnel (ibid.).

Fimrite (1976:204) disputes that alcohol is to blame for the apparent upsurge of violence in the 1970s. As he says, 'there has been beer in the ball parks for years'. He posits that some of the changing trends in baseball violence are due to the increased commercialisation of the sport. From the early part of this century,

> the ball parks grew larger and the players, seen from a greater distance, grew smaller, less familiar, less vulnerable. From afar, they looked like heroes, and for at least 30 years or more there was a general trend toward spectator conformity. The ball diamond was a sanctuary not to be broken into by philistines. Then, too, there was no television to tantalize the show-offs.
>
> (Fimrite, 1976:204)

In recent years, the affective bond between players and fans has weakened. Increasingly, stars are accused of disloyalty to the hometown team for 'callously' seeking transfers to teams in higher leagues; or perceived as just 'another member of the Establishment' for spending too much time haggling over pay and fringe benefits. There has consequently developed 'an alienation of affections between fan and athlete'. This, and the growing trend in American society to express displeasure more vociferously and outspokenly than in the past, is said to lie at the root of recent player-directed violence (ibid.:204–5).

It is evident from the above profile that baseball spectator disorder tends not to involve fighting between opposing groups of disorder. Rather, it typically involves acts of aggression towards players and officials, or over-exuberant celebratory activity including the vandalism of property. As such, it does little to help explain the fighting behaviour of British hooligans.

GENERAL MODELS OF SPECTATOR DISORDER

How far, then, do general models of spectator disorder inform our understanding of hooligan behaviour? There are several such approaches in the American literature. Some researchers emphasise the potentially arousing effect of watching aggressive contact sports (Goldstein and Arms, 1971; Harrell, 1981; Russell, 1983). However, the futility of this approach becomes apparent if we compare the levels of disorder at soccer, boxing and ice-hockey events. Soccer is the least violent sport of the three, but the one most synonymous with crowd disorder (Pilz, 1988:168–9).

A second category of explanations employ functionalist approaches to the study of spectator disorder. Smith (1976), for example, adopts Smelser's framework of analysis (see Chapter 1) as a basis for understanding football hooliganism.

Structural conduciveness, as applied here, deals with those features of a situation which predispose it to disorder. Here Smith (1976) includes 'natural rivalries' between spectators, based on nation, region, religion, ethnicity, etc.; the absence of channels for expressing grievances, as in industrially underdeveloped or politically undemocratic societies; the possibility of communication among the aggrieved (e.g. the 'cheek-to-jowl congestion at soccer stadia' or the dissemination of rumour or hostile beliefs via the media); and the 'accessibility of objects of attack', such as referees or unsegregated soccer fans.

As Smith points out, 'Conditions of conduciveness merely make the hostile outburst possible. The existence of a strain, conflict, deprivation or ambiguity, usually accompanied by stereotyped beliefs assigning responsibility for evils to other groups, is the second structural determinant' (ibid.:206). To illustrate this point, he refers to the Honduras–El Salvador 'soccer war' of 1969 in which a series of hotly contested border disputes provided the context for three riotous soccer matches in the World Cup qualifying rounds.

The growth and spread of a hostile belief is necessary to give meaning to the structural strain, possibly by assigning responsibility and designating a certain response as appropriate. 'Prior to and during the three game Honduras-El Salvador series, for example, the press reported charges of "mistreatment" of Honduras fans at the hands of El Salvadoreans and accusations of "brutality" directed at players on both teams.'(ibid.).

Precipitating incidents, such as rough play or disputed refereeing decisions, have the effect of narrowing hostile beliefs into 'specific antipathies'. It is at this stage that the mobilisation of participants for action begins. Often, the behaviour of one spectator may (however unwittingly) serve as a model for others. From then on, the shape and extent of the ensuing disorder will depend on the prior organisation of the crowd, the ecology (or lay-out) of the stadium, and the response of the police. Smith favours the view that decisive policing will most effectively quell the rioting, but concedes that premature intervention may well generate uncontrollable panic.

An alternative functionalist approach has been attempted by Edwards and Rackages (1977). These authors see the spectating of sporting events as functional for society. During times of economic and political stability, on-the-field sports violence allows for tension release, through vicarious identification with the aggressor. This helps the sports spectator to cope with the frustrations and disappointments of everyday life ('particularly those of instrumental relevance') and helps reaffirm his/her commitment to society's values. However, under conditions of social instability where the individual's deteriorating 'life circumstances' generate acute feelings of anxiety, sport may be incapable of providing adequate relief. Thus there is a potential that 'processes or relationships in the general society may transform on-the-field episodes of violent *or* non-violent sport into a catalyst precipitating violent collective behavior by spectators themselves' (ibid.:13).

Aside from the obvious problems associated with structural–functionalist approaches of this nature – chiefly the dubious assumption that violent behaviour is aberrant or irrational (Pearton, 1986:77) – each of these studies has serious limitations. Smith's application of Smelser's model is forced to rely on an assortment of different examples and there is little sense of how well it applies to separate case studies. The model contributes little to our understanding of why 'hooliganism' is synonymous with soccer, why it is more prevalent at certain times in history than others, and why it is predominantly a male, lower-working-class phenomenon.

Edwards and Rackages base their approach on the highly questionable premise that spectator violence is merely a playing out of tensions external to sport itself. Going by their logic, we would expect to see riotous behaviour by stressed small business owners and financial investors at rugby union or American football matches. But neither of these is common. They fail to consider that the fans' cultural and historical relationship to a particular sport may be significant. Even more damaging to their theory is the fact that sports spectator disorder is not always synonymous with economic problems. Finally, it would have difficulties explaining the disorder accompanying championship victory, referred to above.

The need to differentiate between different types of riot and the contrasting meanings involved for the participants is recognised by Smith (1983). Borrowing from the ideas of Marx (1972), Smith makes the basic distinction between *issue-oriented* riots and *issueless* riots. The former typically involve some sort of 'legitimating belief', i.e. 'a belief, attitude, grievance, ideology, or definition of the situation held by riot participants that directly ties the riot to some problem in the social structure and justifies or explains (their) behaviour, at least to themselves (Smith, 1983:146). By contrast, issueless riots are not usually underpinned by such legitimating belief: 'Protest and demands for social change are not significant elements in the genesis of the issueless riot, nor does the issueless riot tend to result in changes in people's life conditions' (ibid.).

Smith then makes a finer distinction between four types of issue-

Table 6.1 Two typologies of sports-crowd riots

Smith (1983)	*Mann and Pearce (1978)*
(a) Issue-oriented	
Demonstration riot Spectators use a sports event to make a political statement or express a grievance	*Remonstrance disorder* Section of crowd uses a sports arena to express a political grievance
Confrontation riot Hostility is vented on members or symbols of an opposing group to promote a cause or ideology	*Confrontation disorder* A hostile expression of rivalry based on religious, geographical or ethnic division
Entry riot Occurs where fans are denied access to a sports event they hope to or feel entitled to see	*Frustration disorder* Breaks out when sense of injustice arises due to denial of access, or the way the game is played or adjudicated
Defeat riot Stems from bitterness over losing, or an unjust action or decision which contributes to a loss	
(b) Issueless	*Expressive disorder* Results from intense emotions accompanying victory or defeat (especially where match is exciting and outcome is unexpected)
Victory riot High-spiritedness accompanying victory (i.e. revelry, drunkenness, vandalism)	
Time-out riot Accompanies a special occasion (a holiday, carnival or festival) where usual norms of propriety are relaxed	*Outlawry disorder* Where violently disposed spectators use a sports event to act out anti-social tendencies

oriented riots (demonstration, confrontation, entry and defeat riots) and two forms of issueless riots (victory and time-out). As Table 6.1 shows, there is a high degree of correlation between his typology of sports-crowd riots and the five types of violent sports disorder nominated by Mann and Pearce (1978).

Among the most relevant of these categories to the present discussion are Smith's time-out riots, and Mann and Pearce's outlawry disorders. The latter (where sports events provide groups of spectators with an opportunity to act out their violent tendencies) could easily relate to the behaviour of fighting crews. Similarly, Smith maintains that:

> Much of what is called soccer hooliganism smacks strongly of time-out behaviour. Most of the scholarly literature on the subject suggests that hooligans are as much motivated by the desire for fun, excitement, and peer status as they are by ethnic, regional, or other animosities. The latter seem more of a pretext for trouble than a cause of it.
>
> (Smith, 1983:152)

Vamplew (1979:2f) states that, of the five types of disorder classified by Mann and Pearce, 'all but remonstrance can be found at soccer grounds in the nineteenth and early twentieth centuries, though the majority of incidents appear to have been of the frustration or confrontation varieties'. However, most contemporary football hooliganism corresponds to the outlawry of time-out forms manifested in fights between opposing fans and creating mayhem during trips abroad. Thus the principal task of theories which specifically address modern football hooliganism is to account for these dominant forms of behaviour.

ACADEMIC EXPLANATIONS OF FOOTBALL HOOLIGANISM

Theoretical explanations of soccer spectator violence occupy four distinct categories. First, there is the early Marxist approach of Ian Taylor which emphasises that hooligan behaviour is a symbolic attempt by working-class fans to restore some control over a game which they feel increasingly alienated from. Second, there is the ethogenic approach of Peter Marsh and his colleagues which sees soccer spectator violence as a ritual expression of masculine aggression. A third explanation, the ordered segmentation approach of Eric Dunning and his co-workers, highlights the significance of lower-working-class gang structures and early socialisation as the key to understanding the patterns of aggression displayed by football hooligans. A final group of approaches see football spectator disorder as a way of compensating for the loss of community caused by post-war industrial and urban development. We begin by looking at one of the seminal theories of soccer spectator disorder, the Marxist approach of Ian Taylor.

Taylor's subcultural approach

Taylor's (1971a; 1971b) Marxist approach sees contemporary spectator violence as a consequence of the increasing loss of control experienced by working-class football supporters over a game which they previously regarded as theirs. His central premise is that most English football clubs were established by working-class occupational groups. For example, Sheffield United were founded by a group of cutlers (hence, their nick-name, the 'Blades'), while West Ham United (the 'Irons') were formed by workers at the Thames Iron Foundry.

Though these clubs grew and become more formalised, supporters were still able to maintain an illusion of participation in the team's affairs. This was because players invariably came from the local community and, by meeting fans in pubs, clubs and at civic functions, somehow seemed accountable to them. Similarly, managers and directors appeared to share an equivalent value orientation to the fans and were more receptive to their opinions. Supporters could perceive themselves as part of 'a collective and democratically-structured enterprise'. The main reason why working-class youths did not invade the pitch in the 1930s was because the ground was theirs and the playing area was sacred (Taylor, 1971a).

Modern changes in the game – specifically its *bourgeoisification* and *internationalisation* – are held to have undermined this illusion of participatory democracy. By bourgeoisification, Taylor is referring to the increasing emphasis within the game on comfort and entertainment manifested in such developments as the reconstruction of grounds as commercial stadia (with covered stands, seats and floodlights), the payment of large transfer fees and the freedom of contract for players which enabled them to command large salaries. Internationalisation refers to the incursion of English soccer into European competitions. Set against these develop-ments, soccer hooliganism may be interpreted as 'attempts by certain sections of the class to assert some inarticulate, but keenly experienced sense of control over the game that was theirs' (Taylor, 1971a:163). According to Taylor it is the working-class element of the crowd, and not football's new, middle-class supporters, who have the most developed knowledge of, and commitment to, the club (i.e. they possess a true 'soccer conscious-ness'). For this 'subcultural rump',

> To induce a goalkeeper by distraction to kick into touch is to win a symbolic victory which may affect the result and one side's league position. Whereas to invade a pitch when a goal is disallowed may be felt *magically* as a way of reversing the referee's decision. And in the most final sense of all, to be arrested while fighting opposing supporters may

be felt as a way of conveying to the management by means of some psychic process the nature of the 'really genuine supporter', and the character of his identification.

(Taylor, 1971b:369)

There is general agreement that Taylor has oversimplified the traditional relationship which once existed between working-class supporters and their clubs. Whannel (1979) doubts, for example, whether soccer clubs ever were participatory democracies. He points out that, of the sixty-six English clubs founded in the nineteenth century, forty were limited companies before 1900, and there were a further nineteen by 1914.

Dunning's and his co-workers' (1984) historical survey of Football Association minutes and reports contained in the *Leicester Mercury* also provides evidence of pitch invasions and other forms of crowd disorder as early as the 1890s. These outbreaks were typically spontaneous and unpremeditated; there is no evidence of a football resistance movement in action. A further weakness of the theory is that it does not explain why so much hooligan activity is based on fan rivalries *within* the working class; nor can it deal with Wagg's (1984:198) observation that 'the most notable attempts by a club's following to prevent it parting with a popular player or manager have usually been initiated by middle-class people'. In a later subsection, we shall see how Taylor has since reformulated his approach to soccer hooliganism. For the time being, we move on to the second of our theoretical perspectives, the ethogenic approach.

The ethogenic approach

The ethogenic approach looks upon football hooliganism as a ritualised expression of aggression, resulting from a need to demonstrate dominance and masculinity (Marsh *et al.*, 1978). According to this conception, disorder is rule-governed: much of the 'aggro' which occurs is largely symbolic, comprising a relatively harmless repertoire of threats, stares, denigratory chants and gestures (cf. Marsh, 1975:9).

Comfortingly, almost, Marsh and colleagues (1978) explain that aggro seldom results in serious injury. This is because those involved tend to be aware of the unwritten set of rules which determine when it is legitimate to attack and when to desist. Aggro is likely to be considered appropriate in situations where opposing fans attempt a territorial invasion of their rivals' 'end'; where one hooligan fan stares at, or adopts a threatening posture towards an opponent, or calls him a demasculatory name, such as 'cunt', 'wanker', or 'poofta'. Alternatively, some types of incident on the field of play – notably the scoring of a goal, foul play by a member of the opposing team or a bad refereeing decision – may also serve as instigatory cues.

A different set of rules then operate to impose limitations on the expression of aggro. Generally speaking, such rules specify that violence should cease when honour has been satisfied. A 'smack in the mouth' will usually be sufficient, especially if the opponent then backs down or buttons his lip. In situations involving large numbers on both sides, honour will be satisfied by 'running' the opposition supporters (i.e. causing them to flee).

Life on the 'end' offers the actual or aspiring hooligan an alternative career as part of the 'Rowdies': 'This "career structure" gives some young people a sense of individual achievement within a semi-formal setting – opportunities denied to them in most other institutions' (Marsh, 1976:348). The 'Rowdies' are the regular hooligans who routinely chant and denigrate the opposition. Next come the older 'Town Boys' who are content to rest on their laurels and do not usually become involved in the aggro. Of all those present, the 'Aggro Leader' enjoys most status, for he is the one who most commonly leads the sorties into the opposition (though his behaviour stays strictly within the rules). This cannot be said of the 'Nutter', whose conduct is the exception which proves the rules. The fact that other fans recognise his behaviour as deplorable and 'beyond the pale' is seen as proof that most fans have a tacit knowledge of the rules of disorder.

According to Marsh and his colleagues (1978) police intervention is often welcomed by the hooligans in so far as their presence provides a safety valve and prevents the aggro from going too far. However, rules of propriety also apply to police conduct. Should they use what is regarded as excessive or unnecessary force, they, too, might well become the targets of aggression.

The ethogenic approach is open to two major criticisms. First, it makes no attempt to explain the class-specific nature of football hooliganism. And second, the theory grossly underestimates the severity of some forms of spectator violence. Witness Harrison's description of the Cardiff *v.* Manchester United match in 1974:

> At about 2.15, someone from the Cardiff side threw the first stone, then the bricks started flying: if they couldn't get at each other on land, then they could always fight a missile war and there was plenty of ammo flying around: the workmen who put the fence in had not swept up the chunks of broken concrete around the supports. Swathes opened up in the crowds on either side as they saw the brickbats coming. I saw three people hit in the face, one above the eye, one in the ear, one on the

nose, blood streaming down them. Great cheers went up when a hit was scored, or when the police dragged someone out on the opposite side.

(Harrison, 1974:602)

Since the 1980s, football hooligans have displayed a callous cunning and organisation. Pickering (1985:473) points out that members of West Ham United's Inter City Firm once settled an old grudge against Millwall's Bushwackers by throwing a rival hooligan under a passing train and stabbing another before leaving their personalised calling card: 'Nothing personal. The Inter City Firm.' On another occasion, it was the turn of Millwall fans to pursue coaches carrying Bristol City supporters across London. The police had prohibited any confrontation at the game, so the Bushwackers tracked their intended quarry in their cars, communicating with each other on CB-radio (*Observer*, 2 June 1985).

The ordered-segmentation approach

The ordered-segmentation approach shares the Marxist view that hooligans come predominantly from the lower-working class (Dunning *et al.*, 1986; 1988). Arrest statistics show an over-representation of people from a small number of working-class estates noted for their toughness and vandalism (Williams *et al.*, 1984). In order to explain this demographic effect, Dunning and co-workers borrow the concept of ordered segmentation, developed by the American sociologist, Gerald Suttles. This concept focuses on the idea that masculine gang structures, based on age-grading, sex segregation and territorial identification, are a particular characteristic of lower-working-class communities. Though keen rivals, such gangs have a propensity to combine against a common enemy.

In football terms, this implies that little 'segments' of working-class communities, which are normally in opposition, may combine in the name of the local football club to confront the common threat posed by opposition supporters. At a superseding level of conflict, northern fans (from, say, Manchester and Liverpool), may fight side by side against the visiting fans of a southern team (e.g. Arsenal). Taken to its logical conclusion, it is possible that the same three groups of supporters may combine to 'represent' England in an overseas confrontation with continental supporters (Williams *et al.*, 1984).

For Dunning and colleagues, the aggressive predisposition of these youths is linked to a socialisation process known as the *sociogenesis of masculine aggression*. From a very early age, lower-working-class boys engage in rough, exclusively masculine forms of play, free of adult supervision. Unlike middle-class children, they are seldom exposed to a parental emphasis on self-control; instead, there is an accent on physical punishment, and aggressive tendencies are further reinforced by the regular occurrence of intra- and inter-family feuds. In this environment, toughness is valued by both sexes and, as the boys grow into youths, the status and prestige they are unable to achieve via education and employment is derived from their ability to fight (Dunning, 1990:76).

As stated previously, Dunning and colleagues (1984) show how football crowd violence had a low level of incidence in the post-war years, but rose in frequency from the mid-sixties on. This is partly attributable to the increased opportunity for away travel which has increased the contact between rival groups of supporters. However, Dunning and colleagues see the chief reason as the gradual acceptance by increasing numbers of working-class people of middle-class norms of behaviour. From 1914 to the early 1960s, such factors as growing affluence, better education, the rising influence of trade unions and greater female participation in the workforce fostered a 'civilising' process. However, not all sections were 'incorporated' in this way: 'whilst the "respectable" sections of the working class have increased in size, the gap between them and the dwindling lower-working class, including the sections who remain "rough", has widened' (ibid.:237–8). The fact that youths from this category have been drawn increasingly to football since the 1960s is put down to possibilities offered for violence, as revealed by the mass media.

It was in the early 1960s that, parallel to its growing emphasis on the 'disturbing activities' of working-class youth, the media also began to focus on minor incidents of soccer crowd violence. This may have been due to the fact that preparations for hosting the 1966 World Cup Finals were under way and there were fears that, as the English game came under greater international scrutiny, football hooliganism could damage the nation's prestige. It was soon realised that media reporting of crowd disorder boosted the sales of newspapers – a matter of importance in an increasingly competitive industry. Very soon, soccer grounds became 'advertised' as somewhere where a good fight was guaranteed, hence their appeal to the 'rough' sections of society. Alarmed by this influx, many 'respectable' fans vacated their regular places on the end terraces and congregated in the stands. The resulting division of the 'home' and 'away' ends thus became an established feature of the game. As media coverage persisted and grew even more sensational, 'league tables' developed based on reputations for toughness.

Here the masculine ethos of the game and its implications for the reputation of working-class communities becomes relevant.

Given the large crowds, moreover, professional soccer provides a context where it is relatively easy to escape detection and arrest, and last but not least, a group of outsiders, the opposing team and its fans, comes regularly into the home territory where they are perceived as invaders and targets for attack. A corollary is that these fans derive pleasurable excitement from going on away trips and invading the territories of opposing fans. They are engaged in a kind of war game and one of their principal aims is to move with impunity in the sections of stadia favoured by home fans like themselves and to establish momentary control over the city centre pubs and other areas favoured by their home counterparts. It is also their aim to fight and establish physical dominance over their rivals or at least to make them run away.

(Dunning, 1990:77)

Dunning and colleagues do not pretend that football hooligans are drawn exclusively from the lower working class, or that all lower-working-class adolescents and young adults use the game as a context for fighting. They merely suggest that younger elements of the 'rough' working class are 'the most central and persistent offenders in the more serious forms of football hooliganism' (Dunning *et al.*, 1988:213).

The same authors fail to provide an entirely convincing explanation of why non-working-class hooligans (the so-called 'soccer casuals') are attracted to the violence. They can only suggest that their involvement may be due to such personal circumstances as geographical proximity to 'rougher' areas, conflict with parents or school authorities or an opportunity to act out racist tendencies. 'They may even become match-day "organizers" or "planners". However, they are not, typically, regular fighters. nor are they in our experience typically involved in the fighting end of the more seriously violent incidents' (ibid.:214–15).

A participant observation study of Sheffield United fans, purporting to show that hooligan supporters come from a variety of social backgrounds (Armstrong and Harris, 1991) has been justifiably criticised by Dunning and colleagues (1991) for its methodological shortcomings and contradictory presentation of evidence. Nevertheless, anecdotal evidence suggests that Dunning and colleagues may have overstated the extent to which hooligans originate from the lower working class.

Chelsea's Anti-Personnel Firm mainly come from affluent London suburbs, places like Croydon, Harlow, Slough, and new towns like

Bracknell and Milton Keynes. They are from upper-working-class, semi-affluent backgrounds, the *Demi-Semis*. Loyalty to urban football clubs stems from when their parents used to live in inner-city areas. Support for the old team increases, rather than decreases, when the families move out. 'It's my roots. Know what I mean?'

(*Observer*, 2 June 1985)

As we are about to discover, this evidence is more consistent with the next body of explanations to be considered in this section – those which emphasise the loss of working-class community as their key explanatory variable.

The magical recovery of community

A third group of academic theories locate the origins of contemporary football hooliganism in the post-war demise of working-class communities.

These writers have put 'football hooliganism', and developments among working-class youth generally, into the broader context of the social history of Britain since 1945 – in which the breaking up of traditional working-class communities, industrial decline, rising unemployment and periodic panics about unruly youth have all been pre-eminent. Common to much of the literature has been a notion ... that these kids – and many others like them – have been trying to 'recover magically' territory, both physical and cultural, that they have lost and to appropriate in the same way territory that has never been theirs.

(Wagg, 1984:204)

With the gradual decline of established occupations and trades went massive rehousing and the breakdown of community and neighbourhood ties. With the onset of greater affluence and associated higher wages, came the privatisation and commercialisation of leisure. The wages for many teenage and low-paid workers rose correspondingly. These developments led to a changing relationship between many sections of the working class and the game they were once so slavishly loyal towards. For the latest generation of skilled working-class adults and their families, leisure became more privatised: pubs and clubs were no longer a source of attraction unless they catered for couples and promised an evening of entertainment. Likewise, football was to be consumed like any other consumer product – only if it offered the prospect of excitement – often as a TV spectacle in the comfort of one's own home.

Working-class youths now had a new range of 'industries' – notably popular music and clothing – to cater for their needs. However, for one section of youth, the lower-working-class 'roughs', living on housing estates and high-rise flats, for whom the prospect of unemployment was added to the possibility of boring, unskilled work, 'only the football ground remained – stark, dirty, exposed to the elements – as a traditional gathering place for working-class lads' (Wagg, 1984:206–7). For such people, the haven of the soccer ground offered a venue for new coalitions and a rejuvenated sense of community.

As Robins' and Cohen's (1978) study of Arsenal supporters shows, great importance was attached to the defending or taking of ends. But the significance of this terrace solidarity went much further than this.

> It is as if, for these youngsters, the space they share on the North Bank is a way of magically retrieving the sense of group solidarity and identification that that once went along with living in a traditional working-class neighbourhood.
>
> (Robins and Cohen, 1978:137)

According to them, the subsequent involvement of skinhead supporters contributed to the notoriety of the ends.

> Yet the skinheads neither created nor were created by the 'end'. What it gave them was a visible stage, a public platform – and what they gave back to the 'end' was a sense of itself, a common life-style. The skinhead phenomenon rallied the mass of young supporters on the terraces, and brought more kids in.
>
> (Robins and Cohen, 1978:139)

A slightly different slant is provided by Clarke (1978), who maintains that, in developing their earliest relationship to the game, young working-class fans brought with them traditional soccer/shop-floor values, such as partisanship, toughness, masculinity and collectivism. The working-class youth had inherited a traditional way of watching a match,

> seeing it not as a game between two teams but between *his* team and the opposition, a position which not only gave him a particular involvement, but also particular rights of commentary and criticism on the team, the management and the club.
>
> (Clarke, 1978:43)

Recent changes in adult leisure behaviour meant that youths were less likely to be accompanied to the game by older male relatives who had previously 'educated' them in terms of the appropriate way to behave.

Thus previous restraints on terrace behaviour no longer operated. The young, working-class fan had inherited the tradition without some of the controls on behaviour that accompanied it (ibid.:51–2).

Equally important were post-war developments in the game of football. The post-war period had witnessed the growing *professionalisation* of the sport. This was partly a reference to how the game was played: its new emphasis on the professional foul, dossiers on opposition players, new fitness training methods and greater tactical awareness. Equally important, however, was the increasing commercialisation of the game via extra seating, bars, restaurants, social clubs and executive boxes. Alongside this professionalisation was a parallel emphasis on the *spectacularisation* of football – i.e. an attempt to make it more attractive and eye-catching via such devices as pre-match and half-time entertainment and the regular televising of match highlights.

For Clarke, football hooliganism developed at the intersection of these trends: the fans have now taken the traditional values of toughness, masculinity, local identity, collective action and partisanship and made them part of the game's new, more spectacularised style. The collective chanting of slogans and songs, the taking of ends and the solidaristic expressions of violence are merely the 'old ways' manifested in an unrestrained and more spectacular form.

Holt (1989) puts forward a synthesis of these ideas. For him, the breakdown of working-class communities has meant that the traditional means by which men taught their relatives and apprentices how to hold their drink, and how not to allow occasional street brawls to get hopelessly out of hand, have disappeared.

> Since the 1950s the old solidarities of working-class culture have disappeared. So too have many of the communities themselves. Networks of neighbours have been broken up by rehousing. Sons are far less likely to follow their fathers or other male relatives into the same occupations or places of work. Football since the 1950s has come to provide a kind of surrogate community for the young; the club defines their identity and the 'end' is their territory, even if they have moved out to the high-rise blocks miles away.
>
> (Holt, 1989:337)

Holt is not surprised that many football hooligans come, not from lower-working-class housing estates, but from the affluent suburbs and new towns away from the major conurbations: 'When a group have lost their old territory in which their traditions were established, football provides a symbolic substitute for the young in the heart of the old community' (ibid.:339).

Taylor (1982; 1989) has recently recast his views on soccer hooliganism, bringing them closer to other approaches described in this section. His most recent work finds him distinguishing between two separate 'fractions' of the dislocated working class who have become involved in soccer violence as a result of the peculiar material circumstances affecting their daily lives.

Taylor's starting point is the assertion that Britain has the 'worst educated' youth population of any advanced society. The under-resourced state system produces cohorts of unqualified, unemployed or underemployed youths whose 'conditions of existence' are characterised by a moral, cultural and experiential shallowness.

For one section of youth, the 'upwardly mobile, individualistic fraction of the (male) British working class' – epitomised by young dockers and construction workers – the restructuring of British industry over the past twenty years has produced relative prosperity. Despite their lack of formal education and training, they can afford to travel to overseas matches where their crude moral values are reflected in 'nationalistic aggression' towards foreign fans.

A second, more troublesome fraction exists at the lowest end of the working class. This consists of a less affluent underclass of young males who, unlike previous generations, cannot rely on the prospect of a steady job and membership of a well-integrated occupational community to nourish their sense of security and esteem. Involvement in hooligan activity plays a significant part in their lives – by providing its own mechanism of recognition and reward.

Critics of this theoretical approach emphasise that spectator violence existed before the First World War. It therefore seems unreasonable to see it as a result of the fragmentation of working-class communities (Dunning et al., 1984). Moreover, there is documentary evidence that adolescents have always attended the game without the supervision of adults. Dunning and colleagues conclude that authors like Clarke are guilty of romanticising working-class history, 'attributing to it a degree of family, inter-age-group and neighbourhood solidarity it has probably never possessed' (ibid.:237).

DISCUSSION

Contemporary British football hooliganism most commonly takes the form of fighting behaviour between rival groups of fans. Though the American literature on spectator disorder generally contributes few useful insights,

Smith's distinction between issue-oriented and issueless riots helps to highlight the crucial difference between hooligan behaviour and the other forms of public disorder referred to in previous chapters. Whereas the disorder associated with violent demonstrations, riots or industrial confrontation tends to focus on the defence or assertion of 'rights' which are perceived as being violated or denied, football hooliganism is an issueless form of activity, pursued primarily for pleasure and excitement, and to achieve the status and respect of one's peers. The flashpoints model is therefore inapplicable to this form of disorder and other explanations are therefore necessary.

Each of the theoretical approaches outlined above is vulnerable to specific criticisms. Nevertheless, it is possible to combine the most feasible aspects of a number of these theories into a reasonably coherent explanation of football hooliganism. This explanation may be summarised as follows:

1 Football hooliganism is largely engaged in by young males whose position in society leaves them culturally and materially deprived. They tend to receive an unsatisfactory education, harbour poor employment prospects and have few ways of creating a positive self-concept.

2 Hooligans tend to come from social backgrounds where masculine aggression is highly valued. They live in (or their parents once came from) lower-working-class neighbourhoods which use toughness and fighting prowess as a criterion of status and respect.

3 Post-war urban development has meant that occupational communities no longer exist to provide readily available jobs and cater for the social needs of adolescent males. Aggressive tendencies on the part of young men are no longer held in check by the moderating influence of older males.

4 Membership of fighting crews provides a 'surrogate community' and offers a career structure for earning status and esteem.

5 The game of soccer is an ideal vehicle for acts of collective aggression, guaranteeing encounters between rival groups of supporters and providing emotive issues which serve as rallying points for aggressive behaviour.

6 The mass media have helped increase the prevalence of football hooliganism since the 1960s by advertising soccer grounds as places where fighting was likely to occur, and then by creating and enhancing the notoriety of particular groups of fans.

Several of the above points appear to be endorsed by Pearson's cogent account of what makes the hooligan tick:

In a singing community of his peers he comes alive and discovers a sense of membership which is denied him elsewhere: all the more reason to embrace the slightly devilish and glamorous identity which is thrown at you by 'them' and sing along, 'We are the famous football hooligans!'

(Pearson, 1979:215)

Dunning and his co-workers are undoubtedly justified in maintaining that football hooliganism was prevalent in society long before the post-war decline of community life; and that it was common for young males to attend football matches without adult supervision before the 1960s. While these observations undoubtedly discredit Clarke's theory, Holt's position remains intact. His analysis emphasises that, as with the other forms of disorder considered in this book, soccer spectator disorder requires a conjunctural explanation. Football hooliganism *may well* be older than the present century

But the *specific forms* of hooliganism *are* new; football crowds were not segregated by age before the 1960s; youth did not congregate around parts of football clubs as their territory – they had a larger territory and community which they shared with their older male relatives. When there were fights at football matches there was no dramatic media coverage. All of these features have combined to create the contemporary problem; hooliganism exemplifies to perfection the difficulty of disentangling what is new from what is old in social history.

(Holt, 1989:343)

Chapter 7

The 'Troubles' in Northern Ireland

This chapter sits uncomfortably in a book about public disorder. Some might argue that it would be more appropriate to treat the recent 'Troubles' in Northern Ireland (from 1968 to the present) as an example of guerrilla or civil warfare. One reason for including them here is that the bombings and assassinations of today are the legacy of the civil disturbances of the 1960s. As such, the escalating conflict in Northern Ireland offers a useful paradigm for predicting whether a similar process of escalation might feasibly occur on the British mainland. A second reason is to show how recent British security developments are based on precedents set during the containment of the Irish conflict.

The chapter begins by examining the historical roots of the present Troubles. It then traces the development of the conflict from the seminal activities of the Catholic civil rights protest of 1968 to the introduction of the British Army in 1972. A third section documents and analyses the increasingly repressive role played by the security forces and the corresponding violence employed by insurgent civilian paramilitary organisations. Finally, the chapter evaluates the likelihood of recent patterns of conflict in Northern Ireland being reproduced elsewhere in Britain, and briefly explains how the security approach developed in the 'orange state' has served as a model for British police practices.

A TROUBLED PAST

The present Troubles in Northern Ireland are the most recent manifestation of a centuries-old history of conflict. Between the twelfth and seventeenth centuries, a succession of English monarchs made a series of expansionist forays into the neighbouring country of Ireland. As early as AD 1250, Norman leaders had subjugated most of Ireland's Gaelic population. Fifty years of guerrilla-style rebellion by the Gaels gradually reduced the amount of territory controlled by the invaders to a small enclave around Dublin, known as the Pale. There settlers established the earliest English plantation in Ireland.

Further attempts by the English to extend their presence in Ireland were successfully resisted. A fierce uprising in 1534 was suppressed by Henry VIII, who declared himself King of Ireland in 1541. England was a Protestant country, while the Gaels were almost exclusively Catholic. The Church of Ireland was formed in 1560 to convert the Irish to Protestantism. These and other English ways were resisted. In 1579, when the Gaels attempted to forge an alliance with Spain, the English slaughtered thousands of Irish people, destroying their crops and livestock.

As a result, the English jurisdiction over Ireland extended across Leinster, Munster and Connacht, leaving only the remote and troublesome province of Ulster as an unsubdued Gaelic stronghold. However, by 1607, the last of the Ulster chieftains had either been routed or driven into exile and, in six of the nine counties, English and Scottish settlers arrived to consolidate colonial rule and the English monarchy. By 1640, 100,000 planters had arrived in Ireland when the native population numbered only one million inhabitants.

In 1641, the Gaels rebelled again, this time against their most immediate oppressors, the Protestant planters. Further uprisings occurred until 1649 when Oliver Cromwell, fresh from his victory in the English Civil War, brutally put down the recalcitrant Gaels. Many Catholics were banished to the west and south of their country. Some twenty-six of the thirty-two counties of Ireland were subsumed by the English government, with large sections of land being awarded in payment to those who had fought and financed the war.

More conflict followed the arrival of the deposed Catholic King, James II, in Ireland in 1689. The exiled monarch rallied an Irish Catholic army to do battle against his usurper from the English throne, the Dutch Protestant prince, William of Orange. James besieged the Ulster city of Derry, but its 35,000 Protestant inhabitants successfully defended it, due largely to the leadership and example of the 'Apprentice Boys'. One year later, William arrived with his army in Ireland and proceeded to defeat James's Irish troops and their French allies at the River Boyne near Drogheda. These victories at Derry and the Boyne have hallowed places in Protestant folklore.

Following James's defeat, more Catholic land was confiscated, leaving them with a mere 14 per cent share of Irish territory. Then, harsh Penal Laws were introduced, forbidding Catholics from entering public employment, voting in local or parliamentary elections, openly practising their religion and carrying firearms. The law also abolished the principle of primogeniture (the direct passing on of land to the first-born son), save for those cases where the eldest male was prepared to embrace Protestantism. Unless this occurred, the land was divided equally amongst all the male heirs, reducing the size of Catholic plots.

The end of the eighteenth century saw the development of the United Irishmen movement, a body (including many prominent northern Protestants) committed to greater equality for Catholics. Unwilling to allow legal reforms like the Catholic Relief Act 1793 (which repealed some aspects of the Penal Laws) to appease them, the movement rose up in rebellion in 1798. The rebellion was crushed by the British Government, which then passed an Act of Union in 1801, abolishing the Dublin parliament and integrating Ireland with the UK. The Irish – politically and militarily outmanoeuvred – were allocated 100 of the 660 seats at Westminster.

Restrictions on trade were lifted but, due to the expropriation of Irish wealth, only Ulster – and Belfast in particular – was able to flourish under the Union. This growth and industrial expansion of Belfast, and a corresponding famine in the south, facilitated a dramatic rise in the city's Catholic population (from 6 per cent in 1800 to over 30 per cent in 1861). However, because the Catholics had little share in the city's wealth creation, they continued to identify with the nationalist tendencies of the southern Irish majority.

In the 1885 British election, the nationalist Home Rule Party won eighty-five seats at Westminster (including seventeen out of thirty-three in Ulster). Finding themselves holding the balance of power in parliament, they managed to introduce the Home Rule Bill of 1886. This, and a second bill in 1893, were both defeated. However, a third bill was passed in 1914, but not implemented due to the outbreak of the First World War.

Protestant Unionists had begun to respond to this threat to their supremacy by organising a private army, the Ulster Volunteer Force (UVF), said to have had the backing of the Conservative Party and the British military establishment. In the south, recruiting began for the Irish National Volunteers. When war broke out with Germany, many UVF members and National Volunteers joined the armed forces. However, some remnants of the latter (the Citizen Army and Sinn Fein Volunteers) seized Dublin in 1916 and proclaimed it an Irish republic. This 'Easter uprising' was soon put down, its leaders rounded up and shot.

The 1918 General Election heralded the political ascendancy of Sinn Fein (the Gaelic for 'ourselves alone'). The party won seventy-three out of 105 available Irish seats, thus ousting the United Irish League (the old

Home Rule Party) as the major Irish political force. (Though, of the thirty-seven Ulster constituencies, the Unionists won twenty-two.) Sinn Fein's success was built around the pledge that, if elected, they would refuse to take up their seats in Westminster and set up a separate Irish parliament instead.

True to their word, Sinn Fein's newly elected MPs soon convened the first meeting in Dublin of Dail Eireann and declared their independence. Thereafter, a civil war was waged between the re-formed Irish Volunteers (soon to be known as the IRA) and the Royal Irish Constabulary (RIC). Originally fought out in the south and west of Ireland, hostilities then shifted to the north which became the focal point of paramilitary gun battles and sectarian rioting.

The Government of Ireland Act came into effect in May 1921. As a result, two elections were held: one in the six counties of the north, and another for the Home Rule parliament in the south. In the north, there was an 89 per cent turn-out which resulted in forty seats for the Unionists to six each for Sinn Fein and the Nationalist parties. Consequently, on 22 June 1921, the King officially opened the new parliament and Northern Ireland was born. This partition of Ireland into the twenty-six counties of the Irish Free State and the six counties of Northern Ireland has endured to this day. (In 1949, following the Free State's secession from the British Commonwealth, the Irish Republic was formed.)

Within a year of partition, the Constabulary Act (NI) 1922 was passed, which provided for the formation of the Royal Ulster Constabulary (RUC). This was a predominantly Protestant force which soon came to be regarded as repressive and bigoted by the Catholic minority. The 'B Specials' (a part-time force of largely Protestant volunteers) were retained to work alongside the RUC whenever necessary.

Police powers in Northern Ireland were virtually unlimited. The Civil Authorities (Special Powers) Act 1922 enabled the security forces to search and arrest arbitrarily, to detain suspects for up to 48 hours for the sole purpose of interrogation and to break up assemblies of three or more persons on the grounds that their presence might lead to a breach of the peace.

Under authority invested in the Minister for Home Affairs, the Act also provided for internment without trial, the imposition of curfews, the serving of exclusion orders against named persons, the prohibition and distribution of certain forms of literature, the banning of various associations and the death penalty for causing or attempting to cause an explosion likely to lead to injury. As Walsh (1984:328) emphasises, the Special Powers Act remained unmodified until 1972. 'The history of its application throughout this period suggests that its more important function was to suppress all forms of challenge, whether peaceful or violent, to the hegemony of its unionist sponsors.'

The creation of the new state was seen as illegitimate by large sections of the southern population and by Catholics in the north. The contested nature of this political arrangement was evident in skirmishes with the IRA in the 1920s, around the Second World War and in an extended campaign, lasting approximately from 1956 to 1962. The present Troubles have been the most bitter and prolonged in recent Irish history. Though an inexorable development of the centuries-old political struggle, we shall see how the present violence 'was born of the denial of civil rights to the Roman Catholic minority. The conflict itself has given birth to new violations of human rights, which have, in turn, been the impetus for further fighting' (Hewitt, 1982:153).

THE BASIS OF CONFLICT

In Ulster, some two-thirds of the population are Protestant (the Loyalist, or pro-British section of the country), while the remaining one-third is Catholic (Nationalist), defining itself as Irish. The present wave of Troubles has its basis in the Catholic grievances about discriminatory practices which have operated against them ever since the state's inception (cf. Darby, 1983).

To begin with, Catholics objected to religious discrimination reflected in the unfair allocation of jobs, housing and industrial investment. A second serious cause of complaint concerned the heavy restrictions on the local election franchise which was not available to lodgers, sub-tenants and children under 21 living with their parents. This cut out a quarter of people otherwise eligible to vote, the majority of whom were Catholics. Moreover, the Representation of the People Bill 1946 entitled limited companies to up to six votes in local elections, depending on their rateable value. This, too, operated to the advantage of Protestants. A similar complaint surrounded the deliberate manipulation of ward boundaries (i.e. 'gerrymandering') to ensure the greatest possible representation of Protestant local politicians. Finally, there was popular Catholic resistance to the implementation of the Civil Authorities (Special Powers) Act, and resentment at the retention of the B Specials, who were seen as drawn from, and biased towards, the Unionists.

This is insufficient to explain why radical protest suddenly became so salient in the late 1960s. Part of the answer lies in the growth of an Irish Civil Rights movement, stimulated, in turn, by the emergence of a larger, better-educated Catholic middle class, less willing to accept a status of inferiority and blatant discrimination than earlier generations. Two other political factors were pivotal. First, there was the accession to power in Britain of the Labour Party, some of whom were sympathetic to the idea of 'sensible reform' (Bew *et al.*, 1979). Second, there was growing Catholic disaffection from the moderate policies of the Catholic National Party.

The attitude of the Catholic working class was crucially important, not least because:

> while everywhere else (including the Protestant community) the un-skilled section of the working class was diminishing as a proportion of the work-force, in the Catholic community it was actually increasing. No less than a quarter of the non-agricultural work-force was consigned to the residuum of unskilled labour, excluded not only from political life but also from social rewards. This sector constituted an immense reservoir of opposition to Unionism and indifference to moderation.
>
> (Bew *et al.*, 1979:170–1)

The Civil Rights movement was given a major thrust forward by the 'Caledon squatting incident' (20 June 1968). This episode concerned activities in a small village located in the Dungannon Rural District. There a local Northern Ireland MP occupied a council house in protest at the eviction of a Catholic family and reallocation of their house to a Protestant woman who did not rate as a priority for rehousing. The incident received widespread television and press publicity, and prompted a civil rights march on 24 August from Coalisland to Dungannon. The march, the first ever organised by the Northern Ireland Civil Rights Association (NICRA), involved 2,500 protesters and was peaceful from start to finish. This was not true, however, of a similar march in Londonderry 2 months later.

THE LONDONDERRY MARCH AND THE ESCALATION OF VIOLENCE

The Londonderry march of 5 October 1968 was proposed, and initially only supported, by Londonderry left-wing and pro-Republican activists. NICRA had been concerned about the potential for violence which arose when the Apprentice Boys of Derry gave notice of their intention to stage an 'Annual Initiation Ceremony' to coincide with the demonstration. However, they agreed at the last moment to participate. On 3 October, the Minister of Home Affairs prohibited all processions occurring within the city's walls, but the march took place as planned.

The influential Cameron Report, which traces the development of conflict in Northern Ireland from June 1968 to May 1969 (see page 149), acknowledges that NICRA had no intention of staging a disorderly protest. On the other hand,

> The extremists of the left were anxious to ensure that there was a violent 'confrontation' with the police, and to organise opposition in the city on class lines. Since these extremists had been principally responsible for the detailed organisation of the march it is not surprising that there were no serious plans to control it, or to ensure that it went off peacefully. The chief marshal notified to the police appears to have been inexperienced and relatively ineffective.
>
> (Cameron, 1969:27–8)

There were two related problems: first, the organisers greatly over-estimated the size of march (putting the likely turn-out at 5,000 when it was closer to 2,000); and second, the stewards included serving IRA members.

The Report makes it plain that the police 'certainly expected trouble'. They regarded NICRA as a 'Nationalistic' movement and saw the march as being 'effectively in the hands of a small group of left-wing and Republican extremists in Londonderry' (ibid.:26). Usually, only sixty officers were available but, on this occasion, 130 men had been assembled (ibid.:28). It may also have been significant that the local County Inspector was on leave and that the County Inspector in charge of the RUC's Special Branch supervised the operation.

From the outset of the march, the demonstrators observed a different route to that notified to the police. As they set off to cross a bridge already cordoned off as a prohibited area, the police hurriedly re-formed in front of them. Two MPs at the apex of the march were batoned, apparently without instruction from the senior officer. There was great confusion and indignation as the marchers were forced to halt. A senior NICRA member appealed to the crowd to eschew violence, but could not be heard above the din. Thirty more minutes elapsed without any further progress before she and several others appealed to the crowd to disperse.

At this stage, some demonstrators (reputedly, members of 'Young Socialist Alliance') threw placards and stones at the police. Police were instructed to draw their batons and move in to disperse the marchers. However, far from responding in an organised manner, 'the police broke ranks and used their batons indiscriminately' (ibid.:29). A second group of police assembled behind the marchers, effectively hemming them in. Water cannons were then introduced and turned on marchers and innocent bystanders alike (ibid.).

The crowd was eventually scattered but, later that evening, the police tried forcibly to remove a political banner at the city centre's War Memorial. Some protagonists (said to be non-marchers) were chased into the Catholic Bogside area of the city, where barricades were erected, a number of petrol bombs were thrown, and some looting took place. A group of stone-throwers were rapidly dispersed when members of the Reserve Force drove landrovers into them.

The resulting television and press publicity proved harmful to the authorities. On 9 October, students at Queen's University, Belfast, set up the People's Democracy (PD) group, 'a loose activist body committed to civil rights reforms, but with a tough Young Socialist hard core' (Farrell, 1980:247). This movement was the instigator of a series of civil rights marches across the north, many of which provoked violence by Protestant counter-demonstrations. Derry, in particular, seemed to be in a state of constant turmoil as marchers broke the government's ban on processions several times a day. Something clearly had to be done.

On 22 November 1968, the Prime Minister, Terence O'Neill outlined an ameliorative package of reforms which, in amongst its other measures, encouraged local authorities to devise a points system for the allocation of housing; abolished the company vote for local elections; and repealed parts of the Special Powers Act. However, as Farrell explains,

> It was too little too late. It was enough to outrage the Loyalists without satisfying the Civil Rights movement at all. The whole campaign began to centre around 'One man, One Vote' – effectively who controlled the gerrymandered councils. O'Neill wouldn't concede it – it would have split the Unionist Party. The Civil Rights movement wouldn't be satisfied without it.
>
> (Farrell, 1980:248)

Consequently, there were a series of marches across Northern Ireland. The most significant of these was the 4-day march from Belfast to Londonderry, starting on 1 January 1969. This march was modelled on the famous Selma–Montgomery march of the American Civil Rights campaign. As anticipated, it was systematically harassed by Loyalists. (Subsequently, the RUC was accused of leading the marchers into an ambush consisting of stone-throwing, cudgel-wielding assailants, many of them off-duty B Specials.)

The march eventually reached its destination but, on the same night, barricades were erected against an RUC raid on the Bogside. A pattern had now been established:

> Protestants were ready to counter any organized Catholic action with

violence to 'nip in the bud' the violence of rebels. Protestant violent action against Civil Rights marches was seen by Catholics as a threat to their communities. They reacted to the Protestant violence with defensive counter-violence which was in turn interpreted by Protestants as a confirmation of their belief that the Civil Rights movement was a front organization for an armed Catholic rebellion.

(Easthope, 1976:417)

The resounding election victory of 21-year-old Bernadette Devlin, a student member of PD who stood as an anti-Unionist candidate, in the Mid-Ulster by-election on 17 April, was taken as affirmation of the minority's support for Civil Rights movement. Confronted with this reality, O'Neill conceded the principle of 'one man, one vote', and the full parliamentary party voted it in on 22 April. That night, two major water pipes were blown up, depriving Belfast of its water supplies. This was allegedly perpetrated by Protestants intent on panicking the Unionist Party into bringing O'Neill down. If this was their intention, they succeeded – by precipitating his resignation.

The election of O'Neill's successor, Major James Chichester-Clark, resolved nothing. The Catholics, with their new-found self-confidence, were not prepared to accept unjust second-class citizenship, while Unionists were unwilling to relinquish generations of privilege and supremacy. Things came to a head at the Apprentice Boys' parade in Derry on 12 August. The parade was scheduled to proceed through the city and skirt round the walls overlooking the Bogside. The march – an annual commemoration of the siege of Derry – was a provocative symbol of Protestant mastery. It was stoned as it reached the Bogside; Catholics clashed with the RUC; and the Bogside Defence Association erected barricades. Petrol bombs were thrown when the RUC drove armoured vehicles at the barricades. CS gas was fired for the first time in Northern Ireland. This was the prelude to 3 days and nights of conflict.

Several authors agree that the Bogside riot represented the symbolic defence of community (Easthope, 1976; Scarman, 1972). Barricades were erected at the precise boundary of the two religious communities in an area of no-man's-land between a Catholic cathedral and a Protestant church, both rumoured to be threatened by attack. Bayley and Loizos observe that:

> very little fighting in Derry was of the hand to hand nature. Generally in Ulster violence was directed against symbols rather than persons – the burning of an Orange Order assembly hall, police stations, or post offices. For example, people of the 'wrong community' in mixed

neighbourhoods were told to leave their houses, which were then burned; the people were then usually allowed to escape.

(Bayley and Loizos, 1969:278)

They had no desire to progress beyond their barricades: 'Their whole rationale was that they were fighting a defensive battle for the protection of their community against arbitrary attack' (ibid.).

On 14 August, as sympathetic rioting flared up in other Ulster towns and cities, notably the Falls area of Belfast, the B Specials were brought in to replace the RUC on the edge of the Bogside. However, in the early evening, British troops moved into Derry, and negotiations between the British commander and representatives of the Bogside Defence Association resulted in the withdrawal of B Specials. The Catholics were euphoric at this outcome:

> The Bogsiders felt that they had won – not only because they had kept the RUC out of their area but because they had forced the British Army to intervene. They sensed vaguely that direct British intervention re-opened the whole constitutional question.
>
> (Farrell, 1980:262)

THE SPIRAL OF REPRESSION

A brief truce followed the arrival of the British Army, but publication of two major government reports led to a resumption of the conflict. On 12 September 1969, the Cameron Commission (referred to on pages 145–6) reported its findings. The Commission validated the Civil Rights movement's complaints about gerrymandering and discrimination, pointed to evidence of violence and indiscipline among RUC officers, and noted the partisan attitudes and behaviour of the B Specials. The Hunt Report, published on 10 October, recommended the disbandment of the B Specials and the disarming of the RUC. The report also recommended the replacement of the B Specials by an Ulster Defence Regiment (UDR), to consist of a locally raised militia.

This last proposal especially outraged the Loyalist communities who, apparently,

> failed to understand that the UDR would also be charged with policing the border and the countryside and would, in fact, be somewhat more efficient in its vigilance against a dreaded IRA invasion. All that the loyalists knew was that their very own Special Constabulary was going to be dismantled and that this had been one of NICRA's long-standing

demands. The Hunt report was thus seen on the Shankill as a craven cave-in to Fenian rioters. It had to be repudiated before its terms of surrender could take effect.

(Kelley, 1988:123)

On the night of 11 October, a day after Hunt's publication, Protestants gathered on the Shankill Road to attack the Catholic Unity Flats, threw stones and bottles at the British troops who were thwarting their advance, overturned cars and set them ablaze, and, unprecedentedly, directed gunfire at the RUC. This fire was returned by police and army personnel.

The Catholics, too, organised and armed themselves in anticipation of a Protestant backlash or about-turn by the security forces. Having played little part in the August riots (epitomised by the derisory slogan, 'IRA – I Ran Away'), old IRA men came out of retirement (Rose, 1972) and 'there was a steady stream of recruits from young men who had seen houses and streets burnt down by Loyalist mobs and who'd been unable to prevent them' (Farrell, 1980:267). Such action widened the growing split between those Republicans (notably the Provisional IRA and Provisional Sinn Fein) who felt that military action was the key to Ireland's liberation, and those, like the official IRA and Sinn Fein, who considered that political means were still preferable (Hannigan, 1985).

The Army's preference to appear neutral was severely undermined by its role during the Loyalist marching season of 1970. An Orange parade on 31 March was the prelude to 4 days of conflict between Catholics and the British Army in Ballymurphy. Perceiving the Army as a protective cover for Loyalism, Catholics attacked the march as it went past the Clonard and Ballymurphy areas. British soldiers saturated the latter area with CS gas before taking up occupation. Catholics threw petrol bombs, provoking the British Commander to warn television audiences that future petrol bombers would be shot dead.

Escalation was relentless. On 1 July 1970, the Criminal Justice (Temporary Provisions) Bill was rushed through Stormont. This provided for a mandatory 6-month prison sentence for anyone found guilty of rioting. Two days later, the Army raided a house in the Lower Falls where they found a collection of arms. This action provoked another major riot. Again, the Army flooded the area with CS gas. Temporarily withdrawing in an attempt to draw out the IRA, they returned to occupy the area for a further 36 hours (Farrell, 1980:273). A curfew was maintained and soldiers allegedly smashed down doors and destroyed furniture whilst conducting searches. Not just illegal, it was also counter-productive, fuelling further resentment among Catholic families (McCauley, 1989:143).

The IRA responded with a bombing campaign directed at business and commerce. From April to June 1971, there were 134 such bombings. The Army was immediately authorised to shoot 'with effect' at anyone acting suspiciously. This was followed, in August, by the blanket banning of all marches and the sudden implementation of an 'internment policy' (McGuffin, 1973). On 9 August, 349 arrests were made as the military swooped to round up serving and former IRA activists. However, due to poor intelligence and a tip-off to the IRA, most victims were civil rights agitators, not IRA supporters (White, 1989).

In the 4 days of violent rioting which followed, twenty-two people were killed, nineteen of them civilians. The Catholic population was further incensed by revelations that a dozen internees had been beaten and subjected to sensory deprivation techniques while being interrogated. These 'five techniques' (requiring prisoners to wear hoods over their heads unless they were separated from other inmates or being interrogated, having them stand spreadeagled against a wall for up to 43 hours, depriving them of sleep, subjecting them to electronic noise and beating them) were subsequently condemned as 'torture' by the European Rights Commission (Hewitt, 1982:157–8).

The repression of the IRA continued unabated: 650 prisoners were interned by the end of November. Many of these were transferred to an internment camp at Long Kesh near Lisburn. In October, two women were shot dead by the Army for touring the Lower Falls with a siren, warning inhabitants of imminent raids. The 'Provos' responded with an urban guerrilla offensive, consisting of attacks on the Army, RUC and Protestant civilians. As Farrell (1980:287) explains, 'Internment had turned a campaign of pinpricks into an all-out war.'

Things came to a head on 30 January 1971 when a NICRA march in Derry, rendered illegal by Faulkner's blanket banning of all marches the previous August, found its exit from the ghetto blocked by British soldiers, including the Parachute Regiment. The Army and RUC had previously decided that, while the demonstration was too big to be prevented, it should none the less be confined to the ghetto. Thus finding their exit blocked, most of the marchers respected the barriers. Others began jeering and eventually threw bottles and stones. The Army moved in with a water cannon and tear gas, forcing the marchers into hasty retreat.

But then, suddenly and without any warning, the army opened fire. Panicked marchers and onlookers ran for cover. They threw themselves down on the street or took shelter behind cars and in doorways. Still the shooting continued – methodical, aimed, deliberate. People were being hit with live lead bullets and were screaming for help. A priest ran out into the road and knelt beside a body which had stained the street red. A couple of men waved white handkerchiefs frantically above their heads as they walked gingerly to where other forms were lying, deadly still. When the firing stopped, 13 Catholics had been killed and 29 wounded, one of whom would die several weeks later. Several of the original 13 dead were teenagers. It was Bloody Sunday in the Maiden City.

(Kelley, 1988:163)

Official accounts of the shootings emphasised that soldiers responded to heavy IRA nail bombing and gunfire, suggesting that a major battle had taken place. This version was contradicted by British press reporters who personally witnessed the killings (see p. 173). 'Bloody Sunday' provoked a retaliatory campaign of violence by the Provos. This, in turn, prompted a political intervention. In March 1972, the Conservative government suspended Stormont (the Northern Ireland Parliament) and assumed direct rule of the province.

Following the failure of militarisation and a sequence of abortive attempts at political reform, the British reverted in the mid-1970s to a policy based the 'primacy of the police'. This policy involved the 'normalisation' of citizen–authority relations in Ulster, i.e. an attempt to 'portray the six counties as a "normal" part of the UK which needed civil policing rather than military invasion' (McCauley, 1989:144). Henceforward the RUC would play the dominant security role with the Army gradually being phased out.

To facilitate this change, the Special Powers Act was superseded by two new pieces of legislation, the Northern Ireland (Emergency Provisions) Act, introduced in 1973 and revised in 1978, and the Prevention of Terrorism (Temporary Provisions) Act 1974. In Walsh's view,

This legislation is designed not only to counteract the violence by harsh, emergency measures, but also to undermine the political nature of the violence by characterising it as mere criminality; the hope being that it will diminish the level of public support for those involved.

(Walsh, 1984:335)

However, this process 'has produced its own sequel of human rights violations' (Hewitt, 1982:158). To begin with, the Emergency Provisions Act (EPA), established special 'Diplock Courts' where 'scheduled' or 'terrorist' offences (murder, or attempted murder, and explosive-related) are tried by a single judge in the absence of a jury. Other provisions 'abolished the prohibition on hearsay evidence and rendered admissible as evidence "confession" statements which, although involuntary, had not actually been obtained by torture, inhuman or degrading treatment, threats or inducements' (ibid.).

Section 11 of the Act authorises police officers to arrest anyone they suspect of being or having been involved in terrorist activity. It is unnecessary for the suspicion to be reasonable; nor must the person be suspected of having committed an offence. Once arrested, a person may be detained for up to 3 days without knowing what he/she is alleged to have done. Another category of arrest is established under section 12. In this case the initial suspicion must be reasonable, whereupon the person may be held for up to 7 days. The Army has similar powers of arrest under section 14 of the Act, but detention may only last for up to 4 hours. Walsh maintains that,

> In practice, these powers are interpreted as authorising arrest for general questioning. They are primarily used for screening purposes, intelligence gathering, surveillance and harassment. As many as 90 per cent of the persons arrested under these powers are released without charge after having been detained for anything from four hours to seven days. For many individuals the experience is repeated several times a year, thereby constituting a serious infringement of their personal liberty, disrupting the lives of their families, often preventing them from complying with requirements for obtaining welfare benefits and effectively making them unemployable.
>
> (Walsh, 1984:336)

In addition to the aforementioned powers, police and Army personnel may stop and conduct random street searches on pedestrians or motorists for possession of unlawful munitions or transmitters. On the appropriate authority of a senior officer, security personnel may enter a person's home for similar purposes. They can stop people, without prior basis of suspicion, ask them for personal details or question them about their knowledge of recent terrorist incidents.

Another centrepiece of the government's emergency legislation is the Prevention of Terrorism Act 1974 (redrawn in 1976 and 1984), passed in the wake of the Birmingham pub bombings of November 1974, in which twenty-one people died as a result of two bomb blasts. The Act enables the authorities to detain anyone '"reasonably" suspected of being involved in the commission, preparation or instigation of acts of terrorism' (Hewitt, 1982:166) for up to 7 days, and to take out exclusion orders banning British and Irish citizens from leaving or entering Great Britain or Northern

Ireland on the grounds that they have been, or intend to become, involved in acts of terrorism.

> The individual is never informed of what it is he (sic) is alleged to have done to give rise to the suspicion; nor, indeed, is it necessary that he be convicted of any offence. The Secretary of State acts as judge, jury, prosecution and defence.
>
> (Walsh, 1984:340)

A further controversial aspect of Westminster's normalisation programme was the abolition of the 'special category' status previously afforded to those convicted of scheduled offences. Such people were based in separate areas of the prison, wore civilian clothes rather than prison uniforms and organised their daily activities independently of prison routines. These privileges were a recognition of their 'prisoner of war' status.

Special category status was withdrawn on 1 March 1976. In 1977, groups of Republican prisoners begun to campaign for its return by refusing to wear prison clothes or do prison work. Such protesters were refused alternative clothing and lost any remission of their sentence. A year later, the protest took a new form: the 'dirty protest' involved prisoners refusing to exercise or use toilet facilities. Many prisoners spread their cell walls with their own excreta.

In 1980, the protest developed into a series of hunger strikes. One of the strikers, Bobby Sands, was overwhelmingly elected as an MP in the Fermanagh and Tyrone by-election. Sands died soon after his election, and was one of ten strikers to die in this way (Beresford, 1987; Collins, 1986). There were riots in Belfast and Derry following Sands' death. During one night of rioting, two youths were run over by Army landrovers. The two drivers were later charged with dangerous driving, but it was widely suspected that they had been acting on orders.

Despite such setbacks to the normalisation policy, the RUC has continued to fulfil the security role vacated by the Army. Indeed, the RUC has become a well-organised paramilitary force with a range of repressive powers. All RUC officers are trained in riot control and counter-insurgency techniques. Military-trained rapid strike units, known as Headquarters Mobile Support Units and Divisional Mobile Support Units, were introduced in the early 1980s. Partly composed of ex-British soldiers, these units place a priority on 'speed, firepower and aggression' (Weitzer, 1985:48). Brewer and co-workers (1988) report that, in 1981 alone, 30,000 rounds of plastic bullets were fired, compared with 55,000 in the 5 years up to 1975. Since 1974, over a dozen deaths have resulted from such shootings.

Freedom of association and expression have been two further casualties of the government's emergency powers. The Public Order (Northern Ireland) Act 1981 makes it necessary for organisers to give the police 5 days' notice of a march for it to be considered legal. Senior officers may also impose such conditions as a change of route or starting time in the interests of public order. The Secretary of State may also prohibit any march in any area, or impose a blanket ban on all marches or a particular category of marches, for a period of 12 months. These powers were employed with telling effect on a series of 'H-block' marches, when hundreds of people were arrested and convicted for taking part in prohibited marches or not observing the 5-day rule.

The Northern Ireland conflict has become progressively more covert in nature. The RUC has the largest computerised surveillance system in the UK. Strategically located road blocks are used to enforce systematic searches of traffic, and vehicle registration numbers are fed back to central control for checking. Listening devices are used, sometimes involving the technique of monitoring conversations via vibrations made on window panes (Hillyard, 1985:180). Cameras are secretly located in public places and helicopters monitor selected areas with video equipment, day and night (ibid.).

Recent insurgency campaigns have been correspondingly covert:

> The targeting of the security forces by Republican paramilitaries is reflected in a rise in the number of members of the security forces killed as a proportion of total deaths. For example, deaths of members of the security forces were 54 per cent of total fatalities in 1985, compared to only 18 per cent in 1976. As a result of the policy of police primacy, an increasing proportion of these have been members of the RUC and RUC Reserve.
>
> (Brewer *et al.*, 1988:69)

Against this, there have been a series of controversial allegations against special police units engaged in covert action. The most notorious of these centred on an incident in December 1982 when two unarmed members of the Republican paramilitary organisation, the Irish National Liberation Army (INLA), were shot dead after police officers had stopped their car on the edge of Armagh. This, and similar incidents, caused speculation that the RUC was operating a 'shoot to kill' policy. An inquiry was authorised to look into these incidents, but when its chairperson, John Stalker, the Deputy Chief Constable of Greater Manchester Police, was suddenly removed over allegations about his previous conduct as a police officer, it led to speculation that a cover-up was taking place to avoid implicating senior RUC officers in covert and probably illegal operations (ibid.:70).

Covert operations now extend well beyond Northern Ireland and the British mainland. On 6 March 1988, three IRA members were shot dead in Gibraltar by plain-clothed British Special Air Service (SAS) officers. The IRA men parked a car believed to be containing a bomb near to a place where soldiers from the Royal Anglian Regiment usually assembled before the changing of their guard. A ministerial statement issued after the killings claimed that, on parking the car, the three moved off toward the Spanish border where they were challenged by the security forces. Here they behaved in such a way as to convince the SAS officers that their lives and those of others were under threat, hence the decision to fire.

Subsequently, Thames Television's current affairs programme, *This Week*, broadcast a feature, called 'Death on the Rock' (ITV, 28 April 1988), in which witnesses came forward to cast doubt on the official version of events. The Spanish police also maintained that they had kept the suspected terrorists' movements under close surveillance and maintained a constant flow of information on them to British officials in Gibraltar.

> If true, this would have implied either that the police had knowingly allowed a car that they thought was full of explosives to drive into and around the island, or that they were aware throughout the operation that the car was not dangerous.
>
> (Ewing and Gearty, 1990:237)

At the inquest on the killings, one of the witnesses interviewed on *This Week* retracted his evidence. After initial indecision, the inquest jury delivered a verdict of lawful killing. The British government saw this as a vindication both of the SAS killings and its own version of events. However, two major civil and human rights organisations, the NCCL and Amnesty International, were critical of the way the inquest was conducted (ibid.:239–40).

Weitzer (1987) argues that the RUC is now trapped inside a 'legitimacy vacuum'. On the one hand, the force is immensely distrusted by large sections of the Catholic community who still see it as an 'armed wing of unionism', propping up an illegitimate regime. Yet, on the other hand, the RUC now faces increasing hostility on the part of the Protestant population. As recently as 1985, there had been signs of greater even-handedness on the part of the RUC, reflected in more frequent prosecutions of Protestants for 'insurgency offences'. A key catalyst of this development was the signing of the Anglo-Irish Agreement in November 1985 which awarded the Irish government a greater consultative role in Northern Irish affairs. The signing of the agreement led to the immediate withdrawal, resignation, and subsequent reselection of fourteen Unionist MPs. There then followed a General Strike in March 1986, which brought the province to a standstill, a series of sectarian killings and a succession of riotous demonstrations involving confrontation between Protestants and the RUC.

Ulster's Protestants look upon the RUC's changing role as a form of betrayal, a shocking revelation that it is not, after all, a 'Protestant force' dedicated to Loyalism. On the contrary, 'From their point of view the RUC is now being used as a *political* force to impose the Anglo-Irish Agreement on an unwilling majority in the province' (Weitzer, 1987:93). Consequently, RUC officers have been subjected to public degradation ceremonies, and there have been threats and physical attacks on themselves and their families, forcing some of them to relocate. Loyalist protesters have shouted 'SS–RUC' and 'Dublin's lap dogs', whilst some elected MPs have exhorted RUC men to resign or mutiny and warned them of the possible consequences of their 'disloyalty' (ibid.). The policing of Northern Ireland therefore stands at a tense crossroads.

DISCUSSION

The escalating conflict in Northern Ireland is not simply a function of deprivation and discrimination (Hewitt, 1981; Kovalcheck, 1987), but a political response to increasing state repression. Recent research by White (1989) confirms that it was internment, in particular, which galvanised young, working-class Catholics into adopting political violence. The introduction of this policy coincided with an upsurge in 'terrorist' activity (Brewer *et al.*, 1988; Peroff and Hewitt, 1980).

There are important clues that, for the British police, 'Northern Ireland has served as a valuable laboratory, offering important lessons for the control of labour protest and racial unrest at home – some "compensation" for Britain's losses in the provinces' (Weitzer, 1985:41). Hillyard (1985) perceives direct parallels between the behaviour of the legal authorities in Northern Ireland and techniques used in the 1984–5 coal dispute. Aside from obvious similarities in police riot-control manoeuvres, there was a widespread tendency to use roadblocks, a systematic abuse of the statutory powers of arrest and overlaps in interrogation and intelligence methods. As we shall see in Chapter 9, there are broad similarities between provisions embodied in the Northern Ireland emergency powers legislation and the British Police and Criminal Evidence Act 1984 and the Public Order Act

1986. Collectively, these statutes enable the police to stop and search suspects and ask for personal details, to enter forcibly and search private properties, to detain suspects for questioning for up to 72 hours and to use as much discretion as they require to impose bans or conditions on marches or assemblies.

Commenting on the provisions of the 1984 Act, Walsh envisages that:

> They will produce a criminal law enforcement system for Britain which is very unlike that currently prevailing there, but very similar to that to which Northern Ireland has become accustomed. It is not difficult to imagine the exercise of these powers in the inner city areas of Britain producing the same reaction as they provoke in the riot-torn areas of Belfast and Derry. The next step will be to adopt more of the North's repressive emergency measures in order to contain the violence. Bit by bit the ignorance of, and lack of respect for, civil liberties and human rights, prevalent for so long in Northern Ireland, will be transported to Britain.
>
> (Walsh, 1984:345)

Walsh's concern for the future of civil liberties is undoubtedly well-founded, but his prediction that the experience of Belfast or Derry might soon be shared by other British inner-city areas may be unduly pessimistic. The Irish Troubles are recent, but their political roots are centuries old. While the grievances held by British blacks are undoubtedly profound, in many ways equivalent to those of Northern Ireland's Catholics, their political objectives are modest by comparison, certainly not extending to the overthrowal of the state.

The continuing problems of Northern Ireland demonstrate the futility of responding to a deeply ingrained political problem with a law-and-order response. As Weitzer maintains,

> The police have been thrust into the resulting vacuum. The solution is not to revert to Army control once again, but rather somehow to achieve a lasting political settlement that denies both insurgents and the paramilitary police their raison d'être.
>
> (Weitzer, 1985:53)

The key lesson of this case study is that order cannot be coercively imposed, and that some form of political consensus is necessary if escalation is to be avoided. How to create a constitutional forum for political discussion involving, amongst others, the paramilitary organisations, is as yet an insoluble problem. The refusal of successive Conservative governments under Margaret Thatcher and John Major to engage in dialogue with the political supporters of paramilitarism makes it difficult to see how such an objective may be achieved. (Talks instigated in April 1991 by the Secretary of State for Northern Ireland, Peter Brooke, brought together representatives of accredited Unionist and Nationalist parties, but excluded Sinn Fein, due to their unwillingness to denounce violence.) For the moment, it remains inarguable that

> any new constitutional arrangement must provide what the 1920 Government of Ireland Act tragically failed to achieve: tough guarantees of basic rights for the minority as well as for the majority community, together with accessible and representative institutions to enforce them.
>
> (Hewitt, 1982:170)

Chapter 8

Media representations of public disorder

Previous chapters have emphasised how the mass media may contribute indirectly to the potential for public disorder, first, by helping to create an ideological climate which justifies and encourages the use of repressive control tactics against dissenting groups; and second, by 'sensitising' the police and public to the possibility that disorder might occur.

In this chapter, we look in closer detail at the media's relationship to public disorder. In particular, we consider such crucial questions as: what are the characteristic images and explanations of public disorder presented by the media, and why do they take their conventional form? Do the media meet their own criteria of objectivity and balance in such representations, and do they reasonably address the underlying grievances of participants? Are we correct to assume that media coverage helps to excuse or justify police aggression? Does it encourage a 'copycat' effect, or generate the potential for further disorder in other, less obvious ways?

These issues are addressed in relation to media coverage of disorderly episodes referred to in earlier chapters. Thus we look, in turn, at how particular examples of political dissent, urban riots, strike violence, football hooliganism and the conflict in Northern Ireland have been represented by the media. Due to an apparently smaller American literature on this subject, discussion of US news coverage is solely confined to representations of the 1960s riots.

POLITICAL DISSENT

We begin by looking at examples of media coverage of disorderly political dissent, notably Halloran's and his co-workers' (1970) seminal study of the press and television reporting of the anti-Vietnam War march in London on 27 October 1968. Based on research carried out by a team from

Leicester University, this study, and subsequent articles arising from it (e.g. Murdock, 1981), analysed the pre- and post-event media coverage.

Analysis of the pre-demonstration news coverage shows how the press and broadcast media referred obsessively to the potential for violence. Detectives were said to have uncovered a plot by 'militant extremists' to use the march as a pretext for attacking buildings and police officers. Violence was predicted on the basis of disorder at demonstrations in Paris and Chicago earlier in the year. As if to support this prediction, some newspapers underlined that American and French students were planning to take part, and noted that certain organisers were not English and therefore 'outside the consensus' (ibid.:210–11). Far from treating the demonstration as a serious political event, the media portrayed the demonstration as little more than a 'performance', speculating about the possible fashion wear of the participants. The protest was therefore emptied of serious political content.

Post-demonstration coverage also marginalised the political content, focusing, instead, on the activities of the violent minority. This coverage was epitomised by a photograph of a demonstrator appearing to kick a policeman in the head, featured on the front pages of seven out of the ten newspapers analysed. The preoccupation with violence was taken to absurd lengths in discussions of why disorder *failed* to reach its anticipated level. Newspapers agreed that this was primarily due to the customary restraint of the British police and British demonstrators' traditional aversion to violence.

Halloran's and his co-workers' explanation of why the media coverage took this form emphasises the importance of news values. News coverage is 'event-oriented' and therefore unconcerned with the political issues at stake. There is a need to make the news as intelligible as possible to the readership, hence the familiar notion of a militant conspiracy, and analogies with recent political events. Finally, the commercial imperative to make media coverage as entertaining and marketable as possible ensures a priority on the dramatic, violent and spectacular.

The Leicester team noted how, despite the massive publicity the demonstration attracted, it was prevented from registering a significant political statement. Sensing how this might have harmful repercussions, Halloran and co-workers asked: 'How long will peaceful demonstrators seeking a new mode of expression be content to demonstrate peacefully when whatever they do is likely to get the negative treatment?' (ibid.:317).

Other studies suggest that media representations may sometimes be deliberately constructed to achieve a favourable impression of police violence against a politically 'threatening' group. This was evident in press coverage of the activities of women protesters outside the American air base at Greenham Common.

For example, on 12 December 1982, 35,000 women arrived to 'Blockade the Base'. On the first day of the blockade, policing was low-key. But, on the second day, the police mounted a paramilitary-style operation to clear the entrance forcibly. The Greenham women complained of police brutality but, as Johnson points out, 'The press portrayed the blockading women as screaming harridans, contrasting us with what they had presented as the nice, well-meaning middle-class mothers and grandmothers the day before' (Johnson, 1989:167). For the next 2 years, the press systematically attacked the women's political motives, their hygiene standards and their sexual identity (Young, 1990).

Then, on 11 December 1983, a large number of Greenham women attempted to pull down the perimeter fence. Police intervention provoked allegations of brutality, but media coverage focused on the few police injuries, underemphasised the extent of police aggression and exaggerated the women's part in the violence.

> Soldiers from the base struck at our hands with metal rods while Thames Valley police twisted and karate-chopped fingers and wrists, pulled us from the fence by our necks and flung us into ditches and trees. Mounted police rode their horses straight into crowds of demonstrators. When one woman tried to remove barbed wire from the path of a police horse she feared would get hurt, her photograph became the basis for a frenzied attack which ran the headline, 'Horse Whipped With Barbed Wire'. Police acknowledgement that this hadn't actually happened was delayed until after the press coverage. Headlines screamed of this fabricated outrage and ignored the many injuries, including broken bones, that women had suffered.
>
> (Johnson, 1989:168)

THE AMERICAN RIOTS OF THE 1960s

American news coverage of the 1960s riots first came under academic scrutiny in the aftermath of the Watts riot, where it was generally felt that media reporting had exacerbated the conflict. 'The media were accused of giving excessive publicity to the more intransigent blacks, of reporting inflammatory incidents, of provoking violence by their very presence, and, in one instance, of actually encouraging a rioter to throw a brick' (Paletz and Dunn, 1969:328).

Baker and Ball (1969:105–6) also believe that television pictures of the riot conveyed helpful information about police movements to arsonists and looters, and blame some elements of the press for disseminating harmful and unsubstantiated rumour, e.g. that the rioting was orchestrated by muslims.

The most comprehensive study of US media coverage of the riots was carried out by the famous Kerner Commission (Kerner, 1968), which examined the style and content of television and newspaper reports for 1967. The Commission found that the coverage of this period was generally calm, factual and restrained. Far from emphasising violent confrontation and looting activity, both media focused on the steps being taken to quell the immediate rioting or the most effective ways of dealing with future disorder.

In a more critical vein, the Commission observed: 'All media reported rumors that had no basis in fact. Some newsmen staged riot events for the cameras' (ibid.:202). The media, it felt, were over-dependent on 'beleaguered government officials' for estimates of the size and severity of the riots. These estimates were invariably exaggerated. While recognising that coverage of one riot tended to encourage rioting elsewhere ('the principle of cumulative effect'), the Commission dismissed this as possible grounds for censorship:

> Once a disturbance occurs, the word will spread independently of newspapers and television. To attempt to ignore these events or portray them as something other than what they are can only diminish confidence in the media and increase the effectiveness of those who monger rumors and the fears of those who listen.
>
> (Kerner, 1968:202)

The Kerner Commission also criticised the media for creating an impression that the riots were confrontations between black and white civilians, as opposed to attacks on white-owned property in Negro areas. Coverage failed to highlight the wrongful arrests of blacks or excessive use of force by the police; nor did it adequately convey the extent of *pro-social* activity engaged in by black 'counter-rioters', such as helping the wounded or assisting the emergency services.

There was no serious attempt to examine the rioters' underlying grievances – seen as a symptom of the media's customary neglect of the social problems experienced by black Americans. Black respondents interviewed as part of the investigation 'noted a pronounced discrepancy between what they saw in the riots and what television broadcast' (ibid.:207). The media were widely distrusted as agents of the white power structure, too willing to accept the accounts of white officials in preference to accredited black representatives.

Similar themes have subsequently been explored by other American researchers. Knopf (1975) objects to the way that the press often used rumour and innuendo as the basis of 'hard reporting'. She refers, for example, to an issue of the *Baltimore Sun* which showed a picture of an unidentified motorcyclist, a gun strapped to his back. The caption read: 'QUIET, BUT... An unidentified motorcycle rider, armed with a rifle and carrying a belt of ammunition, was among those in the heart of York, Pa., Negro district late last night. The area was quiet for the first time in six days' (Knopf, 1975:257). The obvious implication was that the individual was a dangerous sniper when, in reality, he was a 16-year-old boy off hunting groundhogs.

Knopf is also critical of the media's tendency to characterise disorders as 'meaningless, purposeless, senseless (and) irrational'. Referring to press coverage of riots following the death of Dr Martin Luther King, Jnr in 1968, she observes that,

> No attempt is made to place the violence in a social context. The reference to the assassination of Dr King is perfunctory, with only a passing mention of his funeral and a few shouts about his death. Value-laden words receive unusual emphasis. The participants are 'marauders', not men; they 'rove' instead of run; they move in 'gangs', not groups; they engage in 'vandalism', not simply violence.
>
> (Knopf, 1975:262)

Singer (1970) explored the argument that television coverage encourages subsequent riot participation. He asked 499 people arrested during the Detroit riot of 1967 to recall how they had reacted to television pictures of *previous* US riots. Almost half the respondents said they experienced feelings of disapproval, sadness or disgust; only 26 per cent had felt anger or resentment towards the white authorities or pleasure that rioting was taking place. Singer then asked respondents to say how they first heard about the Detroit riot, and what details they were initially given. He discovered that 48 per cent of them first heard about the riot from another person, 27 per cent by direct observation and only 26 per cent from media coverage. The information received typically referred only to the riot's location, and not specific incidents. These findings suggest that media coverage did not play an influential role in encouraging people to participate in the Detroit riot.

A case study reported by Paletz and his co-workers (Paletz and Dunn, 1969; Paletz and Entman, 1981) emphasises that not all American newspapers were guilty of sensationalist reporting. Some, like the *Winston–Salem Journal*, were deliberately restrained. While other local newspapers produced exaggerated and error-ridden coverage of a small North Carolina riot, the *Journal* was careful to define the precise location of the riot, and reassure its readers that most of the city remained unaffected. All rumours were thoroughly checked and omitted if unverified. In attempting to defuse possible inter-racial antagonism, the *Journal* rarely mentioned that most of the 500 rioters were black. 'The paper did not, of course, blur the issue completely; it was perfectly clear that most of the rioters were Negroes. But the *Journal* stressed that those involved were "hoodlums", atypical of the Winston–Salem Negro' (Paletz and Dunn, 1969:337).

The *Journal*'s editorial policy pre-dates the codes of conduct subsequently adopted by many American radio and television stations (Kueneman and Wright, 1975). However, Paletz and his colleagues remain critical of the journalists' over-reliance on official sources of information about the riot (i.e. the mayor and chief of police) which helped to frame the event as the successful police suppression of a naked spree of lawlessness. There was no attempt to empathise with the rioters or to communicate their grievances. Indeed, 'by handling the event as a police-crime story, not a political one', the *Journal*'s coverage 'probably reduced the political power of already inefficacious poor people' (Paletz and Entman, 1981:117).

THE BRITISH RIOTS OF THE 1980s

Tumber's (1982) analysis of television news coverage of the British inner-city riots of 1981 reveals many similarities with corresponding American coverage of the 1960s. A content analysis of BBC and ITV broadcasts between 4 and 16 July showed that 'Riot Equipment' was the most frequently referred-to theme of the news broadcasts. A rank ordering of the thirty-four most popular themes revealed that 'Rioters' destruction of property', 'Causes', 'Looting, theft', 'Race' and 'Rioters' violence against people' were the next most-common items. 'Police violence' was recorded in thirty-fourth place, being referred to only once.

Interviews with riot participants indicated bitterness at the media's failure to highlight prior police–community relations: 'They do not show people being stopped and searched in their cars, in their homes and whilst waiting at bus stops', one interviewee complained. 'Nothing has been shown about what was going in Brixton before April. The public did not, therefore, understand what was going on or why there was trouble' (ibid.:13).

Tumber generally praised media personnel for adopting a responsible attitude in their reporting. Occasionally, these standards lapsed, as when an ITV *News At Ten* headline asked, 'Was Someone Directing The Riots?', a piece of pure speculation based (like Knopf's Baltimore example) on a brief clip of an unidentified motor scooter rider and passenger.

Senior police officers and media professionals interviewed by Tumber felt that broadcast pictures of violence, looting and destruction in progress helped prevent the dissemination of dangerous or malicious rumour. Both the police and rioters agreed that rioting was not encouraged by the 'advertising' effect of television pictures. 'The speed with which some of the incidents flared up suggests, in fact, that the kids were not sitting indoors, but that they were already out there on the streets – often bored, resentful and waiting for trouble' (ibid.:46).

An interesting contrast has been observed in the way that separate British riots were reported. In commenting on the media coverage of the Brixton riot of April 1981, Gordon and Rosenburg (1989:18) point out that 'the editorial responses of most papers as distinct from their news coverage, while condemning the violence, seemed to show some awareness of the underlying causes of the rioting'. However, when the Toxteth disturbance took place only 3 months later, the media response was couched, almost universally, in a 'law and order' rhetoric, emphasising the wantonness and criminality of the violence, and demanding coercive measures to deal with it (Sumner, 1982). Murdock (1984:78) accounts for the general character of press and television coverage of the Toxteth riot in terms of 'the routine business of news production and the practical and commercial pressures which shape it'. Thus priority is given to the statements of senior police and politicians, partly because they are more readily available and willing to be contacted than rioters or their grass-roots representatives; and partly because they are more able to deliver quotable material – an invaluable resource when strict deadlines must be met. Similarly, for safety's sake, photographers are obliged to stand behind police lines. Hence the impression given is of a 'thin blue line' being attacked by a vicious and threatening mob.

As with coverage of political events, there is a need to ensure intelligibility (which is achieved by evoking stereotypical explanations, such as the role of agitators or 'hooligan youth') and excitement (hence the fixation on the dramatic and spectacular). However, Murdock's account does not explain the variation in the reporting of the Brixton and Toxteth riots referred to above.

Wren-Lewis's (1981/1982) analysis of television news coverage of these riots enables us to understand this contrast. He points out that the reporting of the Brixton riot was marked by a discursive struggle between the 'law-and-order discourse' and a 'contra-discourse', which sought to de-mystify 'the hitherto unproblematic position of the police', by emphasising the possibility that police harassment and brutality lay at the root of the disorder.

Subsequent riots were represented almost unequivocally in terms of the 'law and order discourse'. Wren-Lewis explains that this was because, as successive riots occurred, television's preference for scenes of violence and destruction created an impression of unyielding crisis and chaos. There was simply not the time or space to enter into the detailed sort of discussion which accompanied the Brixton riot. In addition, the progressively violent and pandemonious reality suggested by television's own reports created the very conditions in which a law-and-order rhetoric could flourish virtually unchallenged.

Once established in this way, the law-and-order discourse acquired a lasting pre-eminence. By the mid-1980s, rioting, like the Handsworth and Broadwater Farm disorders of 1985, was being reported as a manifestation of 'criminality, pure and simple' (Gordon and Rosenburg, 1989:20). Some national newspapers portrayed the Handsworth riot as an inter-racial conflict, with Afro-Caribbean youths supposedly attacking both whites and Asians. These reports suppressed the fact that more whites than blacks were arrested during the disturbance, and hardly mentioned that police–community relations had recently deteriorated. The notion of outside agitators (including Libyan *agents provocateurs*) was prevalent in reports of the Broadwater Farm disorder (Benyon and Solomos, 1987). Coverage of this riot made no serious attempt to identify its underlying causes (ibid.).

MASS PICKETING: THE 'BATTLE OF ORGREAVE'

In turning to media representations of industrial confrontation, we focus, once again, on the 1984–5 coal dispute. Green is one of several authors who maintain that media coverage of the strike attempted to denigrate and undermine the miners' case against the government.

> The vilification of Arthur Scargill, the unbalanced emphasis on picket-line violence and intimidation, the failure to explain issues at the heart of the strike, the criminalization of striking miners, the unquestioned assumptions of police neutrality and the fundamental contradiction between the reality experienced by striking communities and the distorted presentation of that reality through the mass media – these

were the key components of the media's ideological policing of the strike.

(Green, 1990:157)

Part of this 'ideological policing' involved the use of particular forms of imagery and discourse to condemn the use of violence by the strikers while justifying police aggression. This section demonstrates how, in its choice of language, film-editing techniques and subtle juxtaposition of images and commentary, television news delivered an entirely misleading and politically biased representation of the Battle of Orgreave on 18 June 1984. The following discussion draws on analysis of the BBC 1 *Nine O'Clock News* and ITN's *News At Ten* bulletins by Cumberbatch *et al.* (1986), Jones (1991) and Masterman (1985). The discussion focuses primarily on Jones's study of how the two main channels described first the instigation, then the escalation of the disorder. A final subsection consolidates the analysis by emphasising a number of points raised by the other authors.

The instigation of disorder

The BBC's *Nine O'Clock News* was obviously the first to describe the episode. According to its narrator, John Thorne,

> The strikers' blockade of Orgreave was a precisely planned operation, but the police responded, sending in riot squad reinforcements to match the 5,000 or more pickets, and that was the trigger for some of the worst violence of this lengthy dispute. It reached a peak as miners surged in against the riot shields. Policemen hit out with truncheons under a barrage of stones and missiles. Mass picketing had turned to rioting. The police didn't give any ground and on the front line they handed out as much physical punishment as they received. Eventually, the senior officer ordered in the mounted police.

Thorne's report establishes that it was the miners who 'called' the confrontation. Theirs, we are told, was 'a precisely planned operation'. The police merely 'responded' to this challenge, 'matching' the picket numbers. The commentary clearly implies that the police aggression was justified: 'hitting out' with truncheons is excusable, given the 'barrage of stones and missiles' they were subjected to. That the police 'didn't give any ground' suggests controlled restraint, while the disclosure that they 'handed out as much physical punishment as they received' indicates that they did not use excessive force. The reference to 'Eventually' in the last sentence implies that it was only after a commendable period of restraint that horses were ordered in.

The ITN coverage of this phase differed in several key respects. Their news reporter, Phil Roman, began by explaining how,

> As the last of the lorries went in, the trouble started. Pickets charged straight into the police riot shields. In seconds, a pack of police, twenty deep, was fighting a shower of stones to hold the pickets back. The first cavalry charge came a few minutes later and it clearly worried the pickets. (Film shows pickets scattering across field.)

Where the BBC commentary suggests that the 'mere presence' of police officers was the trigger for the violence, Roman acknowledges that the arrival of the lorries – not naked hostility towards the police – was the pretext for disorder. In this way, the miners' action appears less vindictive. However, the ITN account emphasises that the decision to introduce the police horses was not taken lightly, but as the result of accumulating pressure ('police, twenty deep... fighting a shower of stones'). Finally, in a classic piece of understatement, viewers are informed that the cavalry charge 'clearly worried the pickets'.

The escalation of disorder

The BBC offered the following account of how the confrontation developed:

> A gap opened in the ranks and the horses galloped in. The horses are the most feared weapon in the police armoury on the picket line and they are very effective. But it's the riot squads that follow up to make the arrests and today, on the fields of battle around Orgreave, the police were involved in some of the most vicious hand-to-hand fighting of the entire miners' dispute. (Film sequence of two policemen swinging at, though apparently not hitting, pickets; picket taking a flying kick at a policeman.) The attacks on policemen were horrific but the riot squads gave no quarter, using their batons liberally. It was a miracle no-one was killed, said one police commander. At all times, the police were in control and there were over one hundred arrests as the fighting ebbed and flowed.

There is a marked contrast here between the description of violence by the pickets ('The attacks on policemen were horrific') and corresponding police aggression (they 'gave no quarter'; they were 'in control at all times'). The linguistic transformation known as *object deletion* is used to ensure that instances of police aggression are rendered more palatable. Thus we are told that 'horses galloped in, but not *who* they were attacking; and though the police 'used their batons liberally', it is not revealed *who* they were used against. In each case, the object of the police action has been intentionally deleted.

A number of euphemisms also help to underemphasise the severity of police violence. The revelation that they 'gave no quarter' helps to soften the fact that the police were beating people with their truncheons. References to the fact that the horses were 'very effective' or that the police 'used their batons liberally' further disguise the extent of police aggression. Finally, the simple assertion that the fighting 'ebbed and flowed' creates a misleading impression that it was a fair and equal contest.

ITN's commentary unfolded thus:

> More police reinforcements – this time taking advantage of the confu-
> sion caused by the police horses. As the horses came back, pickets threw
> half-bricks at them. Then they started on the front line of police. Some
> of the pickets had wrenched riot shields away from the police. When
> they started to gather for another push, the second wave of mounted
> police went in, scattering the pickets right across the field. Tension built
> up. The Assistant Chief Constable warned the pickets to stop throwing
> missiles and disperse. They didn't. More reinforcements – this time with
> short shields and truncheons. After two hours, the police were tired of
> being pushed and pelted with house bricks. The pickets knew what to
> expect: they'd been warned it could turn nasty, and it did. (Film
> sequence of riot police following horses in pursuit of miners; policeman
> repeatedly striking crouching picket about the head; miner taking flying
> kick at same policeman; officer hitting different picket on head with
> baton as he is leading him behind police lines.)

Here there is a greater emphasis on the police violence. The ITN sequence of film shows a close-up shot of a miner being systematically beaten about the head by a policeman which, as we shall see later, was deliberately excluded from the BBC version. Nevertheless, the unmistakable impress-ion created is that the police violence was justified: they were 'tired of being pushed and pelted with house bricks' for 2 hours.

Euphemistic references to police aggression are also apparent in the ITN account, as in 'it could turn nasty, and it did', where the agent and object of the violence (i.e. who did what to whom) remain unspecified. Other instances of police violence (e.g. the batoning incident) are not accompa-nied by spoken commentary, as if the reporter is reluctant to condemn such action. The ITN version suggests that the pickets are still largely to blame for the violence, but the police contribution to disorder is given more emphasis than in the BBC's bulletin.

Other points

Jones concentrated her analysis only on the late-evening news broadcasts. A complementary study by Masterman (1985) demonstrates that the BBC 9 o'clock news coverage had been modified since earlier evening bulletins due to a 'crisis of credibility' between its earlier 6 o'clock news broadcast and corresponding ITV accounts. Masterman's systematic comparison of the two narratives indicates how some aspects of commentary were modified to reduce evidence of bias revealed by comparisons with ITN's almost simultaneous broadcast. However, these modifications were only superficial. 'Though additional references to aggressive police tactics had been woven into the text, there was no explicit condemnation (or even mild disapproval) of police action, and no acknowledgement that unnecessary police violence was the central issue at stake' (ibid.:106).

The BBC had edited out at least one police atrocity. As we saw earlier, ITN coverage showed an incident in which one miner took a flying kick at a policeman who was beating a fellow-picket around the head. The BBC coverage excludes the truncheon blow, but includes the flying kick:

> Close comparison of BBC and ITN footage shows that the BBC film has in shot the man who was most severely beaten by the police, but that *the film has been cut at precisely the point when the policeman begins to set about him with his truncheon*. What we cut away to are miners' retaliatory attempts to help their colleagues. But because the BBC film has not shown any examples of police violence, these de-contextualised images can only signify *unprovoked* violence by pickets.
>
> (Masterman, 1985:103, emphasis in original)

A further indictment of editing practices was provided by BBC 2's *Brass Tacks* programme of 30 November 1985. This programme included extracts from the police's own video of the day's events. The video clearly emphasised that the heightening of tension and resulting hostility was caused, not by stone throwing as the news media suggested, but by the tactical introduction of the mounted police (Cumberbatch *et al.*, 1986).

These examples lend weight to Masterman's assertion that 'news presentation is an ideological construction, rather than a matter of unproblematic reporting' (Masterman, 1985:106). Television news personnel feel duty-bound, in times of social and political crisis, to project a pro-establishment view of industrial conflict. In Masterman's view, the Battle of Orgreave stands as a salutary reminder that 'what is omitted from television's agenda cannot easily enter the *general* consciousness and that the control of information, whether it takes a brutal or sophisticated form, is the very cornerstone of political power' (ibid.:108).

FOOTBALL HOOLIGANISM

British and Canadian press responses to the Heysel Stadium tragedy are considered by Young (1986), who notes how newspapers on both sides of the Atlantic ran the story for a whole month, dwarfing coverage of the Bangladesh cyclone which resulted in many thousands of deaths. Young maintains that, 'As horrendous as the results of Heysel were, the lurid impact- and circulation-oriented headlines suggested an event much worse' (ibid.:260). 'The Killing Field' was the macabre headline chosen by three newspapers.

The most frequently cited media explanations for the Heysel disturbance were the influence of alcohol, the involvement of the National Front, the ineptitude or cowardliness of the Belgian security forces and the hooligan mentality of the Liverpool supporters. This final category of explanation typically included references to the irrational, bestial and militaristic behaviour of the British fans. There was no counterbalancing emphasis on the aggressive and provocative activities of the rival Juventus supporters (which were apparent in the live television coverage of the game), or the fact that there were confrontations between Belgian police and Italian supporters prior to the game.

The references to the bestiality and irrationality of the Liverpool supporters are typical of the themes used by sports reporters to systematically denigrate football hooligans. Whannel (1979) identifies four such themes which commonly depict the hooligans as: 'mindless/senseless', 'maniacs/lunatics', 'foul/sub-human' and a 'minority/so-called supporters'. Whannel believes that the main reason why this terminology has taken such an enduring grip is that it is being used to serve the commercial interests of Football League and club officials as part of a hidden agenda to attract a new type of football audience (the 'family audience') and thereby solve the game's economic crisis. According to this perspective, the demand for all-seater stadia and accompanying leisure and commercial facilities – ceaselessly promulgated as a method of curbing hooliganism – is part of a thinly veiled plan to replace soccer's traditional working-class audience with middle-class consumers.

According to a similar perspective, adopted by authors like Hall (1978) and Taylor (1987), the growing media focus on hooliganism since the

1960s may be seen as a political device to help justify a more authoritarian state response to all forms of social dissidence. Lloyd (1989:261) takes a similar position. She argues that, before the Public Order Act 1986 was passed, 'it was the moral panic surrounding football hooliganism which the government used in its publicity for the new law. The opposition vainly argued that football violence could not be lumped together with political unrest and industrial disputes'.

NORTHERN IRELAND

The media's political role is especially ubiquitous in their reporting of Northern Ireland. Before the Army became involved, media accounts often referred to the political background to the conflict and were sympathetic towards the Civil Rights movement (Hillyard, 1982). By 1975, this had all changed: reports, features and editorials now concentrated on protecting the Army's image and portraying the IRA as 'criminals or mindless psychopaths often manipulated by Godfathers behind the scenes' (ibid.:39).

In addition to banning, delaying or censoring news and current affairs reports (ibid.), the British government and military officials have used a variety of sanctions, notably cutting journalists off from authoritative sources of information, to ensure that recalcitrant individuals and institutions are brought back into line (Elliott, 1978:153). In practice, such measures are seldom necessary: most journalists seem aware of their tacit responsibility to toe the approved ideological line (Schlesinger, 1978:225).

The way that these forms of social control can be mobilised is illustrated by newspaper coverage of the events of Bloody Sunday, 30 January 1972 (see Chapter 5). According to Curtis, 'the British media fudged the events, suppressed investigations and blazened forth the idea that the British army had been "cleared" of guilt' (Curtis, 1984:40).

Eye-witness accounts by British journalists told of the unprovoked and apparently indiscriminate shooting of civilians by British soldiers. According to Simon Winchester of *The Guardian*,

> Paratroopers piled out of their vehicles, many ran forward to make arrests, but others rushed to the street corners. It was these men, perhaps 20 in all, who opened fire with their rifles. I saw three men fall to the ground. One was still obviously alive, with blood pumping from his leg. The others, both apparently in their teens, seemed dead...
>
> Then people could be seen moving forward in Fahan Street, their

hands above their heads. One man was carrying a white handkerchief. Gunfire was directed even at them and they fled or fell to the ground.

(quoted in Curtis, 1984:40)

The Times reporter also quoted a British General urging his men to 'Go on the paras, go and get them', and said that the lower ranks appeared to him to be relishing their work and perceiving the Bogsiders as 'legitimate targets' (ibid.:41).

But there was no general media outcry. *The Times* and *Guardian* reports contrasted with those of other papers. Timely interventions by senior Army officers had already established the 'official view' that the paratroops had fired only at clearly identifiable targets, and only when they came under heavy fire from gunmen, and nail and petrol bombers (Curtis, 1984:41–2). Despite the evidence to the contrary, most of Monday morning's newspapers subscribed to the Army's version. Even the *Guardian*'s own headline seemed reluctant to blame the soldiers: '13 killed as paratroops break riot: "Soldiers were returning Derry sniper fire," says Army' (ibid.:43), and the paper's editorial distanced itself from Winchester's account:

As yet it is too soon to be sure of what happened. The army has an intolerably difficult task in Ireland. At times it is bound to act firmly, even severely. Whether individual soldiers misjudged their situation yesterday, or were themselves too directly threatened, cannot yet be known.

(Curtis, 1984:44

The authorities' 'second diversionary thrust' involved the setting up of a Tribunal of Inquiry under Lord Widgery. This move hindered subsequent investigation into Bloody Sunday and nullified further criticism of the Army – largely because the government's Press Office appealed for the suspension of any media coverage which might prejudice the Tribunal's findings. This, and a veiled threat of prosecution, was enough to deter the publication of a *Sunday Times* article and the broadcasting of a Thames Television programme which were both detrimental to the Army's case. The Widgery Report was published in April. Though critical of the fact that four civilians had been shot dead without conceivable justification, the document generally endorsed the Army's version of events and, in the press view, completely exonerated the paratroops (Curtis, 1984:50).

In the autumn of 1988, the British government made its most overt attempt to date to silence its Republican opponents. On 19 October 1988, the then Home Secretary, Douglas Hurd, issued notices to the Independent Broadcasting Authority (IBA) and BBC, requiring them, under the Broadcasting Act 1981, to refrain from broadcasting any words spoken on behalf of, or in support of, a 'proscribed organisation', excluding anything said in the course of parliamentary proceedings, or in the run up to a parliamentary, European parliamentary or local election.

The government justified the imposition of this censorship on the grounds that the appearance on television of 'supporters of violence' might frighten or offend, or provide sustenance and support for terrorists themselves. Ewing and Gearty are not impressed by such reasons. They argue that it is misguided to pretend that these proscribed organisations (like Sinn Fein) either do not exist or do not carry massive popular support.

> Rather than face up to the horrendous alienation implied by such strong electoral support for Sinn Fein, the Government has closed its eyes and now compels the population to do the same. Such blindness distorts truth; such political irresponsibility stores up trouble for the future.
>
> (Ewing and Gearty, 1990:246)

DISCUSSION

The role of the media in public disorder has been found to be consistent across different historical periods, geographical locations and types of disorder. An ideal type of their operation is offered in Figure 8.1. An important caveat to such generalisations is that the category of the 'mass media' contains a variety of means and forms of communication. The treatment of public disorder in a serious documentary on a public television service is likely to have different preoccupations from the main news bulletin on the same channel. Newspapers, in turn, differ considerably in layout, audience and political slant. Nevertheless, analyses of media coverage of disorder have consistently found more similarities than differences in media coverage. Thus the processes identified in the diagram will be evident in the majority of media outlets, the exceptions being few and far between.

To describe how the media cover disorder is not in itself an explanation of why they should adopt this approach. Those who regard the media as little more than an arm of the capitalist state (Miliband, 1969) will be content with a structural or conspiratorial explanation, emphasising the institutional dependence and ideological role of the media. Cohen and Young (1981) call this the 'manipulative model' and rightly insist that the problem of explanation is more complicated.

Broadly speaking, we can identify four sets of pressures which serve to disable the media from meeting their own criteria of objectivity and balance

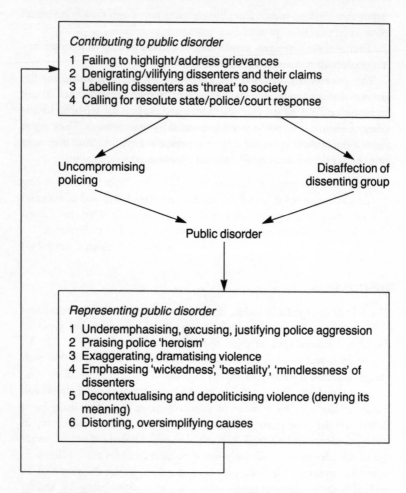

Figure 8.1 is composed of the following labelled boxes:

Contributing to public disorder
1 Failing to highlight/address grievances
2 Denigrating/vilifying dissenters and their claims
3 Labelling dissenters as 'threat' to society
4 Calling for resolute state/police/court response

Uncompromising policing

Disaffection of dissenting group

Public disorder

Representing public disorder
1 Underemphasising, excusing, justifying police aggression
2 Praising police 'heroism'
3 Exaggerating, dramatising violence
4 Emphasising 'wickedness', 'bestiality', 'mindlessness' of dissenters
5 Decontextualising and depoliticising violence (denying its meaning)
6 Distorting, oversimplifying causes

Figure 8.1 The media's relationship to public disorder

in the coverage of public disorder. The first set consists of institutional and professional definitions of what constitutes news. As the classic formulation of Galtung and Ruge (1981) demonstrates, news is a cultural construct. It must fit the institutional demands for the production of news on a regular cycle within predetermined categories and established formats. Thus lead news stories are concerned with the immediate and dramatic, with effects

rather than causes, with surface appearances rather than underlying processes.

The operation of news values constitutes the second set of pressures.
Topics and events are selected as headline news according to their news-
worthiness. Hence the emphasis on the dramatic, unexpected and negative,
the measurement of the significance of negative events in terms of damage
to people and property. Here, too, are sedimented conventions of presentation: the need to personalise the issue by interviewing hapless victims, to
make comparisons with other events classified as similar in kind and, most
obviously in the case of television, to be attracted to that which can be
pictured and distracted from that which cannot.

All this drives the media towards a largely predictable way of selecting
and presenting events: what Tuchman (1974) has called 'routinising the
unexpected'. Another aspect of routinisation reveals a third set of factors:
the need for authoritative opinion. In a constitutional democracy, there
are individuals whose status or office gives them the automatic right to be
heard. Though other accounts may be sought and presented, those in
authority occupy a privileged position in what has been called the 'hier-
archy of credibility' (Becker, 1972). They occupy the role of primary
definers (Hall *et al.*, 1978) whose interpretation of events immediately sets
the agenda within which alternative versions must be cast. Thus the
reactions of politicians, police and employers have a different weight to
those of demonstrators, rioters or strikers.

Thus, by virtue of institutional demands, occupational conventions and
perceived political legitimacy, the media as a whole are predisposed to
adopt a style of coverage which will pay scant regard to analysis of the
causes of protest or the grievances of protesters. Where there is room for
manoeuvre is in the way the media seek to locate the political significance
of disorderly protest. Here the media enter into a directly ideological role,
since they are explaining to us what these events mean. This need to 'define
the situation' is the fourth set of pressures. At its most rampant in the
conservative popular press, the view is likely to be taken that the protesters
– the violent minority by their acts, the majority by their association – have
moved outside the realm of politics and into the area of criminal activity.
More sophisticated versions argue or imply that there can be no excuse for
their actions, that they have lost whatever case they had by their conduct.
More crudely, they are written off as a rampaging mob, victim to primitive
urges or the machinations of conspirators. At this point, dehumanising
language is evoked and inhuman measures of repression advocated.

Not all the media choose or are able to indulge in such ideological
vilification. Laws and conventions constrain the broadcast media, who may

nevertheless reproduce the voices of those who can adopt such a stance. Especially in times of political crisis, the need to delegitimate the form of protest and thus the cause itself may lead the media to slant its coverage towards a version which justifies its own ideological view. Hence the police are assumed to be in the right, capable only of restrained reaction to provocation. If need be, the words and pictures of reporters can be adjusted to fit this version of events. Only at this point is a conspiratorial interpretation of the role of the media justified.

Since, as we have argued, disorder is frequently motivated by the failure to find any other effective voice, media coverage merely perpetuates the problem. By condemning the disorderly symptoms of social conflict and neglecting its causes, the media implicitly endorse further repressive measures. This exacerbates the possibility of further disorder as more protest is aroused by the loss of civil liberties. Too many contemporary social problems are conveniently attributed to the media but, in the case of public disorder, some blame is clearly justified.

Chapter 9

Contemporary policing and its democratic control

Since the inner-city disturbances of 1981, public order policing in Britain has become discernibly more authoritarian and paramilitarised (Jefferson, 1990; Uglow, 1988). This chapter considers these developments, arguing that they have an obvious potential to amplify, rather than reduce, the tendency to public disorder, and assessing their implications for the erosion of civil liberties.[1]

The chapter begins by analysing changes which have occurred in the American style of policing since their riots of the 1960s. This overview, culminating in a recent case study of American police practices, offers a reasonable basis for predicting future British trends. A second section then analyses the corresponding drift towards a more repressive style of policing in this country. It also examines a recent case study of a British police operation which exemplifies current trends. The third section moves on to investigate the nature and effectiveness of British and American mechanisms for exercising democratic control over the police (i.e. influencing their policies and making them answerable for their behaviour). Three such mechanisms are evaluated: community policing arrangements, police complaints procedures and formal systems of accountability.

AMERICAN POLICING TRENDS

General developments

We begin by examining American policing trends over the last 25 years. Fearful of any repetition of the urban riots, the American government took several measures in the late 1960s to strengthen its control capabilities. According to Button (1989:297), it was the Detroit riot of July 1967 which 'marked a turning point in federal policy towards local law enforcement because this upheaval clearly demonstrated the inability of local and state forces to contain disorders'.

Prior to this riot, the Johnson administration's strategy had been to try and eradicate the possibility of further disorder by tackling the chronic social problems highlighted by the riots. One of its key policies was to activate an improvement of police–black relations. A series of conferences were staged for local officials and police personnel from America's 136 largest cities. The Justice Department's Community Relations Service was enlarged to co-ordinate federal programmes aimed at reducing inner-city social problems. With the continuation of the disorders into 1968, the administration shifted its emphasis – to that of riot control.

New legislation was enacted in the form of the Omnibus Crime Control and Safe Streets Act 1968, which established a national police-training centre and provided financial assistance to local police forces to strengthen their riot control capabilities. Most US cities upgraded their riot technology, invested more in training and developed contingency plans for dealing with major disorder. Special 'riot squads' emerged throughout the USA. By 1968, 15,000 men had been trained for handling civil disorder. The US military and intelligence agencies were correspondingly expanded.

The greater emphasis on law-enforcement techniques pushed American urban conflict towards a new phase of 'political or conspiratorial violence' (Janowitz, 1969:332). Between 1968 and 1970, there were numerous violent incidents involving shootouts between the police and members of the Black Panthers organisation. Subsequently, another radical organisation, the Black Liberation Army (BLA) adopted such tactics as ambushing police in the ghetto and bombing police stations.

It was during this phase of conflict between the police and black radicals that,

> With more than 1,000 plainclothes agents, the army gathered information on approximately 18,000 American civilians between 1967 and 1969 in its efforts to assemble data for city and other public agencies preparing for domestic upheaval. Shortly after the election of Richard Nixon to the presidency, and his appointment of a 'law and order' attorney general, the FBI was authorized to engage in electronic surveillance of, and to direct counterintelligence activities toward, black militants and their organizations as way of preventing ghetto violence.
> (Button, 1989:298)

These, and other militaristic tactics, hastened the decline of organisations like the Panthers and BLA. Twenty-four black militant organisations were subjected to 'tax surveillance' as part of International Revenue Service

(IRS) harassment, and FBI agents placed bogus documents into the hands of Panther members which led them to suspect each other of being police informants (McAdam and Moore, 1989:281).

The monitoring of political dissidents was routine during the 1960s (Brodeur, 1983). Sophisticated surveillance techniques were used to control crowds at the 1968 Chicago Democratic Convention (see Chapter 2). Here police monitoring of the large crowds was facilitated by 'sophisticated radio equipment supplied by the Army, hot lines to the White House and the Pentagon, and an 8 by 12-foot map of the city, complete with a zoom-lens television camera for closeups, that could show where every police officer and other security force was located at all times' (Farber, 1988:159). This type of technology now exists in all major American cities. Many city-centre streets are monitored by 24-hour surveillance cameras capable of 'seeing' through apartment windows. New York City has a computerised riot control room which uses closed-circuit television cameras to relay detailed information about the movement of riot participants (Manwaring-White, 1983:90–1).

The police capacity to respond to public disorder has greatly improved since the riots. The National Guard is still available on a standby basis. Organised at state level, the Guard is composed of part-timers who undergo a statutory period of training with the regular Army. During the riots, the Guard was criticised for being panicky and uncoordinated (Brewer *et al.*, 1988:117). Now it has been rendered virtually obsolete by the introduction of quasi-military squads of police officers known as SWAT (Special Weapons and Tactics) units. Such units are specially trained and equipped to deal with a variety of situations, like bomb disposal, undercover surveillance, releasing hostages, riots and disasters. Consisting of permanent teams of officers, SWAT units and other similar agencies now exist throughout the USA. For example, Massachusetts has its own STOP (Special Tactics and Operations Unit).

Since the 1980 Miami riot, the Metro Dade Police Department has deployed a specialist 'field force' in response to public disorder.

> Consisting of a platoon of police officers and sergeants, led by a lieutenant, the 'field force' is formed by six squads – one sergeant and seven officers per squad. The remainder form the Commander's executive squad; provide for specialized 'chemical agent' responses; man a 'prison wagon'; and provide vehicle security.
>
> (McKenzie and Gallagher, 1989:169)

Squad members are equipped with body armour, jump suits, shotguns, smoke cannisters, chemical agent launchers and CS gas. They are specially trained in crowd-control techniques and were effective in suppressing outbreaks of disorder in the early 1980s (ibid.).

A case study: operation 'Hammer'

A heavily militarised style of policing has been deployed recently as part of a moral panic surrounding youth gang violence connected to the trafficking of rock cocaine ('crack') in the Watts area of Los Angeles. Here the 'virtual extinction' of job opportunities for young black males, and competition with immigrant workers in the employment sector allied to discriminatory attitudes among employees, has 'incubated [a] counter-economy of youth crime and drug dealing' (Davis, 1988:49).

It was the accidental shooting of a woman outside a theatre in an affluent part of the city which initially generated a media and political outcry. Black community representatives in Watts were among those calling for a decisive police response. The LAPD chief, Daryl Gates, responded to this outcry by authorising a series of 'anti-gang sweeps', known as the Gang Related Active Trafficker Suppression programme (GRATS).

Nine sweeps, each involving three hundred officers, were carried out in February and March 1988. These resulted in 1,500 arrests and the impounding of 500 cars. However, on Good Friday, gang members shot randomly into a streetcorner crowd in South Central, killing a 19-year-old woman, and operation 'Hammer' was mobilised to finally snuff out the problem. In the space of one single weekend, elite tactical squads, joined by a special anti-drug taskforce and 1,000 extra-duty officers, rounded up scores of Watts teenagers.

> Kids were humiliatingly forced to 'kiss the sidewalk' or spreadeagle against police cruisers while officers checked their names against computerized files of gang members. 1,453 were arrested and processed in mobile booking offices, mostly for petty offences like delinquent traffic tickets or curfew violations. Hundreds more, uncharged, had their names entered on the LAPD gang roster for future surveillance.
>
> (Davis, 1988:37)

As Davis points out, these tactics and the lack of public opposition to them, have ominous implications for the future of civil liberties:

> Those who applaud the Hammer as a necessary evil today will be urging some form of youth internment as a necessary evil tomorrow. The logic of civil libertarians has never been more compelling: the rights taken away from gang members will be rights denied all minority youth; the

walls put around gangs will imprison whole communities; the police state once expanded will not easily be contracted.

(Davis, 1988:59)

BRITISH POLICING TRENDS

As in America, important developments have occurred in the following areas of public order policing: public surveillance, crowd-control training and technology and the extension of legal powers. These changes are separately analysed.

Public surveillance

Finch (1989:290–1) asserts that there has been a progressive growth in the routine surveillance of political 'subversives' over the past decade. In her view, techniques developed in Northern Ireland have become more apparent on the British mainland. Policing at all levels now recognises the need to accumulate and maintain 'low-level intelligence' which may be used to anticipate or pre-empt disorder. Finch points out that the job description of some Scottish police officers requires them to enlist the co-operation of at least one person in every street who is willing and able to pass on useful information. According to her, Neighbourhood Watch schemes have been encouraged with similar objectives in mind (ibid.: 295–6).

In the early 1980s, the Metropolitan police installed Divisional Information Officers to monitor the rise and fall of 'tension indicators' (e.g. violence or abuse towards police officers, increasing numbers of complaints against the police and a decline in public co-operation) in specially targeted local communities and report their findings to the Central Information Unit within the Metropolitan Public Order Branch (Lloyd, 1989:273–4). These indicators are used to identify 'riot prone' areas in London (ibid.). The problem with using them is that they may produce a self-fulfilling prophecy. Small incidents may be over-reacted to in the strong anticipation of trouble, rendering it more likely that confrontation will actually occur.

The surveillance of targeted individuals, organisations or localities may also be achieved via access to computer information. For example, the Police National Computer (PNC) has a Suspect and Stolen Vehicles file which lists cars seen at demonstrations or owned by people who the police simply wish to keep an eye on, as well as vehicles suspected of being stolen or belonging to criminals (Manwaring-White, 1983:58–9). Pounder (1985:76) argues that preliminary information of this nature will encourage officers to place less emphasis on their own personal discretion and more emphasis on the background 'history' of the people involved.

In 1980, the Post Office Engineering Union alerted the general public to the increased prevalence of telephone tapping. The police allegedly 'listened in' to conversations involving members of CND and were similarly active during the national steel and coal disputes (Docherty, 1983; Finch, 1989). Infiltration by Special Branch officers posing as miners is said to have occurred during the coal dispute (McCabe and Wallington, 1988:145). There have been several instances in the late 1980s of undercover operations leading to the rounding up of soccer hooligan offenders (Fielding, 1991:218).

Video cameras were used regularly in the late 1980s for crowd surveillance at soccer grounds, and as a method of enforcing post-match arrests (Uglow, 1988:95). London demonstrations are routinely monitored by sixty cameras placed at symbolic locations, enabling an area of 200 square miles to be covered by the Scotland Yard operations room. In addition, the police sometimes deploy 'Heli-teles' – remote-control TV cameras with a wide-angle lens for scanning and a zoom-lens for focusing in – for use in helicopters. The resolution of these cameras is good enough to pick out number plates or the faces of individual demonstrators. Colour pictures monitored in a control room enable instructions to be relayed to police on the spot (ibid.:68–9).

Police riot training and technology

As early as 1978, one-third of all Metropolitan police officers received riot training (BSSRS, 1985:78). This force now has the most sophisticated riot-training facilities in the United Kingdom, with special training centres at Greenwich and Hounslow. The latter has its own 'small town' where riot simulations are carried out (Lloyd, 1989:270). These arrangements are increasingly being adopted by other forces, all of which put their special units and Police Support Units through public order training.

Crowd-control training is complemented by courses on community and race relations. But a Home Office study by Southgate (1982b) reported that officers saw little value in such training: they quickly forgot the content and saw it as no substitute for direct experience or the advice of senior colleagues. Northam (1988) points out how the Metropolitan police have responded with 'considerable imagination' to the apathy and cynicism of lower ranks by putting them through courses designed to combat sexism, racism and what he calls the John Wayne machismo 'canteen culture'. The main problem is that they are then required to undergo training in paramilitary riot control at Hounslow under the tuition of superfit instructors who convey a militaristic image.

Following the Lewisham disorders of 1977, perspex riot shields were introduced as standard police issue (BSSRS, 1985). After the 1981 riots, improvements were made in the fireproofing of shields and garments and police officers were routinely provided with riot boilersuits (Lloyd, 1989). In addition to these defensive provisions, forces were also provided with a range of offensive technology. By November 1982, twenty-two of the forty-three forces had stocks of plastic bullets, and thirty had supplies of CS gas.

CS gas was used, against Home Office regulations, during the 1981 Toxteth riot, but has not been used since. Similarly, the use of plastic bullets was authorised by the Metropolitan Police Commissioner, Sir Kenneth Newman, during the Broadwater Farm disturbance of 1985. Here, too, weapons were not used, though, afterwards Sir Kenneth put the people of London 'on notice' that plastic bullets and CS gas would be used in the event of future disorder (ibid.:267).

Recent technological developments have enhanced the possibility of fatal shootings. In April 1990, a week after the poll tax disorder, the *Sunday Times* Insight team revealed secret ACPO plans to deploy SAS-trained police marksmen in situations where rioters were thought to possess guns (*Sunday Times*, 8 April 1990). A 'Doomsday scenario', outlined in the Association's Tactical Options Manual, provides for units of officers, equipped with Heckler and Koch machine guns, to be driven into riot situations by armoured landrovers.

In May 1991, it was disclosed that the Metropolitan police area was to be permanently patrolled by special units, known as ARVs (armed response vehicles). These units would consist of three specially trained officers, driving around in Rover 827s, with each unit armed with two self-loading carbines and three handguns. Eight such units were envisaged, and it was anticipated that between three and five would be on the streets at any given time (*The Guardian*, 10 May 1991). As with the Doomsday scenario, this further militarisation of the police occurred without public debate or accountability.

Extended police powers

Provisions embodied in recent legislation, notably the Police and Criminal Evidence Act 1984 (PACE) and the Public Order Act 1986,

represent a quantum leap in police powers, reinforcing the view that the British state is becoming increasingly authoritarian. The public order legislation will mean that the police, besides being charged with the duty to keep the peace, will be enabled to mediate the already constrained ability to engage in protest and dissent on a much wider front.

(Brewer *et al.*, 1988:31)

In so far as they encourage greater police intervention on picket lines or at demonstrations, and enable them to impose their authority on many aspects of community life, the 1984 and 1986 Acts have profound implications for the possibility of disorder.

The PACE enables the police to stop and search any person whom they reasonably suspect of possessing stolen goods, an offensive weapon or items to be used in connection with a burglary or theft. The person may be detained for as long as is 'reasonably practicable' to carry out such a search. Reasonable force may be used against anyone who is uncooperative, and anyone failing to give their name and address when asked is liable to be arrested. The Act also empowers the police to set up roadblocks to discover whether vehicles contain anyone who has witnessed, committed or is about to commit a serious crime. Other provisions enable police officers to enter private property forcibly without a search warrant if they deem such action necessary to prevent a breach of the peace, reach someone who has committed an arrestable offence or search for evidence of an offence by someone they have already arrested. Subject to obtaining a magistrate's warrant, police officers may also enter premises forcibly to look for evidence of a serious arrestable offence (ranging from murder and rape to any act which has led or might lead to public disorder, or, vaguer still, acts which might interfere with the effective administration of justice). Under the Act, persons may be detained for questioning at a police station, without charge, for 36 hours on the police's own authority, and for a further 60 hours subject to successful application for a magistrate's order.

It is evident, even from this brief review of the Act, that its overall effect has been to legitimise and encourage numerous police practices (e.g. stop and search, roadblocks, forcible entry) which have consistently alienated and antagonised large sections of society – notably, black communities and trade-unionists – and had the accumulated effect of generating public disorder. Similar antagonism is likely to be produced by the use of police discretion allowed under the Public Order Act 1986. Several features of the Act which were designed to reduce the possibility of public disorder seem more likely to promote its occurrence. This is most evident in those provisions relating to the policing of static assemblies and marches and processions. The Act states that, in the case of marches and processions, organisers must give written notice, 6 clear days beforehand, of the date, starting time and route of the march, together with their own names and addresses. The police can use their discretion to impose prior conditions on the march, such as when it occurs, its route and numerical strength. They may also prohibit certain activities, such as the carrying of banners or the chanting of particular slogans. These prior conditions may be determined by a chief constable or his deputy, or someone of equivalent rank in the Metropolitan police. Once the march is in progress, the police may impose further conditions as they see fit (e.g. deciding to alter the route). Here conditions may be set by the most senior officer present.

The grounds on which such conditions may be imposed include police perceptions that disorder might otherwise occur, that there exists the possibility of damage to people or property or that the march is likely to intimidate people, or interfere with or disrupt the life of the community. Organisers failing to give notice or not complying with conditions risk arrest, conviction, possible 3 months' sentence or £400 fine. Participants who break any conditions are liable to arrest, conviction or a £400 fine.

The Act retains the power of a Chief Constable or his/her deputy to ban a march under the 1936 Public Order Act. Here the Chief applies to his Local Authority, who then seek the appropriate permission from the Home Secretary. (The Metropolitan Police Commissioner applies directly to the Home Office.) It is an offence to organise, or participate in, a banned march or procession.

The provisions related to public assemblies vary slightly from those for marches and processions. A public assembly is defined as a gathering of twenty or more people in a place which is wholly or partially open to the air (e.g. a mass meeting, picket, demonstration or pop festival). Advance notice is not required in these cases. However, as with marches and processions, the police have the power to impose conditions on the location, duration and size of the assembly on similar grounds to those which apply to marches. Equivalent penalties apply to anyone failing to observe these conditions.

As Lloyd points out, 'In effect it is now up to the police to exercise their political judgement about our freedom to demonstrate' (1989:260). This is bound to result in frequent problems. Frustration will inevitably arise on any march or at any static assembly where participants believe that the police are imposing unnecessary or unreasonable conditions, rendering the protest ineffectual. There is nothing to guarantee that police conditions will be adequately conveyed or heard before or during the march. Events at the anti-poll tax rally showed how confusion and indignation can easily occur when police instructions are inaudible. Given their virtually unlimited powers to dictate what a dissenting group may or may not be allowed to do, there is a danger that police will prove less willing to negotiate arrangements with protest organisers, preferring to impose conditions as the law allows. Obviously, this would be a fragile basis on which to reach a 'contract with the crowd'.

A case study: operation 'Kingfisher'

If the prospect of British 'bobbies' behaving like their LAPD counterparts seems too remote to be taken seriously, we might do well to consider the events of 29 September 1989 when 400 police officers carried out a drugs raid on the Broadwater Farm Estate. Operation 'Kingfisher' followed 2 months of planning, including the 3-week undercover surveillance of a launderette, reckoned to be the focus of drug-dealing activity.

At 5 p.m. – the time established as the peak of illegal activity – 200 officers and a complement of specially invited newpaper reporters and television crews moved in. Teams of officers arrived on the scene in unmarked furniture vans. Under the protection of bullet-proof vests and riot gear, they used axes and sledgehammers to break down doors before seizing twenty-four prisoners and a large haul of cannabis. Afterwards, police distributed 2,500 copies of a letter explaining their actions to local residents. Community leaders were fully debriefed.

Newspaper reports on the following day contained complaints of excessive behaviour by the police: some people claimed that doors throughout several blocks of flats had been unnecessarily destroyed. A community leader had to be removed from the area under police escort when it was alleged that she had been used as a police informer. The raid represented a convergence of the policing trends referred to in this chapter: the use of covert surveillance, including low-level intelligence; hard, paramilitary tactics and the enabling legislation to enforce them. We may have witnessed the 'moment' of the 'technocop' (BSSRS, 1985). It therefore becomes imperative to ask: what are the existing mechanisms of democratic control over the police, and how effective are they?

DEMOCRATIC CONTROL MECHANISMS

The answers to these questions are considered by examining the nature and effectiveness of three methods of exerting democratic influence over police policy and behaviour: community-policing arrangements, the police complaints system and the relationship between police and elected representatives (the formal accountability system).

Community-policing arrangements

Community policing is based on the principle of a working partnership between the police and local community.

> It is the revitalising of the whole tradition of policing by consent by increasing the level of trust by the community in its police, by fostering a deeper understanding by the police of community problems and community needs.
>
> To achieve these ends, police seek to liaise and work with other agencies, consult their public, and stimulate the self-policing capacities of communities themselves. In so doing, police provide initiatives and leadership, draw interested parties together, and tailor their policing to neighbourhood needs.
>
> (Pope, 1985:104)

This philosophy was massively endorsed by the Scarman Report (Scarman, 1981), which advocated the setting up of community liaison procedures and the use of 'beat' officers as the principal ways of ensuring greater trust and co-operation between the police and their public.

The Police and Criminal Evidence Act 1984 made it a legal requirement for Police Authorities to maintain consultative arrangements on behalf of the local community. Though the Act did not specify what form the consultation should take, Home Office guidelines were issued recommending the establishment of police consultative committees.

> These committees have some common features: membership includes representatives from the police, the police authority, constituent councils, and voluntary, statutory and community groups; meetings are held regularly and records kept; each has some sort of constitution; and the proceedings are generally publicly available.
>
> (Brogden et al., 1988:175)

The objectives of these committeees are to facilitate an exchange of views between the police and the wider community on issues of local concern; to help resolve conflict between the police and dissenting sections of the community; to encourage self-help and crime prevention activities; and to educate or inform the public regarding everyday police matters (Morgan, 1989).

The evidence suggests that community policing has not been the panacea that Lord Scarman envisaged. Critics of consultative committeees dismiss them as ineffectual talking shops, dominated by the 'concerned and worthy' middle classes and excluding those members of dispossessed minorities on the receiving end of police policies (Brogden *et al.*, 1988:176).

There are clear signs that many sections of the general public welcome the presence of home-beat officers (Shapland and Vagg, 1988; Waddington *et al.*, 1990). In a study carried out by Morris and Heal (1981), residents felt 'more secure and confident' following the introduction of beat officers. Proponents of community policing often feel dismayed at the recklessness with which carefully cultivated relationships are undermined by the authorisation of 'fire brigade' tactics at the first suggestion of disorder.

Community policing continues to be afforded low priority and prestige within the police force, where it is generally characterised as 'social work' or not 'real' policing (Fielding, 1991:170). As Stephens points out, the 'capture culture', with its in-built preference for tough, reactive policing, still dominates the force. In the meantime, 'community policing has not developed into a partnership between police and public in the fight against crime. It has remained dominated by the police and operates on the police's terms (Stephens, 1988:113).

Community-policing arrangements have not fared much better in the United States. American officers tend to downgrade community policing as 'unmanly' or 'unimportant'. Since it was first introduced in the late 1960s, it has been resisted or treated with indifference by all ranks. Community officers are castigated as 'social workers' or 'Nigger lovers', and community relations departments branded as 'Commie Relations' units. According to most officers, its only value lies in 'selling the police' to the public (Brewer *et al.*, 1988:126; Riley, 1974:191).

Wintersmith (1974:71–7) evaluated the effectiveness of three American approaches to police–community relations (PCR). The first approach involved despatching specially selected officers into 'alienated neighbourhoods' and having them operate from 'storefront' mini-police stations, where they sometimes worked in teams, helping and advising marginal sections of society, like drug addicts and delinquent children. According to Wintersmith, these officers helped to foster an atmosphere of mutual trust and co-operation. However, the less-committed remainder of their colleagues accused them of 'selling out the department' and the resulting tension forced the community police officers to resign (ibid.:74).

The second approach to PCR – establishing citizens' committees (or neighbourhood–council forums) – proved equally ineffective. 'For the most part, the closest the citizens ever came to confronting the police on specific issues was when an occasional individual dominated the entire meeting to register a personal grievance. Those who participated were essentially propolice' (ibid.:72). The third approach, 'police–community attitudinal change', attempted to change officers' attitudes to minority groups via a series of lectures, encounter groups and sensitivity training. This was impatiently rejected by police officers, who saw the methods involved as an attempt to subvert their authority and effectiveness (ibid.:75).

Police complaints procedures

The police complaints procedure provides a formal mechanism for citizens to lodge complaints about instances of police misconduct. It is the Chief Constable's responsibility to see that these complaints are properly investigated and result in disciplinary action where appropriate. The findings of these investigations, together with the Chief Constable's proposed course of action, are passed on to a key monitoring and supervisory body, the Police Complaints Authority (PCA), which may, if it has reason to be dissatisfied, overturn the Chief Constable's decision.

The PCA was established in April 1985 under the Police and Criminal Evidence Act 1984. It was designed as a more effective replacement for the Police Complaints Board (PCB) which the public appeared to have lost faith in due to the fact that few complaints were ever substantiated, and that all investigations were carried out by the police themselves. The 1984 Act sought to make the system more independent of the police by giving the Police Complaints Authority more involvement in the running of 'major' investigations involving death, serious injury, assault, conspiracy and matters of public concern (including the policing of public disorder).

Under the 1984 Act, the PCA is empowered to: (i) choose, or veto the choice, of investigating officers, supervise their inquiries, and receive their final report; (ii)   monitor the speed and efficiency of the investigation and issue a statement to the Chief Constable saying whether it was satisfactorily carried out; (iii)   receive a Chief Constable's decision on what action he intends to take as a result of an investigation and, if need be, overturn the decision (either by preferring disciplinary charges or, if it believes an offence has been committed, referring the case to the Director of Public Prosecutions). In the latter case, the PCA may still choose to bring disciplinary charges even if the DPP decides there are insufficient grounds for prosecution.

The outcomes of successive PCA investigations of episodes of public disorder have cast serious doubts about its independence and effectiveness. A brief summary of the PCA investigation of complaints about police tactics used to clear demonstrators from the steps of Manchester University's Students' Union building during a visit by the then Home Secretary,

Leon Brittan, in March 1985 highlights the origins of this concern. The severity of these tactics (cf. Manchester City Council, 1986) prompted thirty-three specific individual complaints and seventy-one general complaints related to police misconduct. The subsequent 15-month investigation was carried out by officers from the Avon and Somerset Constabulary.

These officers were accused by complainants of failing to remain impartial, of adopting hostile and dismissive attitudes towards them and of using complainants' own statements as evidence against them in court. It was further alleged that some complainants were shadowed, intimidated and, even, assaulted while going about their daily affairs (*Out of Court*, BBC 2, 4 March 1987). The investigation resulted in criminal charges against three police officers (two for perjury and one for assault) but the PCA found insufficient evidence to substantiate the remaining complaints. The authority had intended to publish a full summary of its findings but was prevented from doing so by the DPP who felt that it would prejudice the trials of the three officers. However, sections of the press saw this as an attempt to suppress the investigation's key finding: that police insensitivity and mismanagement was largely to blame for the evening's confrontation (cf. *Observer*, 1 March 1987).

Increasing numbers of potential complainants now prefer to take civil actions against the police (Emerson, 1989:26). An ITN cameraman injured during a police charge at Wapping received an undisclosed out-of-court settlement from the Metropolitan Police after a High Court damages claim (*The Guardian*, 25 January 1989). Such people seem to have grasped the key distinction that:

> The consequence of winning a civil action is compensation in money whereas if a complaint is upheld, you receive nothing beyond the satisfaction of knowing there is a chance that the officer(s) in question will be disciplined or, just possibly, prosecuted.
>
> (Thornhill, 1989:345)

Debates over the possibility of using civilians to investigate complaints against British police officers often contain references to the ineffectiveness of American Civilian Review Boards (Cohen, 1985:262). It is indisputable that such obstacles as poor financing and staffing, and sustained police opposition have made them practically unworkable: 'typically the pressure of police unions and the operation of political manipulation has resulted in these Boards becoming inoperative edifices to the democratic principle, or at best fairly toothless bureaucracies' (McKenzie and Gallagher, 1989:109). Where they survive, Review Boards tend to lack true independence from the police and seldom break down the barriers of police secrecy and their refusal to co-operate (Cohen, 1985:262).

Formal police accountability mechanisms

Police accountability is the constitutional mechanism which makes the police answerable for their actions. The present institutional structure is based on regulations contained in the 1964 Police Act. Under the Act, the British police force is divided into forty-three separate constabularies. In London, the Metropolitan police force is accountable solely to the Home Secretary. The City of London Police (who are responsible only for a square mile at the centre of London) are controlled by a committee of elected councillors. The remaining police forces come under the joint supervision of partially elected police authorities, the chief constable and the Home Secretary. Police forces outside of London receive 51 per cent of their funding from the Home Office and the other 49 per cent from local government via a levy on the rates. Most of the Metropolitan Police's bill is paid by the Home Office because of its many 'national' police services.

The roles and responsibilities of each member of the tripartite system are prescribed by the 1964 Act. The Local Police Authority (made up of twelve elected councillors and six appointed magistrates) is responsible for maintaining an adequate police force (i.e. in terms of finance, equipment, accommodation and personnel), and making arrangements for local consultation. Members may call for a report on policing matters from the chief constable; and can appoint, discipline and fire senior officers. All of these are subject, however, to the Home Secretary's approval.

The chief constable is responsible for the direction and control of the force. He (there are no female chief constables) is, technically at least, the 'sole determinant' of police policy. He has a statutory obligation to submit an annual report to his local authority and may be asked (but need not necessarily deliver) a report on any aspect of police policy required by the authority.

The Home Secretary is legally required to promote the efficiency of the police. She/he may withhold the central grant to any force deemed inefficient by the Home Office Inspectorate. The minister may also call for the retirement of a chief constable. She/he may direct a chief officer to provide mutual aid to another force and, in the event of any disagreement, determine the relative allocation of costs between an aided and aiding authority.

In practice, the LPA may offer advice to the chief constable on matters of policy, but he is under no legal obligation to accept it. It is virtually impossible for a Police Authority to obtain a report from a chief constable contrary to his wishes. The latter may simply reply that he does not feel it is in the the public's interest, or that the Police Authority does not strictly require it to effectively carry out its duties.

By contrast, in addition to the possibility of withholding the central grant, the Home Secretary may use other avenues of influence:

> The Home Office informs local forces of its views by advisory circulars of which there are about 100 a year. These circulars, though advisory in name, are essentially mandatory. They are frequently the result of liaison between the Home Office and Acpo. Although Chief Constables cavil occasionally they treat circulars as commands. But they are not the result of any form of democratic consultation and LPAs are given no right to see them, even though the policy advanced might directly impinge on their financial responsibilities. Nor is there any means for Parliament to discuss these circulars.
>
> (Uglow, 1988:130)

Thus, as Brewer *et al.* (1988:16) point out, the tripartite structure is actually a bipartite system of control. The policing of the coal dispute provided a clear illustration of this point (Uglow, 1988).

Reiner's (1989) interviews with thirty-nine chief constables in England and Wales revealed that most regarded their authorities as 'useful sounding boards', but were prepared to go against their recommendations if it suited them. Conversely, Home Office guidelines were only exceptionally ignored since 'They were seen as having a legitimacy stemming from the fact of representing the authoritative interpretation of the law by the elected government of the day' (ibid.:211). Chief officers continue to oppose any reform of the present system.

> As listening-posts attuned to balancing all shades of community opinion, they see themselves as more representative than formally elected representatives, who may represent a merely temporary or apparent majority. In any event, they claim both a legal and moral mandate to act according to their 'consciences', tempered as these are by professional experience and wide public consultation.
>
> (Reiner, 1989:208–9)

The American system of police accountability bears no relationship to its British tripartite structure. In America, the majority of urban police departments are headed by a chief of police, selected and appointed by the elected local mayor. Less frequently, the chief may be appointed by a city or county manager, or an administrator, appointed by local councillors (cf. McKenzie and Gallagher, 1989). In theory, accountability is exercised when constituents take the mayor's policing record into account in local elections. But this system is inevitably prejudicial against minority sections of the community.

> The close relationship between police chiefs and elected mayors in American cities makes it difficult for the former not to curry favour with what is perceived as the 'majority view' within his (sic) jurisdiction... The police chief fears that his appointment could be terminated if he carries out policies that impinge directly on the interests of the mayor's political supporters: electoral considerations and impartial policing thus make awkward bedfellows.
>
> (Brewer *et al.*, 1988:116)

Nevertheless, some of the tension which existed between the police and black communities in the 1960s appears to have been relieved by an increase in the number of elected black politicians and their moderating influence on police policy: 'The growth of elected and appointed black people in the political system means that racialist and violent police behaviour comes to be more and more criticised and highlighted' (Kilson, 1987:59). Alongside this, the US Supreme Court has expanded citizens' rights to sue police departments or their chiefs for officer misconduct. The individual officer is rarely held personally liable for his or her actions: damages are paid by the city, while legal costs are met by the union. However, such procedures are expensive, encouraging police departments to exercise more discipline over rank-and-file officers (Sherman, 1983:227).

These political and legal developments have encouraged a pronounced shift of emphasis: from a *law enforcement conception* of policing, which 'views enforcement of the law as an end in itself, regardless of its consequences for the social order' to a *peace-keeping conception* which 'views law enforcement as a means towards an end: the highest possible level of public safety, order and preservation of life and property' (Sherman, 1983:230). Sherman believes that, as a result of these changes, police are more likely to talk their way out of a potentially disorderly situation than they were in the 1960s (ibid.:231).

This peace-keeping conception of policing is less likely to apply where democratic influence is too weak to restrain a police chief's commitment to a law-enforcement conception. This is illustrated by the controversy surrounding a highly publicised racial assault by members of the LAPD on a black motorist on 3 March 1991. Here a national outcry was provoked

when fifteen white police officers either stood by and watched or personally took part in the systematic assault of a black man whom they had
stopped after a car chase. The officers struck or kicked the motorist,
Rodney King, more than fifty times, causing serious head, leg and
abdominal injuries. Unknown to them, the whole incident was videotaped
by an amateur photographer and pictures were subsequently broadcast on
nationwide television (*The Guardian*, 22 March 1991).

This prompted civil rights organisations and black politicians to demand
the resignation of the chief of the Los Angeles Police Department, Daryl
Gates. Then, on Tuesday, 2 April, the city's black mayor, Tom Bradley,
publically stated that he had asked Gates to resign from his job. Gates
refused to tender his resignation on the grounds that his 8,300 members
were depending on him to provide strong leadership in a difficult situation
(*The Guardian*, 4 April 1991).

The problem confronting Bradley was that Los Angeles operates according to a structure of authority in which power is devolved between
the mayor, the city council and tenured civil servants. City laws therefore
prevented the mayor from firing his chief. Bradley's personally appointed
police commission suspended Gates from office, only for the city council
to return him to duty via the courts. By May 1991, the issue had not been
legally resolved. In the meantime, a political representative of the city's
black population was asking, 'What if the people of South Central realize
that they cannot remove Daryl Gates?' It was an outcome which, she
ominously predicted, 'could be very dangerous' (*Newsweek*, 20 May 1991).

DISCUSSION

This chapter has provided overwhelming support for Northam's assertion
that police paramilitarism is now a fact of British life:

> Almost every major city in Britain has a police force armed with plastic
> bullets, CS gas and live firearms, and trained to use them to put down
> disturbances. Its policemen and policewomen have undergone a rigo-
> rous course of crowd control techniques modelled on the riot squads
> used throughout the British colonies. The men who walk our streets as
> community bobbies today are equipped and ready to take them by force
> tomorrow. /
>
> (Northam, 1988:130–1)

Developments in police-control techniques have been accompanied by a
major extension of police powers which encourage their intervention, not
only on marches, at demonstrations and mass pickets, but in the everyday

affairs of the community. The recent provision of mobile, armed response units in the Metropolitan area, and police activities like Operation 'Kingfisher' suggest that Los Angeles-style 'street sweeps' are an alarming possibility.

Not that current democratic safeguards could offer much protection. All are ineffectual. Community liaison committees tend to steer clear of contentious issues, and the agenda is usually set by the police. The police complaints procedure remains a 'watchdog without teeth' (Emerson, 1989). Finally, the tripartite system of accountability is 'amenable to a high degree of central influence and control', but operates as a *bipartite* structure with 'occasional genuflections towards the local authority' (Uglow, 1988:130).

Who knows how close the rest of Britain came to resembling Northern Ireland when plastic bullets were introduced at Broadwater Farm, but not used due to a decrease in the violence.

> Had the situation been different and plastic bullets had been fired, the longer-term consequence would have been to have moved the police significantly towards the position where the use of baton rounds was perceived by them as an appropriate method of crowd dispersal during large-scale civil disturbance. Such decisions, however, are taken by the police; the public has no direct say. Indeed, when a police authority has instructed its local constabulary not to purchase stockpiles of baton rounds nor to undertake training in their use, the Home Office has stepped in to circumvent this instruction by allowing police forces to hold such devices on permanent loan.
>
> (Stephens, 1988:85)

Britain urgently requires a mechanism for influencing the policies and behaviour of its police. American democratic and legal structures strong enough to restrain police behaviour have produced a reduction of public disorder. The precise form of the structures required to ensure more effective police accountability in this country is one of several policy recommendations to be outlined in the concluding chapter.

Chapter 10

Conclusions

A FAMILIAR INCOMPREHENSION

I utterly condemn this mindless hooliganism and yobbery for which
there can be no excuse. I hope all local people in the areas involved will
back the police in the difficult job that has faced them.

(Home Office Minister, John Patten, quoted in
The Guardian, 4 September 1991)

This was the forthright denunciation by a government minister of 4 nights
of public disorder on council house estates in Cardiff and Oxford, and a
night of looting in the Handsworth area of Birmingham, which took place
between 30 August and 3 September 1991. The Cardiff riots broke out on
an Ely housing estate when police confronted local youths who stoned an
Asian grocery store. In Oxford, a police operation designed to rid the
Blackbird Leys estate of 'hotters' (people who participated in or watched
the performance of high-speed stunts in 'hot', or stolen, cars) resulted in
similar clashes. Finally, in Handsworth, a crowd of youths took advantage
of a temporary loss of electric lighting in the area to break into local shops.
A police vehicle was stoned and twenty-three arrests were made as the
police reimposed their authority.

The almost simultaneous occurrence of these disorders prompted
people to look around for a common cause. The Chief Constable of West
Midlands Police highlighted two contributory factors: high levels of
alcohol and the exceptionally hot summer weather which was keeping
people out on the streets at night (*News At Ten*, ITV, 3 September 1991).
Several newspaper editorials also emphasised the significance of the 'Indian
Summer' heatwave.

Further rioting broke out in North Shields, Tyne and Wear, on 7
September, after a police crackdown on 'ram raiding' (crashing stolen cars
into shops and looting goods) had resulted in the death of two youths who

crashed their stolen car in a police chase. The Prime Minister, John Major, and the President of ACPO, David Owen, each invoked the notion of a 'copycat' effect to explain the latest disorder. The leader of the main opposition party, Neil Kinnock, referred to the disorder as a criminal attack on the community, while his shadow Home Secretary, Roy Hattersley, insisted that the ringleaders be caught and given severe exemplary sentences.

British society had been revisited by the same sort of incomprehension which characterised responses to the anti-poll tax riot of March 1990. Just as predictable as the knee-jerk explanations of senior police and politicians were subsequent calls for stronger legal measures (this time, the return of the Riot Act) and demands that the police be given better financial resources. It is because such stereotypical reactions and accompanying demands for tougher policies are barriers to effective understanding and tend, in the long term, to exacerbate the problem, that this book has sought to provide a more considered approach to the explanation of public disorder. This conclusion re-emphasises the need to analyse public disorder both in terms of general conjunctural factors and the dynamic processes relevant to a specific episode. This eclectic approach is briefly applied to the summer riots of 1991. Two final sections contemplate the possible future nature of disorder in British society, and recommend a series of preventative measures.

EXPLAINING PUBLIC DISORDER

The context of disorder

Violent disorder is not peculiar to the present era; nor has it been a constant feature of this century. Different forms of disorder have varied in frequency and intensity from one decade to another (Dunning *et al.*, 1987). Specific periods of this century are distinguishable by a relatively high incidence or strong severity of one or more forms of public disorder. In Britain, the most distinctive periods have been: 1910–14, 1919, the early 1930s, and from the mid-1970s to the present day. America has experienced a slightly different pattern: 1917–19, the 1930s and the 1960s. These conjunctural patterns and associated forms of disorder are summarised in Table 10.1.

As the table indicates, the violent confrontations in Britain just prior to the First World War broke out when an increasingly nervous establishment responded coercively to 'subversive activity' by suffragettes and trade unionists, who were both aggrieved by the faltering pace of social reform and, in the latter's case, by rising inflation:

Table 10.1 Twentieth-century disorders in Britain and America: a summary of key conjunctures

Period of century	Dominant conjunctural factors	Principal forms of public disorder
1910–14	**Britain** 1 High inflation 2 Slowing socio-legal reform 3 Rise of Syndicalism 4 Government anxiety: ready to use police/ military suppression	1 Anti-Chinese riot 2 Suffragette agitation 3 Strike violence
1919	**Britain** 1 High inflation 2 Housing shortage 3 Inter-racial/inter-generational conflict over jobs, housing 4 Resentment among demobilised soldiers 5 Police hardened and embittered by war role, loss of strike **America** 1 Inter-racial conflict over jobs, housing	1 Seaport riots 2 London youth riots 3 Rioting by soldiers 4 Rioting/looting during Liverpool police strike 1 Urban riots
1930s	**Britain** 1 Economic depression (high unemployment) 2 Rise of fascism (scapegoating of Jews) 3 Use of special constables **America** 1 Pro-labour legislation (capitalist resistance) 2 Economic depression (high unemployment)	1 Clashes between police and organised unemployed 2 Clashes between police and anti-fascist demonstrators 1 Strike violence 2 Clashes between police and organised unemployed
1960s	**America** 1 State unresponsive to black relative deprivation 2 Government indifferent to student-led anti-war protest 3 Repressive policing policies	1 Ghetto riots 2 Clashes between police and anti-war demonstrators

Table 10.1 (continued)

	Britain	
	1 Catholic Civil Rights movement (led by educated working class)	1 Clashes between Civil Rights marchers and security forces
	2 Catholics seen as undermining state	2 Disturbances in Catholic communities
	3 Repression by RUC/ B Specials/Army	
1981–91	*Britain*	
	1 Economic recession	1 Inner-city riots
	2 Abandonment of consensus politics	2 Strike violence
	3 Police become more paramilitarised but less accountable	3 Disorderly demonstrations

Many in the working classes lost faith in Parliament; so did the militant suffragettes, rebelling against security and incited to violence by the restless spirit of the new century. By 1910 the output of social legislation was slackening. The demand for fresh leaders was strident. Within four years the Liberals found that the immense goodwill that returned them to power in 1906 had vanished, and disorder and violence had returned to Britain on a scale that had not been experienced for generations.

(Critchley, 1970:165)

During the troubled year of 1919, various groups fell victim to the combined effects of soaring inflation, a shortage of accommodation, and intense competition for employment caused by the return of military personnel. Young males, 'demobbed' soldiers and colonial seafarers all had reason to feel disillusioned and embittered by the way that society had let them down. The dockside poor of Liverpool took advantage of the temporary loss of authority resulting from a police strike to loot local shops.

The seaport disturbances of May and June had much in common with the American 'race riots' of 1917–19. In each society, early twentieth-century migration patterns induced by the economic demand for cheap, exploitable labour, had produced small, ostracised, ethnic minority communities in British seaport and American urban areas. After the war, competition for employment, combined with preferential attitudes towards white ex-servicemen, produced a heightened potential for disorder. Other factors, specific to each nation, also played their part. In America, agitation by the National Association for the Advancement of Colored People urged Negroes not to respond passively to their maltreatment; whereas, in Britain, there were the additional elements of a chronic housing shortage, and a rough, white 'dockside culture', heavily subscribing to an imperialist ideology, to foment the readiness for conflict (ibid.).

The 1930s was the next major period of disorder in Britain and America. The depression years of the 1920s and 1930s produced hardship and suffering in both societies. In America, there was a concerted political attempt to deny the existence of a depression. People suffered quietly and in isolation while 'official denials helped to confuse the unemployed and to make them ashamed of their plight' (Fox Piven and Cloward, 1977:48). However, as whole factories closed down and entire neighbourhoods were devastated, people began to realise that it was not themselves, but 'the system' which was to blame (ibid.:49). Communist-led marches took place in numerous major cities. In some cases, localistic anxieties encouraged repressive police tactics; in others, demonstrators were rewarded with relief measures.

In Britain, the levels of suffering varied: working-class people in heavily industrialised regions were subjected to high levels of unemployment, poverty, the humiliation of long dole queues and the detested 'means test', while millions of others, though by no means immune to the depression, were considerably less affected. It was the unemployed hunger marchers, castigated by the press and politicians on both sides as communist-led subversives, and disowned by their own trade-union movement, which engaged in fearful confrontations with an enthusiastic police force.

The mid-1930s also saw the rise of a British fascist movement eager to encourage the scapegoating of the Jews as the group most responsible for unemployment and depression. Brazenly provocative 'Blackshirt' marches through London often resulted in confrontation between the police and counter-demonstrators, many of them members of the NUWM. The police were invariably intolerant and frequently hostile towards the anti-fascists, perceiving them as subversive and unruly, unlike the more disciplined and co-operative British Union of Fascists, who expressed patriotic sentiments and professed a commitment to law and order.

In the late 1930s there was a resurgence of the American industrial violence which had marked the first two decades of the century. This period represented the last, desperate attempt by capital to resist the encroachment of trade unionism, hastened by the post-New Deal era of pro-labour legislation. Vigilance and intervention by the newly formed National Labor Relations Board, and the need for labour and capital to pull together during the Second World War saw an end to widespread opposition to union organisation and the violence it generated.

Following a long quiescent spell, the next major period of disorder in America was the 1960s. First, there occurred the black ghetto 'uprisings'. The post-war northward immigration of American blacks had swollen the ghetto communities at a time when American capitalism was relocating and restructuring its productive base. The ghettos were left impoverished and lacking basic services, their residents powerless and disaffected, ready to reciprocate aggressive police behaviour. The late 1960s then saw the flowering of the student-dominated anti-Vietnam War movements in Britain and America. The New Left counter-cultural reaction to the depravity of consumer capitalism and the coming of the nuclear age was evident in both societies. In Britain, the ground had been prepared for clashes between police and demonstrators in 1967 and 1968 by similar confrontations between peace activists and the police over crises like Suez and Cuba. In America, students had even more reason to feel upset:

> The US government insisted on fighting a war despite the anger and resistance of many of the young people it expected to do the fighting. So it is not farfetched at all to say antiwar protest and its revolutionary offshoots were the results of the temporary unresponsiveness of a democratic government to some citizens' expectations.
>
> (Gurr, 1989:123)

The police suppression of anti-war protests was most unyielding in places like Chicago where there was local public and political antipathy towards demonstrators.

Another feature of the late 1960s was the onset of the latest – and most protracted – phase of the Troubles in Northern Ireland. Protestant (and state) anxiety and indignation caused by the emergence of the Northern Ireland Civil Rights Association lay at the root of confrontations between the security forces and Catholic demonstrators from 1968 onwards. The Catholic minority within the province was sorely aggrieved by widespread discrimination, disadvantage and political disenfranchisement.

The rise of the Catholic Civil Rights movement was due to a convergence of factors: first, the influence of the black American Civil Rights movement of the 1960s; second, the emergence of a well-educated generation of young Catholics who were prepared to take a lead; third, disillusionment with the Nationalist Party, which was increasingly viewed as ineffectual and unresponsive to Catholic sentiments; and finally, the election of a Labour government in Britain, which might prove receptive to Catholic demands. Fierce political condemnation by the Protestant majority, fearful of Catholics' attempts to undermine the state, was influential in determining a harsh policing response.

It is helpful to look upon the present era of public disorder on the British mainland, from the mid-1970s, as resulting from a rupturing of the political consensus (or 'Butskellism') which had prevailed since 1945:

> The shared commitment to full employment, rising public expenditure, a growing welfare ethos and a recognition of the legitimacy of trades unions as political actors, provided the cornerstones of a post-war settlement that promised the reconstruction of a more egalitarian society.
>
> (Brewer *et al.*, 1988:42)

According to Brewer and co-workers, the commitment to Butskellism was rejected in preference for 'a set of political ideals that makes a fetish of individualism and celebrates inequality' (ibid.:43). This had a profoundly detrimental effect on police–citizen relations, provoking unedifying episodes of political, civil and industrial unrest. Writing in the late 1980s, Brewer and co-workers described how

> Protest and dissent is criminalised by changes to public order law, while those who fight back – like the striking miners – are labelled by the Prime Minister as 'the enemy within'. The nature of recent industrial disputes and the fragility of police relations with ethnic minorities are represented as a challenge to the social order alleged to be far more threatening than any that has emerged in the period since 1945 ... In these circumstances, the prior emphasis on policing by consent has been displaced by a stress on police effectiveness. Against the background of continuing economic decline, the failed attempt to resolve Britain's economic problems has created not only mass unemployment on an unprecedented scale but other forms of social discipline in the shape of new police powers and a threateningly authoritarian framework of public order law.
>
> (Brewer *et al.*, 1988:43)

Clearly, in order to understand the motives and meanings underlying particular outbreaks of public disorder, and to appreciate why some forms of disorder were more prevalent in some periods than others, we must consider the key conjunctural factors. The most important of these are: the depth and intensity of social divisions and grievances, the degree of political consensus, the responsiveness of governments to civilian demands and their willingness to sanction repressive state policies (cf. Sherr, 1989:11).

Certain generalisations clearly emerge. As White (1982:14) emphasises,

'Riot has classically been a collective weapon of the politically powerless – to get those with power and wealth to share a little more or to take notice; to effect revenge; and to preserve traditions and rights from attack.' However, we have also seen that disorder may sometimes be 'issueless' (Marx, 1972). In other words, rioting does not always have such a focused central objective, and has often been 'a frequent resort of those who have been denied a substantial identity in the world: it is a vehicle for prowess, assertiveness and a new set of standards for gauging character' (Rock, 1981:20).

Contemporary football hooliganism may be understood from this perspective: as offering those who engage in inter-fan fighting an opportunity for status otherwise denied them. Academic theorists have referred to a variety of contemporary social changes – the breakdown of working-class community, the modern under-funding of the state education system, widening material and political inequality and the advertising effect of the 'new' media – as relevant conjunctural variables. Rival academics may dispute the validity of these assertions. Whatever their authority, they currently offer a superior basis of insight to explanations which merely condemn inter-fan fighting as moronic or animalistic.

Alongside the need to give full consideration to the prevailing socio-political conditions, it is equally important that explanations of public disorder highlight the significance of human agency, by giving due weight to the dynamic and subjective processes involved. It is here that the flashpoints model of public disorder has proven useful to our analysis.

The dynamics of disorder

The flashpoints model identifies a number of particular circumstances most conducive to disorder. These have been referred to more than once in the context of earlier chapters. For the sake of brevity, we may note that disorder is more likely to occur where:

1 *At the structural level*: A section of society perceives that it is being deprived of something (whether materially, or in terms of a 'life chance') to which it feels legitimately entitled. *Ideological alienation* (where people regard certain state policies to be morally repugnant) may also constitute a basis for conflict.

2 *At the political/ideological level*: The group feels alienated from major state institutions (notably the political and legal systems); it finds itself and its demands vilified or ignored by politicians and the media, and its activities criticised or condemned by influential sections of the public.

3　*At the cultural level*: Members of the group engage in forms of behaviour which, though regarded as 'legitimate' within their own culture, are defined as unacceptable by the police; they share the police view of violence as a legitimate form of expression or defence, and subscribe to similar codes of ingroup solidarity as the police. Each side harbours an unflattering stereotype of the other, these being most negative from the police perspective where the dissenting group has been designated by 'respectable society' as 'police property', to be dealt with more or less as they see fit.

4　*At the contextual level*: Encounters with the police are habitually abrasive; violence is routinely anticipated, though expectations are sometimes heightened by rumour, threats, media sensitisation (to the possibility that disorder may occur) or a growing prevalence of negative incidents. Under these circumstances, the police and dissenting group 'tool up' for trouble and overreact to minor incidents. Such a possibility may be offset where liaison (involving negotiation, co-operation, etc.) takes place between representatives of each side.

5　*At the situational level*: Particular locations of the neighbourhood are looked upon by the group as cultural territory to be defended; or regarded by the police as space they must exercise control over to protect from damage, or prevent from becoming a 'no-go area'. The tactical formation or disposition of one or both sides is 'read' by their opponents as indicative of an intention to engage in a sinister or illegitimate form of behaviour. Ineffective police lines of communication and an ill-defined command structure increase the possibility of indisciplined behaviour.

6　Finally, *at the interactional level*: An especially aggressive encounter (a 'flashpoint') occurs which symbolises a lack, or breakdown, of respect between the police and dissenting group and any acknowledgement of the legitimacy of their activities. Such an incident (e.g. a particularly violent attack on the police, or an especially rough or degrading arrest) offers a clear sign that at least one of the parties has no intention of accommodating the other's objectives or definition of appropriate behaviour. Once the incident has ignited, there is no attempt on either side to defuse or normalise the situation. A spiral of mutual recrimination occurs and violence progressively escalates. Crowd members experience sensations of power, liberation and revenge as they temporarily succeed in expressing their sense of grievance.

The significance attached by our model to the precipitating or flashpoint incident seems justified. Such incidents invariably involve the dramatic violation of one or more group's perceived 'rights' relevant to a specific situation. This may relate to a particular expression of dissent, such as the right to stand in a certain area, stop lorries entering a factory gate in order to speak to the driver, or hand in a petition to a political establishment. Alternatively, a broader claim may be involved, such as the rights of members of ethnic communities to smoke ganja or walk the streets of their community without suffering police harassment. Whether or not disorder ignites depends on perceptions of the flashpoint incident as symbolic of a universal grievance which justifies immediate redress. This is what distinguishes actual from potential flashpoints.

Often, disputed claims to rights are accommodated within a tacitly agreed code of conduct, exemplified by the notion of 'a good, clean shove' between police and pickets, and embodied in police 'blind-eye' strategies. Flashpoint incidents typically indicate an absence, or breakdown, of such accommodation, the more so if the acts are especially brutal or uncompromising, or involve attacks on figureheads or vulnerable members (e.g. women) on one side or the other.

Though we have emphasised the pivotal role of the flashpoint incident, it is evident from the 'Martin Luther King, Jnr riots' of April 1968 and the Miami riot of 1980 that emotive outcomes or events may have the same symbolic significance and equally precipitous effect. Other forms of riot are not 'triggered' as such. This was true of the redressive action taken by the dockside communities of Liverpool in 1919. Here looting started on the opening of a floodgate (the withdrawal of police authority), rather than the sparking of a flashpoint. Generally speaking, however, it is possible to speak of a particular incident or event which crystallises grievances, encourages communication and provides an irresistible catalyst for disorder.

HEATWAVE HOOLIGANS? THE SUMMER RIOTS OF 1991

The present chapter has so far highlighted the conjunctural and dynamic factors necessary to explain previous examples of twentieth-century disorder. In this section we update our analysis by exploring possible causes of the summer disorders of 1991. In searching for more incisive explanations than those proffered by prominent public figures, some serious journalists evoked comparisons with the inner-city riots of a decade earlier. For example, *The Economist* (7 September 1991) observed 'striking parallels' with the riots of 1981 and 1985, namely: 'a background of rising unemployment, a spell of hot weather and the end of the school holidays combining to draw bored, fidgety youngsters on to the streets of poor areas

at night'. But these superficial similarities conceal other important differences. Indeed, rearrange the numbers slightly and a more compelling basis of
comparison – the riots of 1919 – comes to mind.

There is an obvious basis of comparison between the opportunistic
looting which occurred in Handsworth and the Liverpool disorders of
1919. Whereas the latter were in response to the withdrawal of local
authority following a police strike, the Handsworth events were encouraged by a temporary loss of illumination when a warehouse fire shut down
a neighbouring electricity generating station. The failure occurred at 9.15
p.m. and, in the 3 hours before lighting was restored, seventeen shops were
looted. To the chagrin of local traders, police waited until 3.30 a.m. before
chasing youths out of the area. As we know from previous chapters,
Handsworth is a severely deprived inner-city area. While this fact does not
justify the looting, it does explain the underlying motivation.

The events in Oxford bear a tenuous similarity to the London youth
riots of 72 years earlier. Both were in response to the heavy-handed
policing of improvised youth leisure activity. For at least 9 months (some
accounts suggest even 2 years), young males aged between 14 and 24 from
the Blackbird Leys estate had been engaging in a late-night pastime called
'hotting', i.e. performing 100 m.p.h. stunts, such as skids and handbrake
turns, in stolen, expensive fast cars. Hotting had become an 'alternative
spectator sport', attracting crowds of 250 onlookers into the area to watch
the so-called displays.

Police had been keeping this activity under constant surveillance and
had recently increased the number of officers into the area in an attempt
to deter those involved. Then, on Thursday, 29 August, police moved in
and arrested twenty hotters. On the following night, police officers in full
riot gear were the targets of stones and petrol bombs in the first of 4
successive nights of confrontation. The police described this as the frustrated reaction to the succcess of their operation. Local residents said that
it was due to resentment caused by the brutal and indiscriminate nature of
the police intervention.

In order to understand the riot, it is necessary to appreciate the cultural
significance of the hotting behaviour to the youths, and the reasons for the
police reaction towards it. Blackbird Leys is a relatively rundown inner-city
council estate, though nowhere near as deprived as (say) Moss Side or
Handsworth. At the time of the riot, the local unemployment rate was 9
per cent, 2 per cent higher than the city average. However, successive
rounds of redundancies in the local car industry, and the prospect of even
more to come, had generated what a local council report, commissioned
9 months earlier, referred to as 'a mounting sense of uncertainty about the

future' (*Independent on Sunday*, 8 September 1991). Local professional workers and clergy further highlighted the growing signs of family tension and demoralisation particularly affecting local teenagers who comprised a quarter of the population. They commented on the absence of investment in much-needed retraining initiatives.

Faced with such uncertainty and stress about the future, local youths – many unemployed, others facing a similar prospect – turned to hotting as a way of bringing stimulation, status and fellowship into their lives. Some youths (the 'stealers') derived their pleasure from the theft of expensive, 'macho' status symbols; for others (the 'scanners'), it was the more cerebral satisfaction of monitoring police activity on their radios; while for the drivers of the cars (the 'dons') it was the 'buzz' they enjoyed from performing their daring stunts, and the folk-hero status conferred on them by their peers.

Unable effectively to give chase to the hotters for fear of endangering the lives of pedestrians and motorists, the police had been forced to play a waiting game, based on covert surveillance. As the rate of car thefts increased and old people on the estate complained more stridently about the noise, danger and disruption, the police determined on a sudden show of strength which provided the setting for the riot.

There are undoubted similarities between the Oxford riots and subsequent events on the Meadow Well estate in North Shields. Here, too, rioting was related to a recent police crackdown on car theft and the associated practice of 'ram raiding', i.e. driving stolen vehicles at shop fronts, then looting the premises. On Saturday, 7 September, a concentrated police attempt to deal with this problem culminated in the death of two local youths who crashed a stolen Renault Turbo into a lamp post during a 125 m.p.h. police chase. Almost immediately afterwards, graffiti appeared on local garden walls accusing the police of being murderers and vowing, 'Dale 'n' Colin, we will not let them get away with it' (*The Independent*, 10 September).

On Monday, 9 September, local youths set fire to an electricity sub-station, blacking out the estate, brought down telephone wires, and set a number of shops on fire in a deliberate attempt to lure the police into their midst. The police chose not to enter, preferring to give three hundred youths a 4-hour free run of the estate, during which time they looted shops and burned down buildings, including a school and community and health centre.

The significance of chronic deprivation was more evident here than in any of the other riots. Poverty was so endemic that each of the 252 children at the local primary school received a clothing grant; housing was so substandard that 27 per cent of dwellings had their windows boarded up; finally, unemployment was over 40 per cent (but estimated at more than 80 per cent in some sections of the estate), leaving local youth with little prospect of finding jobs. Given these environmental conditions, stealing cars to ram-raid becomes more meaningful to the observer – as a source of fun, kudos and supplementing dole money or the 'pittance' earned on a youth training scheme.

The police were never likely to interpret it this way. The rising incidence of car theft, the growing use of Meadow Well as a dumping ground for stolen vehicles and the allied complaints of traders encouraged a legal crackdown. Local youths complained to press reporters of 'years' of heavy-handed policing. One employed resident of the estate stated that to be found wearing a new anorak was to invite police suspicion and risk being told, 'Stop stealing cars, son, or we'll break your finger' (*The Guardian*, 11 September 1991). The disorder which broke out after the death of the two youths was an expression of festering resentment. (So, too, it appears, was subsequent sympathetic rioting in nearby Elswick.) It is a further possibility that such targets of attack as the local community centre – from which the youths had been excluded – and the primary school were the focuses of similar resentment: unsympathetic institutions which had somehow let them down.

The next of the summer riots to be considered lacks an obvious precedent unless, as many believe, deteriorating inter-ethnic relations were at its core. The disorder which broke out on the Ely council estate in Cardiff was related to antagonism between a local Asian shopkeeper and a section of the community. Acute ill-feeling had been generated towards him after he had invoked a legal covenant preventing a neighbouring newsagent from selling cheap bread and dairy products in competition with his own sales. The shopkeeper had also been taking an increasingly hard line towards shoplifters, culminating in the detention of a drunken youth who refused to pay for a bottle of cider. As the youth tried to leave the shop, an electronic locking device was activated, forcing him to make his escape by breaking out of the shop window, injuring himself in the process.

Shortly afterwards, white youths gathered and proceeded to stone the shop and its upstairs flat before the police were called in to remove them. This was the prelude to 4 successive nights of clashes, culminating in running battles between 500 youths and 100 police in riot gear. In between, youths had thrown stones, roof slates and petrol bombs at the police and devastated two council rent offices. Social deprivation was also evident in this example. The Ely council estate had the highest unemployment rate in the area. Houses were shabby and dilapidated, and a recent renovation scheme had been abandoned 3 years earlier due to a lack of council funds. The local secondary school was badly underfunded and had a high truancy rate. Here, too, there was a high incidence of car theft. The MP for Cardiff West ventured the opinion that 'These people have simply lost faith that the future is going to get any better' (*The Independent*, 4 September 1991).

The precise motives for the riot are less clear than in the other examples. The Ely area has a significant ethnic minority population; the initial target of attack was a muslim grocer. Local community spokespersons denied any racist motive, while press reports seemed reluctant to suggest that inter-ethnic conflict was involved (*The Economist*, 7 September 1991). Yet the Director of the South Glamorgan Race Equality Council wrote of the growing frequency of attacks on Asian shopkeepers, and explained how police figures showed a 200 per cent increase in reported cases of racial harassment and attacks from 1989 to 1990.

It is possible that this riot was a throwback to the inter-racial clashes reported in Chapter 4, of which the 1962 Dudley riot provides the most obvious basis of comparison. Local politicians accounted for the rioting in terms of the indignation of a hard-pressed community towards a hard-hearted shopkeeper, allied to justifiable fears for the future. Certainly, the damage to council rent offices indicate feelings of political resentment and frustration.

Despite their obvious dissimilarities, and some confusion concerning their underlying motives, the Oxford, Cardiff and North Shields riots have several important factors in common. Primarily, they involved groups of young, dispossessed people who faced the future with uncertainty, a lack of hope and an absence of conviction that establishment institutions cared about their plight.

On this basis, there is nothing surprising about their reaction for, as Field and Southgate point out,

> where any social group perceives government institutions as being indifferent to its needs, the authority and legitimacy of social controls ultimately promulgated by those same institutions will be increasingly questioned. In such circumstances a riot may occur in which individuals will participate for a great mixture of motives, and some will undoubtedly have no more than material gain in mind. At the root of it will be the failure of the relevant authorities to retain the support of the community.
>
> (Field and Southgate, 1982:33)

Increasingly conditioned to see themselves as having no stake in society and little prospect of acquiring one, and finding themselves denigrated as 'worthless' or 'scum', such youths closed ranks and discovered alternative criteria of self-assessment. Their cultural response was to place an emphasis on toughness and territoriality, and make the motor car the focus of a daring and defiant improvised leisure pursuit. In Cardiff (and possibly in North Shields, as well) racist sentiments flourished as the youths sought explanations and solutions for their predicament.

Soaring crime statistics and complaints by local residents and traders led to increased police activity and the further deterioration of police–community relations. In atmospheres of heightened tension (between local people and the Asian grocer in Cardiff, and the police and local youths elsewhere) incidents occurred which symbolised enduring grievances and erupted into conflict. Instantly, battle lines were drawn involving the defence or seizure of territory.

The correspondence between these factors and our six levels of analysis is too obvious to warrant systematic application of the flashpoints model. What may require more emphasis is that the summer riots of 1991, the inner-city riots of the 1980s and the anti-poll tax disorder of a year earlier had one notable feature in common: the involvement of large numbers of alienated and dispossessed young people. It is pertinent to ask to what extent they, or other sections of society, are likely to be involved in future instances of public disorder.

PUBLIC DISORDER IN THE FUTURE

Throughout the 1980s, the British government responded to the 'challenge' of public disorder, not by trying to reduce the underlying inequality, deprivation and disaffection, but by providing more equipment and resources for the police and extending their legal powers. As we argued in Chapter 9, recent developments have enhanced, rather than attenuated, the potential for political, civil and industrial violence.

Jefferson (1990:136–8) is worried by the possible implications of failing to arrest the progressive growth of police powers and militarisation. Observing the recent rise in the incidence of retaliatory attacks on police personnel and property – including the use of petrol bombs, incendiary devices and, on one occasion (Broadwater Farm), a gun – Jefferson foresees a conflict-ridden future.

If nothing intervenes to alter present trends, we can expect these presently *ad hoc*, occasional and relatively isolated forms of disorder to become more and more organized, regular and widespread – or, in a word, endemic ... (It) does not need much imagination, nor much sense of history, to see how excluded and dispossessed groups move from disaffection, through spontaneous, angry disorder, to organized opposition and resistance. The examples are all around us. So, it should not be difficult to envisage this spontaneous anger coalescing into something more organized and sustained, involving perhaps some form of urban terrorism.

(Jefferson, 1990:138)

Uppermost in Jefferson's mind is the ongoing conflict between the police and black communities, though the 'examples' he refers to are bound to include Northern Ireland. Police tactical and technological developments appear to have been modelled on those of Northern Ireland. Plastic bullets and CS gas are now widely available. Soon, the Metropolitan police may call upon RUC-style armed reserve vehicles to enforce their 'Doomsday' mission.

Nevertheless, Britain's black communities are geographically and numerically smaller than the Catholic communities in Northern Ireland. They do not have the Irish traditions of organised political resistance; nor do they possess the same degree of religious and ideological cohesion. The British authorities may have adopted many elements of Northern Ireland's security approach, but they are unlikely to have to contend with its dominant mode of conflict.

This is not to rule out completely the possibility of escalating violence; merely to suggest that, in the absence of a coherent opposing political ideology, it is likely to remain retaliatory and sporadic. There is a more obvious parallel, here, with the activities of militant black American organisations in the late 1960s and early 1970s. These organisations were eventually outmanoeuvred and overpowered by the combined security and intelligence forces. Given the far smaller size of their communities, it is difficult to foresee how British blacks could be any more successful, and the impact on their civil liberties would be devastating.

Riots have occurred only exceptionally in the northern states of America since the 1960s. Part of the reason for this may well be that some major cities heeded the lessons of the disorders by instigating community urban-renewal programmes (Thomas, 1987). But the fact that blacks are relatively worse off now on most social and economic indices than they were in the 1960s (cf. Darden, 1989; Keith, 1989), has encouraged speculation that other factors are involved.

One possibility is that black communities have developed their own neighbourhood self-help initiatives to ameliorate some of the worst effects of deprivation and discrimination (Gurr, 1989b). Another likely reason is that black political representation has increased since the 1960s, improving the quality of police–citizen interaction (Horowitz, 1983). However, Rubenstein (1989) suggests that other recent developments have been equally, if not more, important. These are worth considering in detail since they may provide a portent of future British trends.

Rubenstein points out that one reason for the decline of 'mass-based racial or ethnic violence' is that influential blacks and Hispanics have been co-opted into the local polity or business community who might otherwise have galvanised grass-roots rebellion. The trend towards greater social mobility has not been accompanied by a general elevation of black living standards. Finding themselves disorganised and just as impoverished as before, the working-class residuum has been deterred from rioting by the fact that previous disorder secured nothing except a list of broken political promises and extra trouble from the police.

Thus there has been a propensity towards 'anomic, intra-group violence'. According to Rubenstein, a repetition of the 1960s riots has been averted by 'the creation of a new industry', the multi-million dollar illicit drugs trade, involving the sale of cheap drugs like PCP and crack-cocaine.

> Indeed, illegal drugs constitute the basis for the largest retail business in history operated by minority youth. Obviously, the growth of this industry increases violence within and against minority communities. While warfare between drug gangs rivals the criminal gang-wars of the 1920s, the spread of the drug trade has provoked both police interventions of increasing scope and intensity, and various forms of vigilantism, as well as a vast increase in anomic violence. To date, the effect of this trade seems to have been to focus minority and ethnic violence inward, that is, to further divide and demoralize oppressed communities.
>
> (Rubenstein, 1989:321)

The gang warfare in Los Angeles described in Chapter 9 is an illustration, *par excellence*, of this phenomenon. In 1965, Watts was the scene of some of the most serious rioting in American history; by 1988, it had become the focal point of police repression surrounding the street trading of 'crack'.

Rubenstein also detects signs of a re-emergence of inter-ethnic conflict, manifested in organised resistance against 'newcomers' (e.g. the Californian 'English only' movement and attacks by blacks on Asian shopkeepers), attacks on blacks in white neighbourhoods (and vice versa), and the rise of black nationalism which has been openly anti-semitic in orientation. As he further points out,

> These developments raise a disturbing possibility: it may be that the

inefficacy of older forms of group rebellion, combined with the persist-
ence of conditions which have generated group violence in the past, are
leading us toward new forms of revolt.

(Rubenstein, 1989:322)

Writing in 1986, Benyon and Solomos set out a similar 'gloomy
prognosis' for the future of Britain's inner-city areas.

The growth of the voluntary sector, with its successful self-help activities, is likely to continue in the inner cities, and an increasing number
of black people will achieve economic and social success and begin to
form a 'black middle class'. Black people will be elected as Members of
Parliament and as local councillors, but will find it difficult to mobilise
national support for inner-city problems.

(Benyon and Solomos, 1987:193)

They subscribe to Harrison's (1983:435) depressing scenario that 'Revolution does not seem likely, rather a chaos of individual and sectional
pathologies and disruptions', where ever-stricter policing methods are
applied and civil liberties are increasingly trampled underfoot.

The riots of 1991 may be signs of this development. Other signs are
certainly apparent. British newspapers have recently focused on police
attempts to eliminate a growing 'crack culture' in the deprived area of
Manchester's Moss Side: 'Police move against gangsters and traffickers to
break spiral of decline and despair in "Britain's Bronx": 23 held in Moss
Side drugs and gun raids' (The Times, 21 August 1991). Is it too fanciful to
believe that the strife-torn streets of New York and Los Angeles offer a
portent of what might soon become commonplace in Britain's inner cities?

RESPONDING TO PUBLIC DISORDER: POLICY RECOMMENDATIONS

In this final section, we consider a range of policies which might help to
reduce the extent of future public disorder. For effective prevention to
occur, action is required in a number of important areas. Politicians need
to be responsive to the material and cultural deprivations experienced by
specific sections of society, notably working-class youths. Society needs to
ensure adequate representation to those currently excluded or alienated
from its political institutions. Media practitioners must recognise that, in
vilifying dissenting groups and systematically ignoring or misrepresenting
their grievances, they are promoting the potential for disorder. The police
should endeavour to to become more sensitive to the different cultures

they come across, to be less 'macho' in their attitudes, and to appreciate the need to avoid provocative shows of force and abrasive encounters when patient negotiation would be equally effective. Many of these objectives could easily be achieved by policy adjustments in the following areas: (i) police–community relations, (ii) media practices, and (iii) government investment. Such possibilities are now considered in more detail.

Police–community relations

The ultimate goal for society has to be the restoration of the type of co-operation and trust between the police and their constituents that will serve as a lasting basis for negotiating their way round difficult situations. In order to achieve this objective, changes must be implemented in three specific areas: police accountability, public-order legislation and the police's institutional approach to handling disorder.

It has been suggested that one possible reason for the decline in American rioting is the gradual increase in black political representation and its implications for democratic influence over local policing (Kilson, 1987). We saw in Chapter 9 how it is in those major American cities like Los Angeles, whose local political structure remains relatively impervious to mayoral influence, that police–community relations are most antagonistic and volatile. Conversely, where black mayors have been able to exert some influence, there has been a shift 'away from the rigidly mechanistic conception of enforcement of every law to a more malleable conception of keeping the peace' (Sherman, 1983:230). The result has been a reduction in public disorder.

As McCabe and Wallington explain,

> The primary purpose of accountability is to ensure that representative views influence or determine policy. Therefore institutions which are representative of the local community should be the primary basis of accountability. This means – despite well-known police misgivings about 'sectional interests' – elected bodies.
>
> (McCabe and Wallington, 1988:149)

These authors rightly insist that the inclusion of magistrates as members of LPAs is 'incompatible with the representative purpose of the Authorities', and should therefore cease (ibid.).

In order to promote effective local accountability, the present tripartite system should be dissolved:

> To ensure real local involvement, police authorities should have more

power to discuss and decide operational priorities, to exercise proper financial controls, to supervise a local complaints machinery, and to establish closer liaison with the electorate. All of this could quite easily be subject to direction by the Home Office if the powers were used unreasonably.

(Uglow, 1988:130–1)

Chief constables must be made truly accountable in the sense of having to legally comply with democratically determined policies, and being required to rigorously explain or justify any departures from agreed policies or procedures. Ideally, the restraining influence of the Home Secretary should be removed or, where it is maintained, he should be answerable to a Parliamentary Select Committee on the police (McCabe and Wallington, 1988:150). In the event of a national dispute or emergency, a Standing Emergency Committee, composed of representatives of Local Police Authorities and the Parliamentary Select Committee, should be authorised to determine policy. The NRC would be responsible to this committee and come directly under their influence. The cost of diverting police from regular duties would be met by national funds (ibid.:150–1).

To complement this structure, revised arrangements are necessary to ensure effective consultation between the police and local community. Such procedures should have the primary objective of:

> Creating a genuine dialogue with the communities and groups being policed. This involves contact *especially* with those on the receiving end of policing, not just 'respectable worthies', *and* being prepared to listen and learn from such groups about what constitutes acceptable forms of policing disorder.
>
> (Jefferson, 1990:144)

These arrangements should ideally involve rank-and-file police officers; not merely beat officers but members of mounted and special units as well. This would help foster a meaningful dialogue between people on both sides of the policing equation, and lead to a 'mutual understanding and a breaking down of entrenched positions' (Kinsey *et al.*, 1986:181).

Effective minority-group representation on consultative committeees would help to make sure that their views were made apparent. However, as the deficiencies of the American system make only too clear, it is vital for any system of accountability to ensure that the civil liberties of the powerless are not overriden by police strategies which merely reflect the majority view (Brogden *et al.*, 1988:192). For this reason, built-in safeguards of the type envisaged by the Council for Racial Equality (CRE) are required.

The CRE's proposals for monitoring the behaviour of Metropolitan police officers – as submitted to the Scarman inquiry – are that an officer of Chief Superintendent level or above should monitor the arrest records of every station and, if necessary, lay charges of discrimination wherever statistics show that disproportionately high numbers of people from ethnic or national minorities have recently been stopped or arrested (ibid.:193).

In addition to the statutory changes required to implement these procedures, the existing public order legislation should also be modified. At present, police powers to impose conditions on marches and assemblies are not counterbalanced by any recognition or protection of the right to meet and protest. The willingness of the police to negotiate and maintain a 'contract with the crowd' is central to the preservation of disorder at demonstrations and on picket lines.

Police powers to impose conditions on marches and assemblies should therefore be repealed and substituted by a *code of conduct*, advising the police and demonstrators to engage in meaningful liaison, and requiring the latter to give adequate notice of their protest and make their own stewarding arrangements in consultation with the police. The self-regulation of the crowd would help avoid the perception that the police were unnecessarily interfering or taking sides, and cut down on the likelihood of abrasive encounters.

The introduction of an American- or European-style Bill of Rights would also help to protect the freedom to assemble and peacefully protest (McCabe and Wallington, 1988:197). Potentially violent forms of protest could still be prohibited by law; but, under the revised system of accountability proposed above, it is anticipated that such adjudication would be exercised more democratically, and not depend on the sole judgement of the 'most senior officer present'.

Another way of reducing potential conflict would be to introduce legislation or codes of conduct which consolidate those citizens' rights which are presently subject to police discretion. The de-criminalisation of cannabis is one admittedly contentious example (Lea and Young, 1982:18). Less controversially, revisions to the Code of Practice on Picketing could legitimise the perceived rights of trade unionists to stop and peacefully communicate with pedestrians or motorists and leave less legal scope for confrontation (McCabe and Wallington, 1988:153).

A final package of proposed reforms relates to the institutional practices of the police. Prominent amongst these is the need for effective training. Jefferson (1990:143) makes the important point that police officers should be encouraged to *analyse incidents*: learning to distinguish, for example, between 'necessary' and 'unnecessary' or crowd-provoking arrests. There should be a continued emphasis on the acquisition of interpersonal skills, such as negotiating difficult encounters, and developing greater awareness of the particular beliefs and political objectives of different cultures.

Senior police administrators and Home Office advisors should strive to cultivate a new philosophy, corresponding to the American commitment to a 'peacekeeping conception' of policing (Sherman, 1983). As Jefferson explains, this philosophy could easily be prioritised by 'Developing criteria of success based on the achievement of trouble-free public order policing – that is, low arrest, complaint and injury rates – and rewarding its successful achievement' (Jefferson, 1990: 143).

Media practices

The legal system is not the only major social institution which needs to review its attitudes and conduct. The media sorely needs to revise its present approach to public disorder. Far from fulfilling a potentially important democratic obligation as champions of the disadvantaged and oppressed, the media respond pejoratively to those groups most chronically denied or disaffected as a result of state policies. Their generally unsympathetic and vilificatory attitude has served as encouragement for hard-line police policies and a heightened potential for violence. Media representations of confrontations between the police and sections of the public invariably favour the former. By concentrating obsessively on the role of agitators, or the criminality or mindlessness of the crowd, such accounts invariably obscure the underlying political meaning of social conflict. Instances of police aggression are habitually played down and set within a narrative which simultaneously justifies and paves the way for more draconian social policy.

Those who call for reform of media practices soon encounter a number of problems. A major one is that news practices cannot easily be reformed within the current system, since they are intricately linked to the structure and organisation of media institutions. Asking for fundamental changes in news-making practices is to strike at the heart of any national TV network, radio station or newspaper. Once the request for local reform has become the demand for global revolution it can be denounced as impracticable.

However, at least in Britain, the potential and machinery for reform may be present. It is now acknowledged that newspapers should not manufacture stories or harass the subjects of them. The voluntary Press Commission is charged with monitoring and encouraging better ethical standards in British journalism. In television, an obsession with sex and violence prompted the establishment of a Broadcasting Complaints Commission where broadcasters must defend themselves against complaints from (generally powerful) groups and individuals who claim to have been misrepresented.

These monitoring institutions are the products of a right-wing hostility towards the excesses of the tabloid press, libertarian attitudes to sex and violence and any kind of investigative journalism. Their effects have been complex and cannot be detailed here. Nevertheless, all of them indicate how media outlets can be made accountable for their actions. What is currently a narrow concern with individual abuses could be extended to questions about media news policy. Editors and journalists could be made accountable for the accuracy of their facts, the representativeness of their sources, the symbolic messages of their pictures or the sensationalism of their headlines.

Such a task would be complex and require sensitive handling. It would, no doubt, be denounced as undemocratic and a threat to free speech. But something of this kind is a viable alternative to inertia or the total reformation of the mass media systems. What is lacking is not principles or model procedures but political will.

Government investment

The ultimate remedy for public disorder is to eradicate the social inequalities which give rise to despair and resentment. Writing in the wake of the inner-city riots of 1981, Lord Scarman insisted that good policing practices were insufficient in themselves to avert further disorder. He emphasised that funds must be made available urgently to attack the social deprivation at the root of the disorders. Thus far, central government has not responded to this requirement.

Benyon (1987) sets out a catalogue of foot-dragging tactics or cosmetic devices which have been used by the government to appease critics whilst enabling them to avoid providing financial assistance to beleaguered inner-city areas. Thus the government has set up a number of regenerative partnership programmes or environmental improvement schemes ('showcase' projects), which cost far less than the amount of investment required to deal with the ingrained problems of poor housing, inadequate education facilities or dire employment prospects.

Alternatively, ministers have committed themselves publicly to attacking inner-city problems, only to delay implementing policy because insufficient funding is available or further consultation is deemed necessary.

'This postponement frequently means abandonment or emasculation of the recommendations. As time elapses the urgency of the action is likely to diminish as public interest switches to new concerns' (ibid.:174).

Those areas visited by the summer riots of 1991 have experienced a massive erosion of their manufacturing industries like cars and shipbuilding. Urban regeneration programmes have not compensated for this decline. On Tyneside, for example, a number of showcase projects conceal an underlying social malaise.

> Glib generalisations about the revival of the Tyneside economy are often based on a flying visit to the splendidly restored Victorian centre of Newcastle, combined with an expedition to the modernistic Me-troCentre shopping complex in Gateshead. But the housing estates which ring the city centre support a poverty-line lifestyle which would be familiar to readers of Orwell's *The Road to Wigan Pier*.
>
> (*Financial Times*, 15 September 1991)

It is feasible to assume that inner-city initiatives which draw together local authorities, community groups, local business and central government agencies will have a beneficial short-term effect, not least in persuading people that something is being done and they have not been forgotten. But it is the ultimate responsibility of central government to ensure that quick fixes or quack remedies are rejected in favour of regenerative policies which promise lasting solutions and give local people a vision they can believe in.

One Meadow Well woman appealed, sincerely and persuasively, for a more compassionate approach to the problems of her community:

> These kids leave school to a hopeless future. They kick out at anything. They see a car parked and they think: 'God, this person's got everything. Now it's my turn'. And they take it and go thieving. I believe that there's nothing worse than losing hope, and that's what's happening to them. The whole problem here is the poverty. We need help.
>
> (quoted in *The Guardian*, 11 September 1991)

To merely dismiss the rioting as 'mindless hooliganism and yobbery' is to remain blind to the true reasons for its occurrence and to guarantee that it will return with shocking devastation to punish us for our indifference and complacency.

Bibliography

ACAB (1990) *Poll Tax Riot: 10 hours that shook Trafalgar Square*. London: ACAB Press.

Allport, F.H. (1924) *Social Psychology*. Boston: Houghton Mifflin.

Anon (1990) 'Sticks and stones', *New Statesman & Society*, 6 April, pp. 10–11.

Armstrong, G. and Harris, R. (1991) 'Football hooligans: theory and evidence', *The Sociological Review*, 39(3):427–58.

Baker, K. and Ball, S.J. (1969) *Mass Media and Violence*. Washington, D.C.: US Government Printing Office.

Barker, P., Taylor, H., deKadt, E. and Hopper, E. (1968) 'Portrait of a protest', *New Society*, 31 October.

Bayley, J. and Loizos, P. (1969) 'Bogside off its knees', *New Society*, 21 August, pp. 277–79.

Becker, H. (1972) 'Whose side are we on?', in J.D. Douglas (ed.) *The Relevance of Sociology*. New York: Appleton-Crofts.

Bell, D. (1954) 'Industrial conflict and public opinion', in A. Kornhauser, R. Dubin and A.M. Ross (eds) *Industrial Conflict*. New York: McGraw-Hill.

Benyon, J. (ed.) (1984) *Scarman and After: Essays Reflecting on Lord Scarman's Report, the Riots and their Aftermath*. Oxford: Pergamon.

Benyon, J. (1987) 'Interpretations of civil disorder', in J. Benyon and J. Solomos (eds) *The Roots of Urban Unrest*. Oxford: Pergamon.

Benyon, J. and Solomos, J. (eds) (1987) *The Roots of Urban Unrest*. Oxford: Pergamon.

Beresford, D. (1987) *Ten Men Dead: The Story of the 1981 Hunger Strike*. London: Grafton.

Berk, R.A. (1974) 'A gaming approach to crowd behaviour', *American Sociological Review*, 39:355–73.

Berkowitz, L. (1972) 'Frustrations, comparison and other sources of emotional arousal as contributors to social unrest', *Journal of Social Issues*, 28:77–91.

Bew, P., Gibbon, P. and Patterson, M. (1979) *The State in Northern Ireland*. Manchester: Manchester University Press.

Billig, M. (1976) *Social Psychology and Intergroup Relations*. London: Academic Press.

Blauner, R. (1973) 'Whitewash over Watts', in P.H. Rossi (ed.) *Ghetto Revolts*. New Brunswick, New Jersey: Transaction Books.

Bonacich, E. (1976) 'Advanced capitalism and black/white race relations in the

United States: a split labor market interpretation', *American Sociological Review*, 41:34–51.

Bowes, S. (1966) *The Police and Civil Liberties*. London: Lawrence and Wishart.

Brake, M. (1985) *Comparative Youth Cultures*. London: Routledge and Kegan Paul.

Branson, N. and Heinemann, M. (1971) *Britain in the Nineteen Thirties*. London: Weidenfeld and Nicolson.

Brewer, J.D., Guelke, A., Moxon-Browne, E. and Wilford, R. (1988) *The Police, Public Order and the State*. London: Macmillan.

Brodeur, J.P. (1983) 'High policing and low policing: remarks about the policing of political activities', *Social Problems*, 30(5):507–20.

Brogden, M., Jefferson, T. and Walklate, S. (1988) *Introducing Policework*. London: Unwin Hyman.

Brooks, R. (1989) 'Domestic violence and America's wars: a historical interpretation', in T.R. Gurr (ed.) *Violence in America, Volume 2: Protest, Rebellion, Reform*. Newbury Park, California: Sage.

Brown, R.M. (ed.) (1970) *American Violence*. Englewood Cliffs, New Jersey: Prentice Hall.

BSSRS Technology of Political Control Group (1985) *Technocop: New Police Technologies*. London: Free Association Books.

Bugler, J. (1968) 'Solidarity with Violence', *New Society*, 21 March, p.405.

Button, J. (1989) 'The outcomes of contemporary black protest and violence', in T.R. Gurr (ed.) *Violence in America, Volume 2: Protest, Rebellion, Reform*. Newbury Park, California: Sage.

Cameron, Lord (1969) *Disturbances in Northern Ireland*. Belfast: HMSO.

Campbell, J.S., Sahid, J.R. and Stang, D.P. (1969) *Law and Order Reconsidered: A Staff Report to the National Commission on the Causes and Prevention of Violence*. Washington, D.C.: US Government Printing Office.

Caplan, N.S. and Paige, J.M. (1968) 'A study of ghetto rioters', *Scientific American*, 219:15–21.

Cashmore, R. (1981) 'After the Rastas', *New Community*, ix(2):173–81.

Clarke, J. (1978) 'Football and working class fans: tradition and change', in R. Ingham (ed.) *Football Hooliganism: The Wider Context*. London: Inter-Action Imprint.

Clutterbuck, R. (1977) *Britain in Agony*. Harmondsworth: Penguin.

Cohen, B. (1985) 'Police complaints procedure: why and for whom?', in J. Baxter and L. Koffman (eds) *Police: The Constitution and the Community*. Oxford: Professional Books.

Cohen, N.E. (1970) 'The context of the curfew area', in N.E. Cohen (ed.) *The Los Angeles Riots: A Socio-psychological Study*. New York: Praeger.

Cohen, S. (1980) *Folk Devils and Moral Panics*. London: Martin Robertson.

Cohen, S. and Young, J. (1981) *The Manufacture of News: Deviance, Social Problems and the Media*. London: Constable.

Collins, T. (1986) *The Irish Hunger Strike*. Dublin: White Island.

Colman, A. (1991) 'Psychological evidence in South African murder trials', *The Psychologist*, November, pp. 482–6.

Crampton, R. and Jenkins, J. (1990) 'Communities charge', *New Statesman & Society*, 16 March, pp. 16–17.

Critchley, T.A. (1970) *The Conquest of Violence*. London: Constable.

Cumberbatch, G., McGregor, R. Brown, J. and Morrison, D. (1986) *Television and the Miners' Strike*. London: Broadcasting Research Unit.

Curtis, L. (1984) *Ireland: The Propaganda War: The British Media and the 'Battle for Hearts and Minds'*. London: Pluto Press.

Darby, J. (ed.) (1983) *Northern Ireland: Background to the Conflict*. Belfast: Appletree.

Darden, J.T. (1989) 'The status of urban blacks 25 years after the Civil Rights Act of 1964', *Sociology and Social Research*, 73(4):160–3.

Davis, M. (1988) 'Los Angeles: civil liberties between the hammer and the rock', *New Left Review*, 170:37–60, July/August.

Docherty, C. (1983) *Steel and Steelworkers*. London: Heinemann.

Dodd, D. (1978) 'Police and thieves on the streets of Brixton', *New Society*, 16 March, pp.598–600.

Drake, St Clair (1969) 'The social and economic status of the Negro in the United States', in A. Beteille (ed.) *Inequality*. Harmondsworth: Penguin.

Dromey, J. and Taylor, G. (1978) *Grunwick: The Workers' Story*. London: Lawrence and Wishart.

Dunning, E. (1990) 'Sociological reflections on sport, violence and civilization', *International Review for the Sociology of Sport*, 25(1):65–81.

Dunning, E., Maguire, J. A., Murphy, P. J. and Williams, J. M. (1982) 'The social roots of football hooligan violence', *Leisure Studies*, 1:139–56.

Dunning, E., Murphy, P., Newburn, T. and Waddington, I. (1987) 'Violent disorders in an English county', in G. Gaskell and R. Benewick (eds), *The Crowd in Contemporary Britain*. London: Sage.

Dunning, E., Murphy, P. and Waddington, I. (1991) 'Anthropological versus sociological approaches to the study of soccer hooliganism: some critical notes', *The Sociological Review*, 39(3):459–78.

Dunning, E., Murphy, P. and Williams, J. (1986) 'Spectator violence at football matches: towards a sociological explanation', *British Journal of Sociology*, 37(2):221–44.

Dunning, E., Murphy, P. and Williams, P. (1988) *The Roots of Football Hooliganism – An Historical and Sociological Study*. London: Routledge and Kegan Paul.

Dunning, E., Murphy, P. Williams, J. and Maguire, J. (1984) 'Football hooliganism in Britain before the First World War', *International Review Journal, Sociology of Sport*, 19 (3/4): 215–39.

Easthope, G. (1976) 'Religious war in Northern Ireland', *Sociology*, 10(3):427–50.

Edwards, H. and Rackages, V. (1977) 'The dynamics of violence in American sport: some promising structural and social considerations', *Journal of Sport and Social Issues*, 1(2):3–31.

Elliott, P. (1978) 'All the world's a stage', in J. Curran (ed.) *The British Press: A Manifesto*. London: Macmillan.

Emerson, B. (1989) 'A watchdog with no teeth', *New Statesman & Society*, 17 February.

Ewing, K.D. and Gearty, C.A. (1990) *Freedom Under Thatcher: Civil Liberties in Modern Britain*. Oxford: Clarendon Press.

Farber, D. (1988) *Chicago '68*. Chicago: University of Chicago Press.

Farrell, M. (1980) *Northern Ireland: The Orange State*, 2nd edn. London: Pluto Press.

Field, S. and Southgate, P. (1982) *Public Disorder: A Review of Research and a Study in One Inner-city Area*. London: HMSO.

Fielding, N. (1991) *The Police and Social Conflict: Rhetoric and Reality*. London: The Athlone Press.

Fimrite, R. (1976) 'Take me out to the brawl game', in A. Yiannakis, T. D. McIntyre, M. M. Melnick and D. P. Hart (eds) *Sport Sociology: Contemporary Themes*. Dubique, Iowa: Kendall Hunt.

Finch, N. (1989) 'Under surveillance', in C. Dunhill (ed.) *The Boys in Blue: Women's Challenge to the Police*. London: Virago.

Fogelson, R.M. (1970) 'Violence and grievances: reflections on the 1960s riots', *Journal of Social Issues*, 26(1):141–63.

Fogelson, R.M. (1971) *Violence as Protest: A Study of Riots and Ghettos*. New York: Doubleday.

Fogelson, R.M. and Hill, R.B. (1968) 'A study of participation in the 1967 riots', in *Kerner Commission Report, Supplemental Studies*. Washington, D.C.: US Government Printing Office.

Fox Piven, F. and Cloward, R.A. (1977) *Poor People's Movements: Why They Succeed, How They Fail*. New York: Pantheon Books.

Fryer, P. (1984) *Staying Power: The History of Black People in Britain*. London: Pluto Press.

Fusfield, D.R. (1973) *The Basic Economics of the Urban Racial Crisis*. New York: Holt, Rinehart and Winston.

Galtung, J. and Ruge, M. (1981) 'Structuring and selecting news', in S. Cohen and J. Young (eds) *The Manufacture of News: Deviance, Social Problems and the Media*. London: Constable.

Gaskell, G. and Benewick, R. (1987) 'The crowd in context', in G. Gaskell and R. Benewick (eds) *The Crowd in Contemporary Britain*. London: Sage.

Geary, R. (1985) *Policing Industrial Disputes*. Cambridge: Cambridge University Press.

Gennard, J. (1984) 'The implications of the Messenger Newspaper Group dispute', *Industrial Relations Journal*, 15:7–20.

Goldstein, J.H. and Arms, R.L. (1971) 'Effects of observing athletic contests on hostility', *Sociometry*, 34:83–90.

Gordon, P. and Rosenburg, D. (1989) *Daily Racism: The Press and Black People in Britain*. London: Runnymede Trust.

Graham, H.D. and Gurr, T.R. (eds) (1969) *Violence in America: Historical and Comparative Perspectives*. (2 Vols) Washington DC: US Government Printing Office.

Grant, D.S. and Wallace, M. (1991) 'Why do strikes turn violent?', *American Journal of Sociology*, 96(5):1117–50.

Greaves, G. (1984) 'The Brixton disorders', in J. Benyon (ed.) *Scarman and After*. London: Pergamon.

Green, P. (1990) *The Enemy Without: Policing and Class Consciousness in the Miners' Strike*. Buckingham: Open University Press.

Griffin, L.J., Wallace, M.R. and Rubin, B.A. (1986) 'Capitalist resistance to the organization of labor before the New Deal: Why? How? Success?', *American Sociological Review*, 51:147–67.

Gurr, T.R. (1970) *Why Men Rebel*. Princeton, New Jersey: Princeton University Press.

Gurr, T.R. (ed.) (1989a) *Violence in America, Volume 2: Protest, Rebellion, Reform*. Newbury Park, California: Sage.

Gurr, T.R. (1989b) 'Protest and rebellion in the 1960s: the United States in world perspective', in T.R. Gurr (ed.) *Violence in America, Volume 2: Protest, Rebellion, Reform.* Newbury Park, California: Sage.

Guttmann, A. (1986) *Sports Spectators.* New York: Columbia University Press.

Hain, P. (1986) *Political Strikes: The State and Trade Unionism in Britain.* New York: Viking.

Hall, S. (1978) 'The treatment of "football hooliganism" in the press', in R. Ingham (ed.) *Football Hooliganism: The Wider Context.* London: Inter-Action Imprint.

Hall, S., Critcher, C., Jefferson, T., Clarke, J. and Roberts, B. (1978) *Policing the Crisis: Mugging, the State and Law and Order.* London: Macmillan.

Halloran, J.D., Elliot, P. and Murdock, G. (1970) *Demonstrations and Communication: A Case Study.* Harmondsworth: Penguin.

Hannerz, U. (1974) 'Soulside, Washington, D.C., in the 1960s: black ghetto culture and community', in C. Bell and H. Newby (eds) *The Sociology of Community.* London: Frank Cass and Co.

Hannigan, J.A. (1985) 'The Armalite and the ballot box: dilemmas of strategy and ideology in the Provisional IRA', *Social Problems*, 33(1):31–40.

Harrell, W.A. (1981) 'Verbal aggressiveness in spectators at professional hockey games: the effects of tolerance of violence and amount of exposure to hockey', *Human Relations*, 34(8):643–55.

Harrison, P. (1974) 'Soccer's tribal wars', *New Society*, 5 September, pp. 602–4.

Harrison, P. (1983) *Inside the Inner City.* Harmondsworth: Penguin.

Hartmann, P. and Husband, C. (1974) *Racism and the Mass Media.* London: Davis-Poyater.

Hebdige, D. (1979) *Subculture: The Meaning of Style.* London: Methuen.

Hewitt, G. (1981) 'Catholic grievances, Catholic nationalism and violence in Northern Ireland', *British Journal of Sociology*, 32:362–80.

Hewitt, C. (1982) *The Abuse of Power: Civil Liberties in the United Kingdom.* Oxford: Martin Robertson.

Hillyard, P. (1982) 'The media coverage of crime and justice in Northern Ireland', in C. Sumner (ed.) *Crime, Justice and the Mass Media.* Cambridge: University of Cambridge Institute of Criminology.

Hillyard, P. (1985) 'Lessons from Ireland', in B. Fine and R. Millar (eds) *Policing the Miners' Strike.* London: Lawrence and Wishart.

Hobsbawm, E.J. and Rude, G. (1970) *Captain Swing.* Harmondsworth: Penguin.

Holdaway, S. (1983) *Inside the British Police.* Oxford: Blackwell.

Holt, R. (1989) *Sport and the British: A Modern History.* Oxford: Oxford University Press.

Horowitz, D.L. (1983) 'Racial violence in the United States', in N. Glazer and K. Young (eds) *Ethnic Pluralism and Public Policy: Achieving Equality in the United States and Britain.* London: Heinemann.

Hundley, J.R. (1968) 'The dynamics of recent ghetto riots', in R. A. Chikota and M. C. Moran (eds) *Riot in the Cities: An Analytical Symposium on the Causes and Effects.* Rutherford: Fairleigh Dickinson University Press.

Hytner, B. (1981) *Report of the Moss Side Enquiry to the Leader of the GMC.* Manchester: Greater Manchester Council.

Jacobs, J.B. (1982) 'The role of military forces in public sector labor relations', *Industrial and Labor Relations Review*, 35(2):163–80.

Janowitz, M. (1969) 'Patterns of collective racial violence', in H. D. Graham and

T. R. Gurr (eds) *Violence in America: Historical and Comparative Perspectives*, Vol. 2. New York: Praeger.

Jefferson, T.J. (1990) *The Case Against Paramilitary Policing*. Milton Keynes: Open University Press.

Jefferson, T. and Grimshaw, R. (1984) *Controlling the Constable*. London: Frederick Muller.

Johnson, P.B., Sears, D.O. and McConahay, J.B. (1971) 'Black invisibility, the press and the Los Angeles riot', *American Journal of Sociology*, 76:698–721.

Johnson, R. (1989) 'Greenham women: the control of protest', in C. Dunhill (ed.) *The Boys in Blue: Women's Challenge to the Police*. London: Virago.

Jones, K. (1991) 'The limits of protest: media coverage of the Orgreave picket during the miners' strike'. Paper presented at the Coal, Culture and Community Conference, Sheffield City Polytechnic, September 1991.

Joshua, H., Wallace, T. and Booth, H. (1983) *To Ride the Storm: The 1980 Bristol 'Riot' and the State*. London: Heinemann.

Kahn, P., Lewis, M., Livock, R. and Wiles, P. (1983) *Picketing: Industrial Disputes, Tactics and the Law*. London: Routledge and Kegan Paul.

Keith, M. (1989) 'Riots as a "social problem" in British cities', in D. T. Herbert and D. M. Smith (eds) *Social Problems and the City: New Perspectives*. Oxford: Oxford University Press.

Kelley, K.J. (1988) *The Longest War: Northern Ireland and the IRA*, 2nd edn. London: Zed Books.

Kerner, O. (1968) *Report of the National Advisory Committee on Civil Disorders*. Washington, D.C.: US Government Printing Office.

Kettle, M. and Hodges, L. (1982) *Uprising: The Police, the People and the Riots in Britain's Cities*. London: Pan.

Kilson, M. (1987) 'Politics of race and urban crisis: the American case', in J. Benyon and J. Solomos (eds) *The Roots of Urban Unrest*. London: Pergamon.

Kinder, D.R. and Sears, D.O. (1981) 'Prejudice and politics: symbolic racism versus racial threats to the good life', *Journal of Personality and Social Psychology*, 40(3):414–31.

Kinsey, R., Lea, J. and Young, J. (1986) *Losing the Fight Against Crime*. Oxford: Blackwell.

Knopf, T.A. (1975) 'Media myths on violence', in A. Wells (ed.) *Mass Media and Society*, 2nd edn. Palo Alto, California: Mayfield.

Kovalcheck, K. (1987) 'Catholic grievances in Northern Ireland: appraisal and judgement', *British Journal of Sociology*, 38:77–87.

Kritzer, H.M. (1977) 'Political protest and political violence: a nonrecursive causal model', *Social Forces*, 55(3):630–40.

Kueneman, R.M. and Wright, J.E. (1975) 'News policies of broadcast stations for civil disturbances and disasters', *Journalism Quarterly*, 52:670–77.

Ladner, R.A., Schwartz, B.J., Roker, S.J. and Titterud, L.S. (1981) 'The Miami riots of 1980: antecedent conditions, community responses and participant characteristics', in L. Kriesberg (ed.) *Research in Social Movements, Conflicts and Change*, Vol. 4. London: JAI Press.

Lavalette, M. and Mooney, G. (1990) 'Undermining the "north–south divide"? Fighting the poll tax in Scotland, England and Wales', *Critical Social Policy*, 10(2):100–19.

Lea, J. and Young, J. (1982) 'The riots in Britain 1981: urban violence and political marginalisation', in D. Cowell, D. Jones and J. Young (eds), *Policing the Riots*. London: Junction Books.

Lewis, J.M. (1982) 'Fan violence: an American social problem', in M. Lewis (ed.) *Research in Social Problems and Public Policy*. Greenwich, Connecticut: JAI Press.

Lieberson, S. and Silverman, A. (1965) 'The precipitants and underlying causes of race riots', *American Sociological Review*, 30:887–98.

Lloyd, C. (1989) 'Public Order: Political Policing', in C. Dunhill (ed.) *The Boys in Blue: Women's Challenge to the Police*. London: Virago.

McAdam, D. and Moore, K. (1989) 'The politics of black insurgency, 1930–1975', in T. R. Gurr (ed.) *Violence in America, Volume 2: Protest, Rebellion, Reform*. Newbury Park, California: Sage.

McCabe, S. and Wallington, P. with J. Alderson, L. Gostin and C. Mason (1988) *The Police, Public Order and Civil Liberties*. London: Routledge.

McCauley, C. (1989) 'Nationalist women and the RUC', in C. Dunhill (ed.) *The Boys in Blue: Women's Challenge to the Police*. London: Virago.

McCone, J. (Governor's Commission on the Los Angeles Riots) (1965) *Violence in the City: An End or a Beginning?* Los Angeles: College Book Store.

McGuffin, J. (1973) *Internment!* Tralee: Anvil.

McKenzie, I.K. and Gallagher, G.P. (1989) *Behind the Uniform: Policing in Britain and America*. Brighton: Wheatsheaf.

Manchester City Council (1986) 'Leon Britton's visit to Manchester University's Students' Union, 1 March 1985', *Report of the Independent Inquiry*. Manchester: Manchester City Council.

Mann, L. and Pearce, P. (1978) 'Social psychology of the sports spectator', in D. Glencross (ed.) *Psychology and Sport*. Sydney: McGraw-Hill.

Manning, P.K. (1977) *Police Work*. Cambridge, Massachusetts: MIT Press.

Manwaring-White, S. (1983) *The Policing Revolution: Police Technology, Democracy and Liberty*. Brighton: Harvester.

Mark, R. (1977) *Policing a Perplexed Society*. London: Allen and Unwin.

Marsh, P. (1975) 'Understanding aggro', *New Society*, 3 April, pp. 7–9.

Marsh, P. (1976) 'Careers for boys: nutters, hooligans and hardcases', *New Society*, 13 May, pp. 346–8.

Marsh, P., Rosser, E. and Harre, R. (1978) *The Rules of Disorder*. London: Routledge and Kegan Paul.

Marx, G.T. (1970) 'Civil disorder and the agents of social control', *Journal of Social Issues*, 26(1):19–57.

Marx, G. T. (1972) 'Issueless riots', in J.F. Short, Jr and M.R. Wolfgang (eds) *Collective Violence*. Chicago: Aldine-Atherton.

Mason, G. (1991) 'Making sense of mayhem', *Police Review*, 8 March, pp. 476–7.

Massey, D.S. (1985) 'Ethnic residential segregation: a theoretical synthesis and empirical review', *Sociology and Social Research*, 69:315–50.

Massey, D.S. and Denton, N.A. (1987) 'Trends in the residential segregation of Blacks, Hispanics and Asians: 1970–1980', *American Sociological Review*, 52:802–25.

Massey, D.S. and Denton, N.A. (1988) 'Suburbanization and segregation in U. S. metropolitan areas', *American Journal of Sociology*, 94(3):592–626.

Masterman, L. (1985) 'The Battle of Orgreave', in L. Masterman (ed.) *Television Mythologies*. London: Comedia.

Meier, A. and Rudwick, E. (1969) 'Black violence in the 20th century: a study in rhetoric and retaliation', in H. D. Graham and T. R. Gurr (eds) *Violence in America: Historical and Comparative Perspectives*, Vol. 2. New York: Praeger.

Melnick, M.J. (1986) 'The mythology of football hooliganism. A closer look at the British experience', *International Review for the Sociology of Sport*, 21(1):1–19.

Metropolitan Police (1991) 'Trafalgar Square Riot Debriefing, Saturday, 31 March, 1990', London: The Metropolitan Police.

Miliband, R. (1969) *The State in Capitalist Society*. London: Weidenfeld and Nicolson.

Monti, D.J. (1964) 'Patterns of conflict preceding the 1964 riots', *Journal of Conflict Resolution*, 23(1):41–69.

Morgan, R. (1989) '"Policing by consent": legitimating the doctrine', in R. Morgan and D. J. Smith (eds) *Coming to Terms with Policing: Perspectives on Policy*. London: Routledge.

Morris, P. and Heal, K. (1981) *Crime Control and the Police: A Review of Research*. London: Home Office Research Unit.

Muncie, J. (1984) *The Trouble With Kids Today*. London: Hutchinson.

Murdock, G. (1981) 'Political deviance: the press presentation of a militant mass demonstration', in S. Cohen and J. Yound (eds) *The Manufacture of News*. London: Constable.

Murdock, G. (1984) 'Reporting the riots: images and impact', in J. Benyon (ed.) *Scarman and After: Essays reflecting on Lord Scarman's Report, the Riots and their Aftermath*. Oxford: Pergamon.

Nally, M. (1984) 'Eyewitness in Moss Side', in J. Benyon (ed.) *Scarman and After: Essays Reflecting on Lord Scarman's Report, the Riots and their Aftermath*. Oxford: Pergamon.

Navarro, P. (1983) 'Union bargaining power in the coal industry, 1945–1981', *Industrial and Labour Relations Review*, 36(2):214–29.

Northam, G. (1988) *Shooting in the Dark: Riot Police in Britain*. London: Faber.

Oberschall, A. (1971) 'The Los Angeles riot of August 1965', in D. Boesel and P. H. Rossi (eds) *Cities Under Siege: An Anatomy of the Ghetto Riots, 1964–1968*. New York: Basic Books.

Olson, M. (1965) *The Logic of Collective Action*. Cambridge, Massachusetts: Harvard University Press.

Paletz, D.L. and Dunn, R. (1969) 'Press coverage of civil disorders: a case study of Winston–Salem, 1967', *Public Opinion Quarterly*, 33:328–45.

Paletz, D.L. and Entman, R.M. (1981) *Media, Power, Politics*. London: Collier Macmillan.

Parry, G., Moyser, G. and Wagstaffe, M. (1987) 'The crowd and the community: context, content and aftermath', in G. Gaskell and R. Benewick (eds) *The Crowd in Contemporary Britain*. London: Sage.

Pearson, G. (1979) 'In defence of hooliganism, social theory and violence', in N.Tutt (ed.) *Violence*. London: HMSO.

Pearton, R. (1986) 'Violence in sport and the special case of soccer hooliganism in the United Kingdom', in C. R. Rees and A. W. Miracle (eds) *Sport and Social Theory*. Champaign, Illinois: Human Kinetics Publishers.

Peroff, K. and Hewitt, C. (1980) 'Rioting in Northern Ireland: the effects of different policies', *Journal of Conflict Resolution*, 24(4):593–612.

Pickering, P. (1985) 'Fathers tell sons about the police', *New Society*, 28 March, pp. 472–74.

Pilz, G.A. (1988) 'Book Review: A. Guttmann (1986) *Sports Spectators*. New York, Columbia University Press', *International Journal for the Sociology of Sport*, 23 (2):167–71.

Pope, D.W. (1985) 'Developments and problems in police–community relations', in J. R. Thackrah (ed.) *Contemporary Policing*. London: Sphere Books.

Popplewell, O. (1986) *Committee of Inquiry into Crowd Safety and Control at Sports Grounds: Final Report*. London: HMSO.

Porter, B. and Dunn, M. (1984) *The Miami Riot of 1980: Crossing the Bounds*. Massachusetts: Lexington Books.

Pounder, C. (1985) *Police Computers and the Metropolitan Police*. London: Greater London Council.

Raeburn, A. (1973) *The Militant Suffragettes*. London: Michael Joseph.

Ragin, C.C., Coverman, S. and Hayward, M. (1982) 'Major labor disputes in Britain, 1902–1938: the relationship between resource expenditure and outcome', *American Sociological Review*, 47:238–52.

Ramdin, R. (1987) *The Making of the Black Working Class in Britain*. Aldershot: Wildwood House.

Ransford, H.E. (1968) 'Isolation, powerlessness and violence: a study of attitudes and participation in the Watts riot', *American Journal of Sociology*, 73:581–91.

Reicher, S.D. (1984) 'The St. Paul's riot: an exploration of the limits of crowd action in terms of a social identity model', *European Journal of Social Psychology*, 14:1–24.

Reiner, R. (1985) *The Politics of the Police*. Brighton: Wheatsheaf.

Reiner, R. (1989) 'Where the buck stops: chief constables' views on police accountability', in R. Morgan and D. J. Smith (eds) *Coming to Terms With Policing: Perspectives on Policy*. London: Routledge.

Review Panel (1986) Report: *A Different Reality*. Birmingham: West Midlands County Council.

Rex, J. (1987) 'Life in the ghetto', in J. Benyon and J. Solomos (eds) *The Roots of Urban Unrest*. London: Pergamon.

Riley, D.P. (1974) 'Should communities control their police?', in A. Platt and L. Cooper (eds) *Policing America*. Englewood-Cliffs, New Jersey: Prentice-Hall.

Roadburg, A. (1980) 'Factors precipitating fan violence: a comparison of professional soccer in Britain and North America', *British Journal of Sociology*, 31(2):265–76.

Robins, D. and Cohen, P. (1978) *Knuckle Sandwich*. Harmondsworth: Penguin.

Rock, P. (1981) 'Rioting', *London Review of Books*, 17–30 September, pp. 19–20.

Rollo, J. (1980) 'The Special Patrol Group', in P. Hain (ed.) *Policing the Police, 2*. London: Calder.

Rose, R. (1972) 'Discord in Ulster', *New Community*, 1(2):122–27.

Rossi, P.H. (1971) 'Urban revolts and the future of American cities', in D. Boesel and P. H. Rossi (eds) *Cities Under Siege: An Anatomy of the Ghetto Riots, 1964–1968*. New York: Basic Books.

Rossi, P.H., Berk, R.A. and Edson, B.K. (1974) *The Roots of Urban Discontent: Public Policy, Municipal Institutions and the Ghetto*. London: John Wiley.

Rubenstein, R.E. (1989) 'Rebellion in America: The fire next time?', in T. R. Gurr (ed.) *Violence in America, Volume 2: Protest, Rebellion, Reform*. Newbury Park, California: Sage.

Russell, G.W. (1983) 'Psychological issues in sports aggression', in J. H. Goldstein (ed.) *Sports Violence*. New York: Springer-Verlag.

Sahid, J.R. (1969) *Rights in Concord: The Response to the Counter-inaugural Protest Activities in Washington, D.C.* Washington, D.C.: US Government Printing Office.

Scarman, Lord (1972) *Violence and Civil Disturbances in Northern Ireland in 1969.* London: HMSO.

Scarman, Lord (1981) *The Brixton Disorders, 10th–12th April, 1981.* London: HMSO.

Schlesinger, P. (1978) *Putting Reality Together*. London: Constable.

Scraton, P. (1985a) *The State of the Police*. London: Pluto Press.

Scraton, P. (1985b) 'From Saltley Gates to Orgreave: a history of the policing of recent industrial disputes', in B. Fine and R. Millar (eds) *Policing the Miners' Strike*. London: Lawrence and Wishart.

Sears, D.O. and McConahay, J.B. (1973) *The Politics of Violence: The New Urban Blacks and the Watts Riot*. Boston: Houghton Mifflin.

Shapland, J. and Vagg, J. (1988) *Policing by the Public*. London: Tavistock.

Sherman, L.W. (1983) 'After the riots: police and minorities in the United States, 1970–1980', in N. Glazer and K. Young (eds) *Ethnic Pluralism and Public Policy: Achieving Equality in the United States and Britain*. London: Heinemann.

Sherr, A. (1989) *Freedom of Protest, Public Order and the Law*. Oxford: Blackwell.

Singer, B.D. (1970) 'Mass media and communication processes in the Detroit riot of 1967', *Public Opinion Quarterly*, 34:236–45.

Skolnick, J.H. (1966) *Justice Without Trial: Law Enforcement in Democratic Society*. New York: John Wiley.

Skolnick, J.H. (1969) *The Politics of Protest*. New York: Simon and Schuster.

Sloane, A.A. and Witney, R. (1985) *Labor Relations*, 5th edn. Englewood Cliffs, New Jersey: Prentice Hall.

Smelser, N. (1962) *Theory of Collective Behaviour*. New York: Free Press.

Smith, M.D. (1976) 'Hostile outbursts in sport', in A. Yiannakis, T.D. McIntyre, M.M. Melnick and D.P. Hart (eds) *Sport Sociology: Contemporary Themes*. Dubique, Iowa: Kendall Hunt.

Smith, M.D. (1983) *Violence and Sport*. London: Butterworth.

Southgate, P. (1982a) 'The disturbances of July 1981 in Handsworth, Birmingham: A survey of the views and experiences of male residents'. Paper presented at the 20th International Congress of Applied Psychology, University of Edinburgh, 28 July 1982.

Southgate, P. (1982b) *Police Probationer Training in Race Relations*. London: Home Office.

Stark, R. (1972) *Police Riots*. Belmont, California: Wadsworth.

Stephens, M. (1988) *Policing: The Critical Issues*. Brighton: Wheatsheaf.

Stevenson, J. and Cook, C. (1979) *The Slump: Society and Politics During the Depression*. London: Quartet.

Sullivan, T.J. (1977) 'The "critical mass" in crowd behaviour: crowd size, contagion and the evolution of riots', *Humboldt Journal of Social Relations*, 42:46–59.

Sumner, C. (1982) '"Political hooliganism" and "rampaging mobs": the national press coverage of the Toxteth "riot"', in C. Sumner (ed.) *Crime, Justice and the Mass Media*. Cambridge: University of Cambridge Institute of Criminology.

Taft, P. and Ross, P. (1969) 'American labor violence: its causes, character and outcome', in H. D. Graham and T. R. Gurr (eds) *Violence in America: Comparative and Historical Perspectives*, Vol. 1. New York: Praeger.

Talamini, J.T. (1987) 'Social problems in major league baseball', *Free Inquiry in Creative Sociology*, 15(1):65–70.

Taylor, I. (1971a) 'Football mad: a speculative sociology of football hooliganism', in E. G. Dunning (ed.) *The Sociology of Sport*. London: Cass.

Taylor, I (1971b) 'Soccer consciousness and soccer hooliganism', in S. Cohen (ed.) *Images of Deviance*. Harmondsworth: Penguin.

Taylor, I. (1982) 'On the sports violence question: soccer hooliganism revisited', in J. Hargreaves (ed.) *Sport, Culture and Ideology*. London: Routledge and Kegan Paul.

Taylor, I. (1987) 'British soccer after Bradford', *Sociology of Sport Journal*, 4:171–91.

Taylor, I. (1989) 'Hillsborough, 15 April 1989: some personal contemplations', *New Left Review*, 177 (Sep/Oct):89–110.

Taylor, Lord Justice (1989) *The Hillsborough Stadium Disaster (15 April 1989), Final Report*. London: HMSO.

Thieblot, A. and Haggard, T.R. (1983) *Union Violence: The Record and the Response by Courts, Legislatures and the NLRB*. Philadelphia, Pennsylvania: Industrial Relations Research Unit: University of Pennsylvania.

Thomas, R. (1987) 'Looking forward: the Detroit experience after the riots of 1943 and 1967', in J. Benyon and J. Solomos (eds) *The Roots of Urban Unrest*. Oxford: Pergamon Press.

Thornhill, T. (1989) 'Police accountability', in C. Dunhill (ed.) *The Boys in Blue: Women's Challenge to the Police*. London: Virago.

Tuchman, G. (1974) 'Making news by doing work: routinizing the unexpected', *American Journal of Sociology*, 79:110–31.

Tumber, H. (1982) *Television and the Riots*. London: Broadcasting Research Unit.

Uglow, S. (1988) *Policing Liberal Society*. Oxford: Oxford University Press.

Vamplew, W. (1979) 'Ungentlemanly conduct: the control of soccer crowd behaviour in England, 1888–1914', in T. C. Smout (ed.) *The Search for Wealth and Stability*. London: Macmillan.

Venner, M. (1981) 'The disturbances in Moss Side, Manchester', *New Community*, 9(3):374–7.

Viorst, M. (1979) *Fire in the Streets: America in the 1960s*. New York: Simon and Schuster.

Vogler, R. (1991) *Reading the Riot Act: The Magistracy, the Police and the Army in Civil Disorder*. Milton Keynes: Open University Press.

Waddington, D.P. (1987) 'The summer of '81 revisited: an analysis of Sheffield's Haymarket fracas', in A. Cashdan and M. Jordin (eds) *Studies in Communication*. Oxford: Blackwell.

Waddington, D.P., Jones, K. and Critcher, C. (1987) 'Flashpoints of public disorder', in G. Gaskell and R. Benewick (eds) *The Crowd in Contemporary Britain*. London: Sage.

Waddington, D.P., Jones, K. and Critcher, C. (1989) *Flashpoints: Studies in Public Disorder*. London: Routledge.

Waddington, D.P., Wykes, M. and Critcher, C. (1990) *Split at the Seams? Community, Continuity and Change After the 1984–5 Coal Dispute*. Milton Keynes: Open University Press.

Wade, R. (1978) 'Violence in the cities: a historical view', in R. Lane and J. J. Turner, Jr. (eds) *Riot, Rout and Tumult: Readings in American Social and Political Violence*. London: Greenwood Press.

Wagg, S. (1984) *The Football World: A Contemporary Social History*. Brighton: Harvester Press.

Walker, D. (1968) *Rights in Conflict: A Report Submitted by Daniel Walker, Director of the Chicago Study Team, to the National Commission on the Causes and Prevention of Violence*. New York: Dutton.

Wallace, M., Rubin, B.A. and Smith, B.T. (1988) 'American Labor Law: its impact on working-class militancy, 1901–1980', *Social Science History*, 12(1):1–19.

Walsh, D.P.J. (1984) 'Civil liberties in Northern Ireland', in P. Wallington (ed.) *Civil Liberties 1984*. London: Martin Robertson.

Walvin, J. (1986) *Football and the Decline of Britain*. London: Macmillan.

Weitzer, R. (1985) 'Policing a divided society: obstacles to normalization in Northern Ireland', *Social Problems*, 33(1):41–55.

Weitzer, R. (1987) 'Policing Northern Ireland Today', *Political Quarterly*, 58(1):88–96.

Whannel, G. (1979) 'Football crowd behaviour and the press', *Media, Culture and Society*, 1:327–42.

White, J. (1982) 'The Summer Riots of 1919', in *New Society* (ed.) *Race and Riots '81: A New Society Social Studies Reader*. London: New Society.

White, R.W. (1989) 'From peaceful protest to guerrilla war: micromobilization of the Provisional Irish Republican Army', *American Journal of Sociology*, 94(6):1277–1302.

Williams, J., Dunning, E. and Murphy, P. (1984) *Hooligans Abroad: The Behaviour and Control of English Fans in Continental Europe*. London: Routledge and Kegan Paul.

Wilsher, P., Macintyre, D. and Jones, M. (1985) *Strike: A Battle of Ideologies; Thatcher, Scargill and the Miners*. London: Coronet.

Wintersmith, R.F. (1974) *Police and the Black Community*. Lexington, Massachusetts: Lexington Books.

Women of Broadwater Farm (1989) 'Broadwater Farm Defence Campaign', in C. Dunhill (ed.) *The Boys in Blue: Women's Challenge to the Police*. London: Virago.

Wren-Lewis, J. (1981/1982) 'The story of a riot: the television coverage of civil unrest in 1981', *Screen Education*, 40:15–33.

Wright, S. (1978) *Crowds and Riots*. Beverly Hills, California: Sage.

Young, A. (1988) '"Wild women": the censure of the Suffragette Movement', *International Journal of the Sociology of Law*, 16:279–93.

Young, A. (1990) *Femininity in Dissent*. London: Routledge.

Young, K. (1986) '"The Killing Field": Themes in mass media responses to the Heysel Stadium riot', *International Review for the Sociology of Sport*, 21 (2/3):255–65.

Zimbardo, P.G. (1969) 'The human choice: reason and order deindividuation, impulse and chaos', in W. J. Arnold and D. Levine (eds) *Nebraska Symposium on Motivation*. Lincoln: University of Nebraska Press.

Index